CONNECTICUT RETIREMENT GROUP, LLC
P.O BOX 100
NORTH BRANFORD, CT 06471
(203) 484-5056

156/90

LONG-TERM CARE

Your Financial
Planning Guide

CONNECTICUT RETIREMENT GROUP, LLC
P.O BOX 100
NORTH BRANFORD, CT 06471
(203) 484-5056

LONG-TERM CARE

Your Financial Planning Guide

Phyllis Shelton

KENSINGTON BOOKS
http://www.kensingtonbooks.com

KENSINGTON BOOKS are published by

Kensington Publishing Corp.
850 Third Avenue
New York, NY 10022

All Kensington titles, imprints and distributed lines are available at special quantity discounts for bulk purchases for sales promotion, premiums, fund raising, educational or institutional use.

Special book excerpts or customized printings can also be created to fit specific needs. For details, write or phone the office of the Kensington Special Sales Manager: Kensington Publishing Corp., 850 Third Avenue, New York, NY, 10022. Attn: Special Sales Department. Phone: 1-800-221-2647.

Kensington and the K logo Reg. U.S. Pat. & TM Off.

ISBN 0-7582-0553-8

First Kensington Trade Paperback Printing: April, 2003
10 9 8 7 6 5 4

Printed in the United States of America

Table of Contents

Introduction   xi

Chapter 1
Long-Term Care and Your Financial Security   1
  The Odds Are 1 out of 2   5
  An Aging America   6
  All Ages Need Long-Term Care   8
  Families in Transition   9
  The Caregiver's Glass Ceiling   12
  Technology and Lifestyle   13
  Why Doesn't Private Insurance Pay More?   14
  Why Doesn't Medicare Pay More?   15
  You Can't Count on Medicaid   16
  Prospects for Government Help   18
  Tax Incentives for Long-Term Care Insurance   19
  IRS-Approved Medical Expenses   22
  The Private Sector Solution   27

Chapter 2
Features of a Good Long-Term Care Insurance Policy   34
  Level of Care   36
  Home Health Care   36
  Adult Day Care   42
  Assisted Living   43
  Guaranteed Renewable   44
  Prior Hospitalization   45
  Daily or Monthly Benefit   46
  Benefit Period/Benefit Maximum   48
  Restoration of Benefits   53
  Joint Policies   55

Elimination Period (Waiting Period)   56
Mental Conditions   58
Waiver of Premium   59
Inflation Protection   59
Miscellaneous Benefits   67
Alternate Plan of Care   67
Hospice   68
Respite Care   68
Homemaker Services   68
Alternate Payer Designation   69
Impairment Reinstatement   69
Bed Reservation   69
Care Coordination   69
Survivor Benefit   70
Worldwide Coverage   71
Coordination with Medicare and Other Insurance   71
Additional Benefits   72
Rates vs. Ratings   72
The True Cost of Waiting   78
Savings vs. LTC Insurance   80
Underwriting   81
Pre-Existing Conditions   83
"Free-Look" Period   83
Non-Forfeiture Options   84
Assets   88
Claims   89
Tax-Qualified or Non-Tax-Qualified   92
Getting a Claim Paid   95
Policy Improvements   96
Your Customized Benefit Selection Process   98
The Bare-Bones/Best Value Policy
    for the Premium Conscious   103
Some Parting Advice   104

Chapter 3
Long-Term Care: The New Employee Benefit   **105**
Productivity Insurance   **109**
Lifestyle Insurance   **116**
Long-Term Care Insurance Is Not
   "Senior Citizen Insurance"   **124**
Tips for Benefit Choices in Group Plans   **126**
The Federal Long-Trem Care Insurance Program   **129**
Eligibility   **130**
Benefits   **132**

Chapter 4
The Partnership for Long-Term Care   **140**

Chapter 5
The Medicaid Benefit for Long-Term Care   **151**
The Problem   **151**
Income Eligibility Criteria   **152**
Asset Eligibility Criteria   **157**
Transferring Assets—The Myth   **160**
Estate Recovery   **164**
Why Transferring Assets Can Be a Bad Idea   **165**
The Bigger Problem—The Criminal Side Revisited   **168**
The Biggest Problem   **170**
Long-Term Care Insurance—A Better Way   **172**

Chapter 6
Alternatives for Financing Long-Term Care   **174**
Accelerated Death Benefits   **174**
Traditional Viatical Settlements   **177**
The Viatical Settlement Process   **179**
Viatical Settlements vs. Accelerated Death Benefits   **181**

Viatical Settlements vs. Long-Term Care Insurance   **182**
Life Settlements   **183**
Single Premium Life/Long-Term Care Policies   **185**
Effect of the 1996 Health Insurance Portability and
    Accountability Act (HIPAA)   **189**
Long-Term Care Insurance and Estate Planning   **190**
Long-Term Care Annuities   **192**
Reverse Mortgages   **196**
Critical Illness Insurance   **202**
People Who Do Not Qualify for Long-Term Care
    Insurance   **205**
Where Do I Go From Here?   **208**

APPENDIX A: Senior Benefits   **210**
Medicare Benefits   **211**
Enrolling for Medicare   **211**
Two Parts of Medicare   **212**
The Medicare Gaps   **214**
Medicare-Approved Charges   **216**
Be Informed   **218**
Appeals   **218**

2003 Medicare Benefits   **219**
Medicare Part A   **219**
Medicare Part B   **221**
Expenses Not Covered by Medicare   **223**

Medicare Supplement Policies   **224**
Do You Need a Medicare Supplement?   **224**
Can You Self-Insure Balances to Medicare?   **226**
Disabled Individuals Under Age 65   **227**
Federal Guidelines for Medicare Supplements   **227**
Standard Plans   **229**

Features of a Good Medicare Supplement Policy   **230**

Guaranteed Renewable   **230**

Rating of the Insurance Company   **231**

Pre-Existing Conditions   **231**

Underwriting   **231**

Open Enrollment   **232**

Premiums   **233**

"Free-Look" Period   **234**

Multiple Policies   **234**

Benefits   **234**

Excess Physician Charges   **234**

Miscellaneous Benefits   **235**

Claims   **236**

Appeals   **237**

Managed Care for Medicare Supplements   **238**

Medicare Select   **238**

Managed Care Medicare Plans   **240**

New Medicare+Choice Plans   **242**

Enrollment and Disenrollment   **242**

What Kind of Choices Will You Have?   **243**

You Do Not Have to Switch   **246**

Benefits   **246**

What If I Don't Like a Medicare+Choice Plan?   **247**

Want to Know More?   **248**

The Silver Lining in the Managed Care Opportunity   **249**

APPENDIX B: Who to Call for Help   **250**

Directory of State Insurance Departments,
Medicaid and Aging Agencies   **251**

Useful Web Sites   **268**

APPENDIX C: Sources   **271**

Sources for **Introduction**   **271**

Sources for **Long-Term Care and Your
    Financial Security**   **271**

Sources for **Features of a Good Long-Term
    Care Insurance Policy**   **280**

Sources for **Long-Term Care: The New
    Employee Benefit**   **283**

Sources for **The Partnership for Long-Term Care**   **290**

Sources for **The Medicaid Benefit for Long-Term Care** **291**

Sources for **Alternatives for Financing Long-Term Care** **294**

Sources for **Appendix A: Senior Benefits**   **296**

INTRODUCTION

Christopher Reeve's tragic accident spotlighted a reality that many Americans have never faced. A long-term care need can hit at any time, at any age. At age 43, "Superman" fell into this huge category: 40% of people needing long-term care in this country are working-age adults, ages 18–64.[1]

Private health insurance doesn't cover long-term, chronic care for younger people and Medicare doesn't cover it for older people. Medicaid pays only if you spend most of your assets. So we have to take care of ourselves.

Are you a small business person, entrepreneur, or climbing the corporate ladder? If you are working 60+ hours per week as many of us do, and out of the blue, your spouse or parent or parent-in-law has an accident or stroke and needs long-term care, what will happen to your career? At an average of $60,000–$120,000[2] per year (depending on where you live) for daily home health care or nursing home care, most families don't know where to turn for help.

The American female today is projected to spend more years taking care of aging family members than her own children,[3] and by 2005, 37% of U.S. workers will be more concerned with caring for a parent than children.[4]

There's a solution, and a good one, for this dilemma, but it's not for everyone.

This book is dedicated to helping you determine if long-term care insurance is appropriate for you, your spouse and/or your parents. Since it is the fastest growing insurance product in the country, many people want information such as:

1. What are the chances for a government-funded program for long-term care? (See Chapter 1, *Prospects for Government Help*, p. 18.)

2. What are the tax advantages for long-term care insurance? (See Chapter 1, *Tax Incentives for Long-Term Care Insurance*, p. 19.)

3. I've read several articles that advise me to wait until I'm 53 to buy long-term care insurance. Is this a good idea? (See Chapter 2, *The True Cost Of Waiting*, p. 78.)

4. I'm only 40. Wouldn't I be better off just saving the premium and paying for my own long-term care? (See Chapter 2, *Saving vs. LTC Insurance*, p. 80.)

5. What can you tell me about the new group long-term care insurance plan for federal employees? (See Chapter 2, *The Federal Long-Term Care Insurance Program*, p. 129)

As an insurance consultant and former LTC insurance agent, I am especially committed to providing current, meaningful information about long-term care insurance that is not available in any other publication. This book also will explain the other major programs that are impacted by the issue of long-term care, such as Medicare, Medicare supplement and the Medicaid (MediCal in California) benefit for long-term care, in addition to alternatives such as life insurance/LTC policies, accelerated death benefits, viatical and life settlements, long-term care annuities, critical illness insurance, and in some states, a special Partnership program between private LTC insurance and Medicaid.

Please, let me caution you. This booklet is only a summary of the highlights of the various programs. It is not a legal description of benefits and should not be used as such. If you have questions about specific benefit features, you should consult an insurance agent you trust or your state's insurance department (See **Who to Call for Help**, p. 250), and any appropriate insurance policy contracts.

I hope you find this information helpful.

Phyllis Shelton
Nashville, Tennessee
April 2003

Chapter 1

Long-Term Care
and Your Financial Security

"Families are not asking to be free from caregiving duties, but it is clear that without large-scale improvement, most will not have the endurance or money to do the job. Advancements in medicine have made the prospect of caregiving inevitable for nearly all households."

—- Proceedings of a Caregiver Empowerment Summit,
The National Alliance for Caregiving, July 2001

I was three when my grandparents moved in with us. My grandmother died unexpectedly two years later after gall bladder surgery. My grandfather was so sad. I still remember him crying after the funeral.

Born in 1886, my grandfather was blind, a diabetic who had to have a shot every day, and most importantly, my best friend. He listened with endless patience while I laboriously read the adventures of Nancy Drew, Cherry Ames, the Dana Girls, and

1

Trixie Belden, none of which I ever finished. I think he also heard excerpts from Black Beauty and Beautiful Joe, my favorite animal books. Sometimes he returned the favor by telling me stories about his logging days in the East Tennessee mountains.

My mother was a nurse, worked nights while my father could be with us, and cared for my best friend almost ten years in our home, with my help of course. I didn't give him his daily insulin shot or plan his special diet or bathe him or dress him. But I gave him hours upon hours of my time, partially because I took the caregiving responsibility my mother assigned to me very seriously, but mostly because of how much I loved him. We had to be quiet while she slept, so I read him story upon story and fetched many glasses of water and led him to the bathroom when he asked me to. Sometimes I just crawled up on his lap to let him make whatever problem I encountered during the day go away. As I grew older, his room was my first stop when I got home from school.

My best friend went to a nursing home when I was 12. He never asked for help, but I knew my mother was struggling between giving him her best (he was incontinent by then) and caring for me and my three-year-old brother. She was also working double shifts at the hospital for extra money. We moved him to another nursing home once because she didn't think he was getting the best possible care. When he passed away two years later, I was devastated. My best friend was gone.

Twenty years later, my mother lost a two-year battle with cancer at age 54. I thought about my best friend and finally realized that what was a normal lifestyle for me as a child must have been a tremendous sacrifice for her.

Home and community-based care and nursing home care represent the largest out-of pocket expenses facing older Americans.[1] Unfortunately, it is one of the only health care expenses that is not covered by group and individual health insurance, HMOs, retiree health plans or Medicare and Medicare supplements. This chapter presents information about why long-term care has become a national concern. Have you ever known anyone whose assets were totally destroyed by prolonged home health or nursing home care? A friend, a neighbor, a relative—or even you—could be one of the many, many Americans who face this plight each year.

The average annual cost nationally for nursing home care is about $62,000, or $171 per day for total costs, including semi-private room and board, drugs and medical supplies.[2] A ten-hour shift for a home health care aide through a home health agency costs even more at $180.[3] (In some parts of the country, the cost is an astronomical $385 per day, or over $140,000 per year, and home health care can easily cost $27+ per hour.)[4] Using the growth rate of 5.8% projected by the Center for Medicare and Medicaid Services for the period 2001-2011, these costs will at least triple in the next 20 years.[5] This means that the 50-year-old of today can expect to spend at least $320,000 (or over $720,000 in the highest cost areas) per year if he or she requires nursing home care at age 80. If both spouses need the care, the figure grows astronomically.

Do you find these projections hard to believe? The average semi-private nursing home cost in a 1990 Nashville, Tennessee cost survey was $60. That figure in the same survey published in January 2001 was $117—an average yearly growth rate of 6.25%.[6]

The average caregiving time in a national home care survey was five years.[7] The most recent national nursing home survey showed that although two-thirds of nursing home stays were three years or less, 13% of the patients stayed longer than five years.[8] Forty-seven percent of people over age 85 have some type of dementia, most commonly Alzheimer's[9] and an Alzheimer's patient can live an average of eight years and as many as 20 years.[10] A recent study showed that the annual cost to U.S. businesses for Alzheimer's patients and their working caregivers is $61 billion.[11]

> *Shaun Mabry, an independent insurance agent in Dallas, Georgia, knows these statistics firsthand. His grandmother spent 11 years in a nursing home with Alzheimer's until her death at age 83. His knowledge goes far beyond an extended duration of care, however. He also watched as his grandmother went from a "saintly, churchgoing person to a sailor"—Shaun's term for someone with very salty language and a totally unfamiliar, very unpleasant personality, a heartbreaking transition for Shaun's family.*

This extremely high incidence of Alzheimer's coupled with 85+ being the fastest growing segment of the population make it easy to see why a national survey said that caregiving directly affects one out of four families in the United States, with just over 23% of all U.S. households containing at least one caregiver in the decade 1986–1996. Twenty-two percent of these caregivers provided care to two people and 8% to 3 or more![12]

> *Shaun Mabry's other grandmother provides an extreme example of multiple caregiving. At age 77, she is caring for her 78-year-old husband, Shaun's grandfather, who has*

Alzheimer's, her 50-year-old daughter who had a stroke last year, and three grandchildren, all two-years-old, born two months apart. Her mother is still alive in Florida at age 106!

Combine this staggering volume of caregiving with a 2001 survey that reports that two-thirds of Americans say it would be impossible to afford three years of long-term care at $60,000 a year and almost half said they couldn't pay for one year.[13] Given these statistics, it's no surprise that more than half of all nursing home residents run out of money within the first year and qualify for welfare (Medicaid).[14] As you can see, **long-term care is a family crisis for the 21st century.**

The Odds Are 1 out of 2

While the general population perceives the risk of needing long-term care services to be less than 25%, the actual risk for needing long-term care (either home care or nursing home care) is **greater than 50%.**[15] For most of us, that won't be nursing home care, as most people will never be in a nursing home. But home care can cost just as much or more than being in a nursing home, depending on how much you have.

The increasing demand for long-term care is the result of several factors—the aging population, a shortage of caregivers in the home due to women working and children locating away from parents, and technology that prolongs life for victims of heart attacks, diabetes and the like, only to make it that much more likely the survivor will experience a stroke and need long-term care.[16] All these factors combine to make the need for long-term care escalate at a dizzying pace.

An Aging America

Consider this rapidly unfolding social phenomenon. In a little over 200 years, life expectancy has doubled in this nation. In frontier America only one in ten people could expect to see age 65, and today 10% of people over 65 have children over 65![17] Today, almost 80 percent of Americans will live past 65 and life expectancy is another 15 years for men and 19 years for women.[18] Currently, there are 35 million people over 65, some 13% of the population. By 2030, the number will grow to 70 million, or one-fifth of the population.[19] There are 72,000 Americans over the age of 100, and that number is expected to triple in 20 years.[20] And the real shocker? Based on projected trends, the Social Security Administration estimates that 12 million Americans alive today will bring in the NEXT century in 2100![21]

You may have heard of Jeanne Louise Calment of Arles, France, who lived longer than any human on record. She was 122 when she died August 5, 1997. She never lost her saucy personality, evidenced by a humorous anecdote from an interview she did at age 115. The reporter asked her how she saw the future, and she replied without hesitation, "Short, very short!" She was wrong, though, wasn't she? She still had another seven years to go![22]

One-third of all Americans (77 million people) were born between 1946 and 1964—a group we affectionately named the baby boomers. We are about to exchange that well-worn term for another. Instead of having a baby boom, we are on the verge of the country's first Senior Boom. One out of four people in the United States is already over 50. Movies and television over the last twenty years reflect this phenomena: *Space Cowboys, Grumpy Old Men I* and *II, Diagnosis Murder, Murder She Wrote, Matlock,* and the Oscar-award winning *Driving Miss Daisy.* Magazines like *Senior Golfer* and *Modern Maturity* enjoy readerships of millions. You can frequently see 50+ models like Lauren Hutton in fashion magazines and talent acts like Rod Stewart, The Rolling Stones and Tina Turner are still rocking audiences around the world.

In Akron, Ohio you can go to work for Mature Services, a successful employment agency specializing in workers in their 50's, 60's, 70's, and up to meet the community's demand for older workers. It's a win-win: Older workers tend to already have a pension and Medicare, so working part-time without benefits creates a low-maintenance, highly trained labor pool for grateful employers. *National Geographic* reports that by 2005, workers 55 and over will comprise nearly 20 percent of the workforce.[23]

Ray Crist, a 102-year-old professor of environmental science at Messiah College in Carlisle, Pennsylvania was honored as America's Oldest Worker in 2002 by Experience Works, a national nonprofit organization that provides training and employment services for mature workers. Fifty-two other older workers over 100 years old were also honored.

We have managed to prolong life by overcoming a variety of contagious diseases, by utilizing sophisticated technology with heart, cancer and other catastrophic health conditions, and by taking better care of ourselves with diet and exercise, etc. While our great-grandparents would have been glad to have seen 60, Americans are now seeing ninth and even tenth decades. Dr. Robert Goldman, founder of the National Academy of Sports Medicine and the American Academy of Anti-Aging Medicine predicts that "quantum leaps in medical technology will see many baby boomers and their children reach the grand old age of 120!"[24] Unfortunately, as one author put it, we may be buying ourselves a slow death, because long life doesn't guarantee long quality of life.[25] In reality, the longer we live, the greater the chance we will need long-term care. *And the people who take care of themselves the best will probably need long-term care the most, because they won't die suddenly of a massive heart attack or stroke—they'll just wear out slowly!*

All Ages Need Long-Term Care

Since long-term care is defined as care that simply takes care of people who are in chronic conditions with little or no progress, it can happen to people at any age. Few people realize that regular health insurance will not pay for a thirty-two-year-old who winds up in a coma with no progress after an automobile accident. A tragic example is "Superman" actor Christopher Reeve who is almost totally paralyzed after a horseback riding accident at age 43. After almost a decade of battling Parkinson's disease, thirty-eight-year-old actor Michael J. Fox announced his departure from his popular television series *Spin City* to spend time with his family and raise money to search for a cure. This adds him to the list of well-known victims of Parkinson's disease—a list that includes Muhammad Ali, former three-time world heavyweight champion, and U.S. Attorney General Janet Reno.

Forty-five-year-old Bob Dancey is paralyzed from the neck down after suffering the same spinal injury as actor Christopher Reeve, after getting knocked off his surf board by a wave and striking his head in shallow water.[26]

It's very important to realize that long-term care is not just an issue that affects older Americans. Over 40% of Americans receiving long-term care are *under* 65 years old.[27] Only about ten percent of nursing home patients are in this younger age category[28]—the rest of the younger people are cared for in the community, mostly at home. Younger people need long-term care for automobile and sporting accidents, disabling events such as brain tumors, and disabling diseases such as muscular dystrophy, multiple sclerosis, Parkinson's and Lou Gehrig's disease. The federal government estimates up to 2 million Americans suffer some kind of traumatic brain injury each year—50,000 die, but 70,000 to 90,000 are disabled.[29] One-third of the 700,000 stroke victims in the United States each year are under 65![30]

At 52, Marla Everett* leads a simple life in a one bedroom Airstream trailer on her sister's wooded property in Tennessee. Unable to drive or work fulltime, Marty still suffers residual damage from an aneurysm at age 30 that left her unable to care for her two young sons. Fortunately, her ex-husband kept the boys. She lived off and on with parents and friends for several years, then finally alone, until enough of her memory came back to support herself with occasional landscaping or domestic work. She tried a full-time job with the state food-stamp program once, but found the stress too much to continue. Combating a constant struggle to remember lyrics, her musical talent also landed her an occasional low-paying gig with local bands. Today she barely plays her guitar due to an increasing lack of concentration. She also battles agoraphobia.

Families In Transition

Another factor contributing to demand for long-term care is that the caregiving system in the home has experienced a significant

*name has been changed to protect anonymity

decline. The bulk of caregiving is performed by women, and two-thirds of the caregivers are employed full or part-time.[31] Dr. Ken Dychtwald, an expert on the aging population, projects that the average 21st century American will actually spend more years caring for parents than children.[32] A well-known think tank for employee benefits predicts that by 2005, elder care will replace child care as the #1 dependent care need, as more than 37% of U.S. workers will be more concerned with caring for a parent than a child.[33]

Often the need to care for aging parents coincides with the need to pay college tuition for dependent children. Even if college tuition needs are satisfied, the "empty nest" becomes filled with frail parents or in-laws and saving for retirement is compromised. The conflicting priorities for the ways both money and time are spent have to be carefully weighed. A national study found that 12 percent of families who help elderly relatives dip into college funds and 26 percent use money allocated for retirement to pay for this care.[34]

Also, children now live extended distances from parents as our society becomes increasingly mobile. The impact of this mobility? Today, less than 15% of people over 65 live with relatives. The rest live independently, either alone or with a spouse.[35]

Of course, it is only fair to recognize that sometimes we simply cannot be cared for at home due to physical or mental conditions, even when someone is at home to provide the care. An Alzheimer's patient, for example, usually requires 24 hour care, which is extremely difficult for most families to manage.

Forty-one-year-old Julie Endert of Murfreesboro, Tennessee, quit a job she loved with the local school system to care for her aging father, who suffers from dementia. Her decision to quit was undoubtedly influenced by her husband and two teenaged children, one in college. Her only respite time to do grocery shopping and run other errands is made possible by an adult day care program that cares for her father three days a week.[36]

Since almost half of nursing home patients have some type of dementia,[37] this may help explain why a national survey showed that 55% of severely disabled people with both spouse and children receive some formal care.[38] So even though you and your children may want you to live with them when you need long-term care, it's just not always possible when you need continuous caregiving 24 hours a day. On the other hand, if you require lighter caregiving, a home health aide may be able to stay with you for an eight- to ten-hour shift while your children work. This assistance can postpone and even eliminate entering a nursing home for some people.

But few Americans realize how precious a few hours a day of home health care can be to a distraught, exhausted caregiver until they are in the situation themselves, and even fewer Americans realize that those few hours which may mean the difference between sanity and insanity, to quote one caregiver, are not covered by health insurance. Consider these real-life situations:

A rare neurological disorder called primary lateral sclerosis has robbed Gary Nulty at age 43 of his ability to walk or feed himself. His 41-year-old wife and childhood sweetheart, Vivian, has lost 30 pounds in the past year trying to care for him and their two daughters. An environmental geologist, Gary had excellent health insurance, but just as with other health insurance plans, it will not pay custodial care. Gary's mental capacity is excellent, but he cannot even pick up the telephone or right himself in his wheelchair if he slumps over. Vivian manages a part-time job, which she desperately needs since Gary can no longer work, so that he is alone only about two hours a day until their 11-year-old daughter gets home from school. Otherwise she provides him with constant care, since he can't even go to the bathroom by himself. Vivian is desperate for help. "There's 24 hours in a day," she said. "I'm willing to work 20. I'll take four [hours of help]. That's the minimum I need to not go insane.[39]

*Actress Emma Thompson (*Sense and Sensibility, Howard's End*) helped her mother and sister care for her actor/writer/ director father Eric Thompson, after his stroke in her teens. With a combined family effort, he was able to live until age 52, which meant about 15 years of caregiving. The good side, Emma notes, is it caused her and her sister to skip the normal teenage rebellion years because her mom needed so much help.*[40]

The Caregiver's Glass Ceiling

As of 2002, there are an estimated 6.2 million majority-owned, privately-held women-owned firms, accounting for 28% of all privately held firms in the United States. Women-owned firms employ 9.2 million people and generate $1.15 trillion in sales. Between 1997 and 2002, the number of women-owned employer firms grew by 37% — four times the growth rate of all employer firms![41] It's fair to say, women have made monumental progress in the workforce in the last twenty or so years. What can stop them now?

Caregiving can slow and even stop many talented women. Since two-thirds of primary caregivers are women and over half of these women work outside the home[42], caregiving may turn out to be the biggest threat to the women's movement in this century. The amount of time that caregivers spend caring for someone who needs help with two or more Activities of Daily Living (bathing, dressing, transferring, eating, etc.) is 40 or more hours per week. Sixty-four percent of these most intense caregivers had to make changes to their daily work schedule to accommodate caregiving. Ultimately, 30% had to give up work entirely, 15% took early retirement and 26% had to take a leave of absence.[43]

How do you function in an executive position or grow your own business with those kinds of hours?

Technology and Lifestyle

A benefit from enhanced medical technology is increased survival from medical disorders such as heart attack, diabetes, brain tumors . . . things that 30 years ago people would have died from. A downside to prolonging life for these individuals is they may now be at risk of stroke. Stroke is the third leading cause of death in the United States, but is the #1 cause of disability.[44]

And as much as we like to think that we have healthier lifestyles, obesity is rampant in America. The risk of stroke is exacerbated when obesity is combined with one or more health problems such as high blood pressure or high cholesterol or lifestyle choices such as smoking or lack of exercise.

Competing with the highest demand for long-term care ever experienced in the United States is the low level of financing available for long-term care.

Together, conventional health insurance and Medicare pay barely over a fourth of the nation's bill for home health care and nursing home care of almost $150 billion annually, and that small payment is mostly for short-term care that lasts less than three months, not long-term care which can last several years.[45]

Why Doesn't Private Insurance Pay More?

Conventional insurance, including individual and group health insurance for people under 65 or retiree health plans restrict coverage to **SKILLED CARE**—and that's why conventional health insurance does not pay for long-term care, as was illustrated in the real-life stories of younger people needing long-term care in the previous section, *Families in Transition.* HMOs, the new managed care programs for people of all ages, are even more restrictive than regular health insurance and pay very little for home health and nursing home care.

What is meant by skilled care? *Skilled care has nothing to do with how sick you are.* A person can be totally paralyzed or in a coma and still not be receiving skilled care, in which case private insurance will not pay. Skilled care is care to get you better— IVs, dressing bedsores, providing physical and speech therapy after a stroke, etc. Once progress stops, however, the care is "chronic," or "maintenance" and is no longer skilled. Daily cleaning of a colostomy drain or a catheter, or even oxygen or respiratory therapy needed regularly for an emphysema patient, are examples of care that is not skilled. Here's a real-life example of a family who did not understand the concept of skilled care at all:

The once-vibrant 39-year-old Guity Manteghi lies in a nursing home in Walnut Creek, California. Her heart failed with no warning in January, 1996, cutting off oxygen to her brain and sending her into a coma. After eight weeks, the insurance plan said she no longer needed skilled care and stopped payment to the nursing home the next day. With two young daughters, the 50-year-old husband, Maleck Manteghi, doesn't know where to turn. "I thought I had the most adequate health coverage you could buy," he is quoted in the Contra Costa Times as saying, "When you get insurance, who knows what custodial care is, what skilled nursing is?"[46] (Editor's note: Mrs. Manteghi passed away in 1997.)

Why Doesn't Medicare Pay More?

Medicare can approve up to 100 days in a nursing home per benefit period but patients usually collect less. Why? Because Medicare pays only for *skilled* care and the majority of nursing home care is not skilled. In fact, **the average number of days that patients collect for Medicare for nursing home care is only about 23 days,** because most people don't have very many days that qualify as skilled care under Medicare guidelines.[47] Medicare pays nothing for eight-hour shifts at home and only pays home health care visits, when some skilled care is being done. An Alzheimer's patient is a classic example of someone who needs little or no skilled care and would likely not benefit from Medicare. Medicare supplements and Medicare HMOs won't pay a dime unless Medicare pays first, so they won't pay either.

Due to recent legislation to promote cost containment in the Medicare program, restricted access to Medicare payments for home health care and nursing home care is expected to continue. (See *Medicare Benefits* in **Appendix A.**)

As you can see, a 30-year-old with private health insurance is not much better off for long-term care than an 80-year-old on Medicare.

You Can't Count on Medicaid

Medicaid, the federal and state welfare program for the poor, pays 40% of the annual long-term care bill, and at least a fourth comes out of private pockets—maybe yours.[48] It is easy to get Medicaid if you're almost broke. About a quarter of the patients paid for by Medicaid did not enter a nursing home on Medicaid.[49] They spent down, exhausted their resources, then became Medicaid patients as described in Chapter 5.

You should beware of anyone who advises you to transfer assets to your children or trusts in order to qualify for Medicaid. Children may misuse or lose the assets (i.e., in the event of a lawsuit or divorce). Also, many nursing homes no longer accept Medicaid patients because a Medicaid patient represents a financial loss to most nursing homes. A Medicaid patient is at the mercy of the system and may have nowhere to go if nursing homes are full, or may have to go to a rural area if urban homes are full. It's not unusual for a Medicaid patient to be placed hours away from family members. Denise Gott, an Ohio insurance agent, related this story of a family who found this out the hard way:

I conducted a workshop for a AAA Club in Canton, Ohio in September of 1999. I had finished the program and was taking questions. A young gentleman in his late thirties sitting with his wife raised his hand and asked if he could share a story. He proceeded to explain to the crowd of about 40 people that both his mother and father were in nursing homes; they had been there for 2 and 4 years respectively. Unfortunately for this family, they spent nearly all of their assets on the first two years of nursing home care for the father. When the mother went into the nursing home, the family home was sold, the remaining assets totaling $50,000 and the income that the mother was receiving from her retirement plan were all redirected to the nursing home to pay expenses. All funds ran out after the first year and a half that Mom was in the facility. To make matters worse, both parents are now on Medicaid. The saddest part of this story is that due to the fact that there are very few available Medicaid beds in Ohio, Mom lives in a nursing home in Cleveland while Dad lives in a nursing facility in Toledo, a full two hours away. The couple lives in Canton, making visits to both nursing facilities difficult, both physically and emotionally.

Also, in most states, being on Medicaid means being in a nursing home. The option for home care is eliminated because most Medicaid programs pay very little for home health care and nothing for eight hour shifts in the home. Less than 22% of home care costs in 2001 were paid by Medicaid.[50] To have options for home care, assisted living, adult day care, and to be able to choose any nursing home, a number of adult children are purchasing long-term care insurance policies for parents, even though financially the parents will either immediately or in a short time qualify for Medicaid.

> *A 69-year-old woman and her 30-year-old daughter certainly felt that way. When my client purchased her policy in 1993, her only asset outside of her home was a $30,000 annuity and she was a widow. Her daughter attended the appointment and expressed how strongly she felt about keeping her mother off Medicaid if at all possible. We all cried around the kitchen table with the emotion of planning ahead for something no one wanted to happen, but if it did, that night's action of purchasing a long-term care insurance policy would make the way a lot easier by providing money to pay for choices that would make nursing home care a last resort.*

Prospects for Government Help

Because of the serious nature of the long-term care crisis, some people advocate that a new benefit program be created by the federal government to pay for long-term care for everyone.

The answer to this question arrived January 1, 1997 with a new health care reform package that provides tax incentives for individuals and employers to purchase long-term care insurance. Basically, the government is saying there isn't enough money for any type of public program to pay for long-term care for everyone.

Consider that in 1945, in the early days of the Social Security program, there were 42 workers for each retiree. In 2000, the ratio was 3.4 workers for every Social Security beneficiary. By

2030, the ratio is projected to decline to 2 to 1.[51] With costs of home health and nursing home care almost $150 billion per year and expected to increase at least five times in the next 30 years, from where will the taxes originate to pay the tab? We are already spending 44 percent of total federal revenue for net interest but primarily for the "Big Three" entitlements - Social Security, Medicare and Medicaid - and if we do nothing, the U.S. Comptroller General predicts it will be nearly 75% by 2030, and that's without a new prescription drug benefit under Medicare![52] A long-term care program for the 77 million baby boomers could be a larger entitlement than these existing programs, which are already facing insolvency.

Tax Incentives for Long-Term Care Insurance

To encourage Americans to plan for their own long-term care needs and to ensure that long-term care insurance has great value for the future, the federal government has passed legislation to provide tax incentives for long-term care insurance policies issued on and after January 1, 1997,* and to standardize the benefits somewhat to offer the best value for the consumer. For "qualified" policies that meet these criteria, the following apply for 2003:

▲   Benefits will not be taxable income, as long as benefit payments above $220 per day (or the monthly equivalent) do not exceed the actual cost of care. Conversely, benefit payments in excess of $220 per day that do exceed the actual cost of care will be taxed as income.

---

* Policies purchased 12/31/96 and earlier were "grandfathered" and are considered qualified for the new tax treatment. Also, this section is not intended in any way to give tax advice. Please see your tax advisor for a final determination of how this legislation applies to you.

▲ A portion of a long-term care insurance premium based on the age of the policyholder now counts as a medical expense. Since medical expenses in excess of 7½% of adjusted gross income are tax deductible, this means that a portion of your long-term care insurance premium will help you reach that threshold and may even put you over it to receive a tax deduction. Here are the amounts that count in 2003, and they are allowed to increase each year based on the medical Consumer Price Index:

Age at End of Taxable Year	Amount of LTC Insurance Premium That Counts as a Medical Expense:
40 and younger	$250
41–50	$470
51–60	$940
61–70	$2,510
71 and older	$3,130

While younger people generally don't have enough medical expenses to gain a tax deduction from long-term care insurance premiums, this provision may make it worthwhile for older Americans to itemize.

Let's look at an example. Bob is 74 and Martha is 71. Their long-term care insurance premiums are $3,200 and $2,800 respectively. Based on the above table for the year 2003, Bob gets to count $3,130 as a medical expense and Martha gets to count her entire premium, for a total of $5,930. They have an additional $4,500 in other medical expenses for retiree health insurance premiums and their deductibles and co-payments for that plan. Together with the $5,930 deduction for their long-term care insurance premium, they have $10,430 in total medical expenses.   For tax purposes, they can count the amount of medical expense that exceeds 7½% of their adjusted gross income. Their income is $50,000 and 7½% is $3,750, so they can count $6,680 in medical expenses.

They also have $1,500 in charitable contributions and $2,900 in state and property taxes, so their total itemized deductions equal $11,080. Since this exceeds the standard deduction of $9,850 for 2003, they are better off to itemize. Combined with the personal exemption of $3,050 per person that everyone is entitled to, their total deductions equal $17,180 ($3,050 x 2 = $6,100 + $11,080). Therefore their taxable income is lowered from $50,000 to $32,820. If they just took the standard deduction of $9,850 and didn't itemize, their taxable income would be $34,050. The difference of $1,230 in a 15% tax bracket means they will save $184 in income tax. (See chart on next page)

Proposed legislation in Congress will make the age-based amounts of long-term care insurance premium an "above-the-line" tax deduction, which means your taxable income would be lowered by the premium amount allowed for your age and you wouldn't even have to itemize your tax return. The premium would no longer be subject to the 7½ medical expense threshold. You can help get this important piece of legislation passed by writing your congressional representatives. Tell them we need an "above-the-line" tax deduction for long-term care insurance premium in order to make it more affordable for all Americans.

	With LTC Insurance	Without LTC Insurance
Adjusted Gross Income for Married Couple	50,000	50,000
Personal Exemptions	6,100	6,100
Itemized Deductions:		
Medical Expense	6,680	750
Charitable Contributions	1,500	1,500
Taxes	2,900	2,900
Total Itemized	11,080	5,150
Standard Deduction	9,850	9,850
Total Deductions from AGI	17,180	15,950
Taxable Income	32,820	34,050
Marginal Federal Rate	15%	15%
Total Federal Taxes	4,923	5,107
Tax savings with LTC insurance = $184		

IRS-Approved Medical Expenses

It is surprising how many things count as a medical expense in the eyes of the IRS. A partial list includes: contact lenses, eyeglasses, hearing aids, false teeth, artificial limbs, wheelchairs, oxygen and oxygen equipment, prescription drugs and insulin, medical and hospital insurance premiums, cost and care of guide dogs or other animals aiding the blind, deaf, and disabled, medical fees from doctors, dentists, surgeons, specialists, and other medical practitioners, hospital fees, wages and certain taxes for nursing services for chronically ill people, transportation for needed medical care, stop-smoking programs, meals and lodging provided by a hospital during medical treatment. Contact your local Social Security office for a complete list.

▲ The allowable percentage of an LTC insurance premium is now treated like a health insurance premium for the self-employed tax deduction, which provides a first-dollar tax deduction of 100% for tax years 2003 and beyond. "Self-employed" means sole proprietors, partnerships and "greater than 2% shareholders" of S-Corporations and Limited Liability Corporations.

Mary owns an S-Corporation, so she is considered self-employed by the IRS. Her health insurance premium is $1,500 per year and her long-term care insurance is $1,000 per year. Based on her age of 48, she is allowed to add $470 of her long-term care insurance premium to her $1,500 health insurance premium for a total premium of $1,970, of which she will receive 100% as a first-dollar tax deduction for tax year 2003. Therefore, her adjusted gross income for 2003 will be lowered by that amount.

▲ Employers who are defined as a C-corporation will receive a tax deduction for any portion of the long-term care insurance premiums paid for employees, regardless of ownership in the company. Other employers who are self-employed (see previous bullet) must count a long-term care insurance premium as part of their salary. This makes it taxable income if they allow the premium to be paid by the business, and deductible only in the form of salary or compensation.

Premium paid for their employees, on the other hand, does not count as income for the employees and the entire premium is 100% deductible as a business expense to the company. Even though it has to be counted as taxable income, some self-employed owners want the business to pay the premium for cash-flow purposes, and they do still get the first-dollar self-employed deduction described in the preceding bullet, which is 100% for tax years 2003 and forward.

▲   Premium contributions made by all types of employers are not taxable income to employees.

▲   Long-term care insurance premiums are an acceptable medical expense under the new Medical Savings Account (MSA) experiment for the first 750,000 workers who set them up and who are either self-employed or who work for small businesses with 50 employees or less. The experiment ran through 2000 but has been extended through 2003. Hopefully MSA's will apply to companies of all sizes in the future. Check with a health insurance agent for specific availability in your area, but here's a general description of how it works (the dollar amounts cited below for 2003 are subject to change each year):

Individuals must purchase a deductible of $1,700-$2,500 and families must purchase a $3,350-$5,050 deductible. Individuals can put 65% of the deductible into the MSA, and families are allowed to deposit 75% of the family deductible. MSA's are funded with pre-tax dollars, and unused money at the end of the year grows tax-deferred—this is not a "use it or lose it" model. Funds can be used at age 65 for any reason without penalty. Prior to age 65, a 15% penalty is imposed for funds withdrawn for other than an acceptable medical expense (see a partial list of IRS-approved medical expenses on p. 22.) Premiums are typically 30%–50% lower than managed care or traditional health insurance plans. (The contribution can be made by either the employer or employee, but not in combination. Therefore some employers pay the MSA premium, then make a savings contribution into each employee's account equaling the difference between the MSA premium and the amount that would otherwise have been paid for health care coverage.)

▲ Qualified long-term care insurance premiums are eligible expenses in a Section 105 Medical Reimbursement Plan, which is available to small businesses and farms to deduct family health insurance premiums and medical, vision and dental expenses not covered by insurance. To be eligible, a sole proprietor must be married and be legitimately able to employ his/her spouse.

▲ The age-based LTC insurance premiums on p. 20 are an acceptable medical expense under a Health Reimbursement Arrangement, the employer-provided medical care expense plan in which reimbursements for medical care expenses made from the plan are exclud-able from employee gross income. (Rev. Rul. 2002-41)

▲   Unreimbursed expenses for "qualified" long-term care **services**—the cost of long-term care itself, not LTC insurance premiums—will count toward the itemized medical deduction, if paid on behalf of yourself, your spouse or your dependents. (See *Claims* in the next chapter for a definition of "qualified" care.)

This means unreimbursed "qualified" care, as well as long-term care insurance premiums that you pay for a parent, will count as long as you contribute more than 50% of your parent's support. The allowable portion of long-term care insurance premiums that count is based on the parent's age, not yours. Sometimes children form a "multiple support agreement," which means collectively they provide more than 50% of a parent's support. In this case, one child each year can take the tax deduction as long as that child individually provides at least 10% of the parent's support.

▲   Certain benefit provisions are required, which will be discussed in the next chapter, **Features of a Good Long-Term Care Insurance Policy.**

What is this law really saying? The message is loud and clear: **Take care of your long-term care needs with private insurance,** because there isn't enough money to create a new entitlement program for everyone.

Apparently many states agree. The following states have implemented state tax incentives for long-term care insurance: AL,

CA, CO, HI, ID, IN, IA, KY, ME, MD, MN, MO, MT, NY, NC, ND, OH, OR, UT, VA, WV, and WI. Several states offer private long-term care insurance to state employees. In 2002, the strongest message of all emerged when the Federal government introduced long-term care insurance to active and retired civilians, postal workers and military personnel and their qualified family members. With no employer contribution, the FLTCIP sends an especially strong message that Americans need to take personal responsibility for planning for long-term care since there isn't enough public funding to pay for it. (See *The Federal Long Term Care Insurance Program* on p. 129)

The Balanced Budget Act of 1997 implemented several drastic changes in the Medicare skilled nursing facility and home health benefit that will result in restricted access to these benefits for many years to come. (The Balanced Budget Refinement Act of 1999 and the Medicare and Medicaid Benefits Improvement and Protection Act of 2000 restored some of the funds that were taken away by the original act, but these were temporary measures. Medicare provisions totaling $3 billion were allowed to sunset October 1, 2002.[53] Legislation like this makes LTC insurance policies more meaningful as government shifts costs away from Medicare to private LTC insurance.

The Private Sector Solution

Over eight million Americans have turned to private long-term care plans to protect their assets.[54] Over 5,000 employers offer group long-term care coverage, and the number of employer plans in force has tripled in five years.[55] With new tax incentives for employers, this trend should continue to explode in the 21st century. Many buyers are in their 40's and 50's as most insurance companies target these age groups with attractively low premiums. Long-term care insurance is the private sector's solution to what an increasing number of people are calling "the *real* health care crisis" in the United States. Right now, private health insurance only pays 11% of long-term care costs, and welfare (Medicaid) is paying a little over 40%.[56] If private long-term care insurance doesn't flip those percentages for the baby-boomer generation, the tax consequences to all of us will be unprecedented. Sweden, for example, has a government-funded long-term care program -- and an average tax rate of over 50%![57] Most importantly, long-term care insurance for many represents the best opportunity to retain a sense of dignity—in the form of purchasing power—which all too many people who thought they were affluent have lost to the merciless financial demands of long-term care.

People who are not affluent also are buying long-term care insurance. About a third of purchasers in 2000 had assets less than $100,000, and an income of less than $35,000.[58] These statistics are not so surprising when you look at the most frequently cited reasons for purchasing the insurance—**to maintain independence and choice** by guaranteeing affordability of care in order to avoid depending on others for care. Asset protection was only the second most important reason for purchase.[59]

Based on today's current economic environment with lower investment earnings, it is strongly advisable for individuals to consider LTC insurance when their asset base ranges between $50,000 and $2 million, not counting the home and automobile. *Fortune* magazine reports:

In fact, for anyone with a household income ranging from $40,000 to $250,000 . . . there's long-term care insurance or nothing.[60]

A prominent national group of financial planners who specialize in wealth preservation and wealth transfer extends the asset figure to $5 million for its clients. Many people in the "several million" asset range plan to self-insure their long-term care risk. If you are in this category and self-insuring is a viable option, you may want to seriously consider the single premium/life insurance or annuity LTC policies, since these types of policies will pass any money you don't use for long-term care on to the beneficiary of your choice (heirs, church, charity, your estate, etc.), but if you do need long-term care, your dollars are maximized for long-term care coverage. (See Chapter Six, **Alternatives for Financing Long-Term Care**, for a description.)

It's difficult to box appropriate purchasers for long-term care insurance into a range of assets and income, because people buy things for different reasons. Consider this story:

David Miller, an Ohio insurance agent, sold long-term care insurance to a man who owns ten McDonald's. Mr. Miller was understandably shocked that this gentleman wished to purchase insurance and asked why. With tears in his eyes, the client pointed to an oil painting of a young man, and said, "That's my reason for wanting to do this. That is our son who was killed in an automobile accident 17 years ago and I want to make sure his children will be taken care of for college and someday buying their own homes, and I want to take care of my other kids and grandkids. I don't want one dime of my money ever going to a nursing home!" Mr. Miller understood quickly that here was a man who was determined to spend his money on his family just as much as it was in his control to do so and sold him and his wife long-term care insurance policies.

People with larger estates especially need to determine the amount of liquid assets that can be used upon demand. Otherwise a long-term care need may require the sale of investments or property at a loss. If you are "house rich and cash poor," you may want to consider a reverse mortgage, which will allow you to leverage the money from your home to pay for long-term care insurance instead of paying premiums out of the income you use for living expenses. (See **Reverse Mortgages,** p. 196.)

But think about it, affluent people don't usually spend their own money when they don't have to. Seventy-five percent of Americans over 65 have private health insurance in addition to Medicare, at a time when there is very little left to pay after Medicare pays. The average out-of-pocket expense, excluding home care and nursing home expenses, for someone with no supplemental insurance of any type to Medicare is less than $2,000.[61]

Affluent people also have homeowners' policies even when the mortgage is paid off, yet the odds of needing long-term care, at 1 out of 2 are much higher than losing a home. Just think, if you looked out of your window and saw one out of two houses burning in your neighborhood! We can't sleep at night without a homeowners' policy, yet losses for long-term care can be much greater than the cost of replacing our house. This is probably why an educational insert in a recent issue of *Fortune* magazine contained a highlighted block that said:

Long-term care is more important than car and homeowners insurance, since the statistical probability of using it is higher.[62]

People with assets greater than $50,000 who believe in Medicare supplement policies and homeowners' policies are well advised to consider long-term care insurance. This means that the $500,000 or more they might spend on long-term care could go to a favorite charity, church or be split among the grandchildren.

The following chart shows that a couple with $500,000 will spend down to nothing in less than five years, with only one spouse needing long-term care at $60,000 per year. Another consideration is that affluent people may be interested in around-the-clock home health care, which can triple these costs.

Year	Assets at Start of Year	Income Needs	LTC Expense	Investment Yield	Assets at End of Year
1	$500,000	$59,703	$60,000	$40,000	$420,297
2	420,297	61,494	63,000	33,624	329,427
3	329,427	63,339	66,150	26,354	226,292
4	226,292	65,239	69,458	18,103	109,699
5	109,699	67,196	72,930	8,776	21,652

Note: "Income Needs" is the portion of household income needs that the assets had been relied upon to provide and assumes annual inflation of 3%. "LTC Expense" is for nursing home care, based on a typical rate, and is subject to 5% annual inflation. "Investment Yield" is assumed at 8% annually after taxes.

People with lower assets are purchasing long-term care insurance to maintain independence and receive the same treatment as private pay patients if care is needed, or their children are buying it for them for the same reason.

Most of us can imagine the consequences of walking into a hospital or doctor's office with no health insurance! Mary Vanac of the *Akron Beacon Journal* writes, "That's why many legal and financial professionals are advising their middle-aged clients to plan for their own long-term care, as well as for the care of their parents, and such planning involves the whole family . . . Although it's a hard topic to broach, planning for long-term care can keep a tough family situation from becoming a disastrous one." [63]

> *Margie White of Plano, Texas, bought a long-term care policy at the advice of Joan Gruber, a Dallas financial planner who specializes in helping adult children with aging parents, after caring for both parents and losing her marriage as a result. "There was a definite lack of foresight and planning on my parents' part," she says. "I can understand. They never expected to live that long. But it took five or six years out of my life. I don't want my sons to have to do this for me."* [64]

Parents who buy long-term care insurance are taking care of their children far into the future. As many caregivers can attest, caregiving takes a phenomenal toll mentally, physically and even spiritually. Exhausted caregivers may become care recipients themselves, leading to a further, often preventable, drain on resources. Carol Levine, a nurse who has been caring for her husband, who is totally disabled and requires 24-hour care after a severe brain-stem injury in a car accident ten years ago, wonders,

"Does my managed-care company realize that during the past year it paid more for my stress-related medical problems than for my husband's medical care?"

In addition to accidents and other traumas that cause younger people to need long-term care, our rapidly aging population is putting insupportable demands on families in this century. Families simply can't shoulder this monumental burden alone. They have to have help.

LTC insurance means choices and options when that help is needed. For most of us, long-term care insurance may be the main key to not outliving our money—a very real fear that a number of people have as life spans continue to increase.

Chapter 2

Features of a Good Long-Term Care Insurance Policy

~~~~~~

E ffective January 1, 1997, new health care legislation required insurance companies to offer new "tax-qualified" policies that contain certain standardized benefits that were recommended by the National Association of Insurance Commissioners (NAIC), the regulatory body composed of all of the state insurance commissioners. Most of these guidelines were already being followed by the insurance companies and simply provide extra protection for the consumer to ensure high value for premium dollars.

Congress ruled that long-term care policies issued prior to 1/1/97 will count as qualified policies and do not have to be exchanged for a new policy. This includes employer-sponsored plans that were set up prior to 1/1/97, so that new enrollees after 1/1/97 have a "grandfathered" plan. However, if you materially change a policy that you purchased prior to 1/1/97, the policy will lose this "grandfathered" status and will no longer be considered tax-qualified by the IRS. An example of a "material change" would be adding an inflation rider, which is a benefit increase for additional premium. A partial list of changes that are not considered a material change and therefore would not affect the grandfathered status are:

▲ Premium modal changes; e.g., changing an annual payment to monthly payments.

▲ A class rate increase or decrease, which means a rate increase or decrease that applies to an entire segment of policyholders.

▲ Discounts that you receive after the original issue date of your policy due to other family members purchasing a policy; for example, if your spouse purchases a policy at a later date than you do.

▲ Premium decreases due to a reduction in coverage:

▲ Provision of alternate forms of benefits that do not increase the premium; for example, companies sometimes add coverage for new forms of care, like assisted living, without increasing your premium.

▲ Allowing policyholders to continue group coverage if the policyholder is no longer part of the group; for example, because he or she terminates employment with an employer who offered a group long-term care insurance plan.

(*Caution:* Some insurance companies are still marketing non-qualified policies. Please be aware that if you purchased a non-qualified policy in 1997 or later, there is a chance that the IRS will say that benefits received from the non-qualified policy will be taxable income to you. A quick way to see if your policy is tax-qualified is to check the first page of your policy. All tax-qualified policies issued after 1/1/97 have a sentence that says the policy is intended to satisfy the requirements for a tax-qualified policy. As you read this chapter, you also will learn how to check the benefits to ensure that you have a tax-qualified policy.)

To provide you with a measuring stick for value if you already have a long-term care insurance policy or if you are currently shopping for a policy, this section will explain each feature of a long-term care policy in detail to give you an in-depth understanding of how long-term care insurance works. If you are shopping for a policy, you will find helpful recommendations for appropriate benefit selections that you can apply to your situation. An insurance agent who sells long-term care insurance can help you finalize your choices.

Level of Care

Make sure the policy pays all levels of care—skilled or non-skilled—in any setting: the home, in an assisted living facility, in an adult day care center, or in a nursing home. (Sometimes you will hear non-skilled referred to as intermediate or custodial care. "Intermediate" means some skilled care but not every day, and "custodial" means no skilled care at all. These terms are old and just refer to non-skilled care.) Benefits should not be reduced because the level of care is less than skilled. Also, the policy should not require skilled care before non-skilled benefits are paid.

Home Health Care

More than 12 million Americans need some type of long-term care and only about 1.6 million are in nursing homes.[1] This means that most people are being cared for at home or in a community setting like assisted living or adult day care and that less than 15% of long-term care is in a nursing home. The number of nursing home patients has actually declined in recent years due to an increased availability of home health and other community services[2]. Understandably, coverage for home health is a popular addition to long-term care insurance policies. Here are some points to keep in mind when choosing a policy:

▲   The home health care benefit is not intended to be 24-hour per day home health care because around-the-clock care at home is more expensive than nursing home care. The home care benefit is most helpful when you have someone to live with; i.e. a "primary caregiver," such as a spouse, son, daughter, or other family member or friend. If you qualify for benefits under the policy, a home health aide can stay with you for an eight- to ten-hour shift while your primary caregiver is at work, for example. The aide can do the heavy caregiving, such as giving you a bath (something you may not want a family member to do), washing your hair, changing your bed, preparing meals, supervising your medicine, and maybe light housework and laundry. Then perhaps your family can take care of you at night. Even if you have a primary caregiver who doesn't work, no one can provide 24-hour care, so home health care can make it possible for your primary caregiver to get adequate rest.

A common statement is "I'm not buying long-term care insurance because I'm never going to a nursing home."

The irony is that a long-term care policy with great home health benefits may be the only thing that keeps you out of a nursing home by providing financial and emotional support to the people who care about you so they can keep you at home.

Judy Geck, Chattanooga, Tennessee, has seen both of her parents in long-term care. Her father had a major stroke six years ago, which was magnified by complications from the diabetes he had suffered with since his early 40's. After almost two years of caregiving, he passed away within weeks prior to being admitted to a nursing home. Her mother had a severe stroke three months after his death which, coupled with dementia, made it necessary for her to move in with Judy and her husband, Richard. Having a very solid position with the same company over fifteen years, Judy was loathe to give up her job for financial reasons, especially since she had a new grandchild to buy for! In order to keep her demanding job and get adequate rest at night, it has been necessary to have home health aides 16 hours a day, from 7 a.m. till 11 p.m. Judy sleeps in a chair four nights a week next to her mother and has an additional home health aide the other three nights.

It's been four years since the stroke, and her mother still can't be left alone. In addition to the dementia, she is unable to speak and cannot respond to verbal commands to move her body due to damaged motor skills from the stroke. Judy is home every evening and activities or even vacation ideas that would take her away from home have been out of the question. The time when the paid home care is cut back, and her mother's savings run out, could be as soon as a year.

▲   If you want to design your policy to pay 24-hour home care, work with your insurance agent to determine the cost for that service in your community so you can select a daily or monthly benefit that is high enough to accomplish your goal. This selection will substantially increase the premium.

▲   Home health coverage is automatically included in some policies—these policies are usually called "comprehensive" policies—and optional in other policies. If the coverage is optional and you really have no one to live with when you need care, you might consider putting your premium dollars toward a policy that covers just assisted living and nursing home benefits. This is called a "facility only" policy. You can use the additional premium of 30%-40% that you would have spent on home health benefits to buy a higher daily benefit to help you afford a private room, for example, or a longer benefit period such as five years or even a lifetime (unlimited) benefit period.

▲   There are a handful of policies that pay only for home health care with no coverage for assisted living or nursing home care. No policy can guarantee that you will never need nursing home care, so a policy that focuses 100% on home care may not be a wise choice. (It's doubtful that very many of the 1.5 million Americans in nursing homes today "planned" to be there!)

▲   The most valuable home health benefit pays the same level of benefit for home care as for nursing home care, or at least 75%-80%, instead of paying home care at a lower amount such as 50% of the nursing home benefit, as many policies offer. Why? Because an eight-hour shift of home health care costs almost the same as a semi-private day in a nursing home, and a ten-hour shift costs more.

▲ If the policy allows family and friends to provide the care, a lower benefit can work since these people may charge less. A policy like this has a higher premium which buys you additional flexibility. The policy will pay a monthly benefit to you, and you can hire anyone you like, or use the money for other needs because you don't have to provide proof of services or file claims in any way as long as you qualify for benefits. No surprise, additional flexibility usually brings additional responsibility. There are two cautions to this type of policy, which some refer to as a "disability-based" policy:

1) Since this is a cash benefit, the temptation can arise in a family to use the money for a purpose other than for which it was intended; i.e. why not buy a big screen TV for the whole family or a trip to Disney World?

2) If you hire caregivers and pay them yourself, the IRS probably will view you as an employer, which normally means you are responsible for the employer's contribution for the caregiver's Social Security, unemployment, Medicare and state employment taxes. The good news is these expenses are deductible medical expenses for you.[2] Your accountant can help you understand any employer responsibilities you may have in this capacity.

▲   Some policies, however, require care to be provided by a licensed home health care agency and do not pay for family and friends (unless the family member is a licensed health care professional and services are billed through a third party, such as a home health agency).

▲   Most new policies do not require that the care be provided through a home health agency. A policy like this will pay "professionals operating within the scope of their license," such as a Registered Nurse (RN) or Licensed Practical Nurse (LPN) who is freelancing his or her services. It is possible to find a policy that will pay for a family member, friend, or other person of your choice, except for an immediate family member, to obtain the necessary license or certification in your state to be paid as a freelancer. This can be helpful if you live in a rural area without a strong network of home health care agencies. (To find out more about your state's home care licensing and certification training program, call your state's Agency on Aging in **Appendix B** of this book and ask for the telephone number of your state's association for home health professionals.)

▲   To help family members who are willing to be free caregivers, most policies pay for caregiver training to teach a family member how to provide care in the most effective and safest way for both patient and caregiver; e.g., lifting techniques, patient positioning to avoid pressure sores, insulin injections, changing bandages, and so forth. The benefit amount for this feature is usually five times the daily benefit.

▲   The policy should not require a nursing home stay prior to providing coverage for home health care.

▲   The policy should pay for non-skilled care at home (bathing, dressing, helping the patient get in and out of bed, etc.) with no requirement for skilled care (care performed by nurses, physical therapists, speech therapists, etc.) Many policies also pay for companion care and homemaker services like cooking, cleaning and laundry.

Adult Day Care

The policy should cover adult day care in addition to home health care. A December 19, 2002 *Wall St. Journal* article[3] does an excellent job of pointing out the important role adult day care can play in the long-term care continuum. Aging adults who might otherwise succumb to isolation and depression if kept at home with an aide, sitter or companion can blossom in the socially more active setting provided by adult day care. It says there are about 3,407 centers now, well under the number needed in the country, and only 39% of them offer the extended hours that working caregivers need, but the industry is growing. Dollars from long-term care insurance policies will stimulate this growth as more families have funds to pay for adult day care.

The average cost of adult day care is cited at $56 per day, much less than assisted living at $500/week or home care or nursing home care which can easily reach $1,000 a week.

To locate adult day care centers, an eldercare locator can be reached at 800-677-1116 or www.eldercare.gov. Other resources are the National Adult Day Services Association (www.nadsa.org) local senior centers, Area Agency on Aging, and of course, the Yellow Pages.

Assisted Living

Sometimes people may need help with one or two Activities of Daily Living (ADL), such as bathing or dressing, but may not need total 24-hour care in a nursing home. Retirement centers and nursing homes often have special sections for people who need just slight assistance. This type of assistance is called "assisted living." This type of care also is available in some independent facilities such as personal care homes or bed and board homes. Assisted living is a popular form of long-term care because the setting is more like a home setting and costs less than nursing home care. (Compare the cost of about $82 a day for assisted living vs. $143 a day for semi-private nursing home care, both for just room and board—miscellaneous charges like drugs and medical supplies will bump both figures up about 20%.)[4, 5]

Assisted living is a wonderful alternative to nursing home care and consequently may be the fastest growing form of long-term care. To further explain the difference, nursing home residents typically need help with 3–4 Activities of Daily Living, while assisted living residents only need help with 1–2 ADLs and are certainly not bed bound. So assisted living provides a place that looks like independent living to many people who can't stay home anymore because they need extra help. Also, assisted living facilities make it possible for spouses to remain together, whereas nursing homes usually do not, at least in the same room.

Although many assisted living residents would not qualify for benefits under long-term care insurance policies because they don't need very much help, the National Center for Assisted Living reports that about sixty percent of assisted living residents need help with two or more Activities of Daily Living and probably would qualify.[6] Others may qualify under the cognitive impairment benefit trigger as half of the residents have significant cognitive impairment.[7]

Many policies provide assisted living benefits at a percentage of the nursing home benefit, and most newer policies provide equal benefits. Some policies pay assisted living under the nursing home benefit and some under the home health care benefit. If you want the assisted living coverage and can do without home care benefits, you can save about 30%-40% in premium by considering a "facility only" policy that covers only assisted living facilities and nursing homes.

Guaranteed Renewable

Policies today are "guaranteed renewable", which means the policy cannot be cancelled as long as premiums are paid, even if the insurance company stops selling long-term care insurance. However, if the insurance company you bought your policy from goes out of business you can still lose your coverage, so it pays to consider large, reputable companies (See *Rates vs. Ratings* on p. 72).

Beware of anyone who tells you not to worry about the stability of the insurance company because the state guaranty fund will bail you out. This is a special pool of money that assumes responsibility for claims of policyholders from failed insurance companies. You have to be "on claim", which means receiving benefits, on the date the company becomes insolvent to receive help from the guaranty fund. The guaranty fund is funded from assessments made by the insurance department on the other insurance companies in the state that sell similar insurance policies, and its liability does not extend to claims past the date of insolvency, so it doesn't pay for future claims.

In addition to meaning the policy can never be cancelled, "guaranteed renewable" also means the rates can increase only if they go up on a "class" basis, not just on your policy. A "class" is usually defined as a specific policy form number, perhaps in a specific geographical area. Some policies offer rate guarantees from three to 20 years. Additional premium is normally required for rate guarantees longer than three years. (See *Lowering or Eliminating Long-Term Care Insurance Premiums in Retirement* on p. 76.)

Prior Hospitalization

It is illegal today to sell a policy that won't pay nursing home benefits without a prior hospital stay. Many older policies were sold with this restriction, and their premiums are lower because these policies screen out a large number of claims. With strict hospital admission guidelines set forth by private insurance and Medicare, doctors can no longer admit patients just to satisfy an insurance requirement such as this. For example, Alzheimer's patients or the frail elderly usually do not need hospitalization. Less than half of the nursing home patients in the last major survey came directly from a hospital.[8]

Daily or Monthly Benefit

Some long-term care policies pay a flat amount per day or per month for nursing home care with selections ranging from $40–$500 per day or $1,000–$15,000 per month. Other policies will not pay more than the actual charge, regardless of the daily benefit you select. Many of these policies will allow the amount of daily benefit not used to carry over, thus extending your benefit period. Knowledge of local nursing home costs is helpful in making this selection. Costs nationwide average $171 per day for semi-private nursing home care plus prescription drugs and care-related supplies, both of which are usually billed separately from the room and board charge.[9] If home health care benefits are offered, the benefit ideally will equal the nursing home benefit but could be a percentage of the nursing home benefit, if it's at least 75%.

A policy with a monthly benefit will pay if home care for a particular day exceeds a normal daily benefit. For example, a therapist and an aide could come on the same day and charges for both might total $150. A $100 daily benefit would pay no more than $100 for that day, but a $3,000 monthly benefit would pay the entire $150 or whatever the daily charges are until the $3,000 is used up for that month. Some policies provide a weekly benefit instead of monthly for home care. This can be helpful because there is less risk of using up all of your home care benefit in the early part of the month. Some newer policies give you a weekly or monthly benefit if you use a care coordinator at claim time (See **Care Coordination** on p. 69).

Note: Some applicants intentionally select a benefit lower than area charges to merely supplement their assets and income. For example, someone with $2,100 in monthly income may figure that he would use $1,000 of his income to pay toward his care, which is the equivalent of $30 per day. He then might purchase a policy that will pay $150 per day, which results in a potential $180 per day available for an eight- to ten-hour shift of home health care or for semi-private nursing home care. Just be careful when you do this calculation to consider how much of your income you will need to pay your living expenses, which will be higher if you are receiving home care vs. nursing home care.

Some people prefer a private room and purchase a daily or monthly benefit to accommodate private room costs (i.e. $150+ daily benefit or $4,500+ monthly benefit). The daily benefit usually applies just to room and board. Additional charges, such as laundry, personal items (TV), hairdresser, etc. aren't covered, and miscellaneous charges like drugs and medical supplies can average 20% more than the room and board charges. Selecting a benefit fairly close to the average cost in your area probably means you will still be self-insuring some of the costs, especially if you have no other coverage for prescription drugs. Make sure the policy will pay the percentage of costs you expect so you won't be surprised when the bills start coming in.

The advantage of a policy that pays the daily benefit regardless of charge—an "indemnity" policy—is to provide extra money to pay for these incidental or miscellaneous charges. The advantage of a "reimbursement" policy, one that pays no more than the actual room and board charge, is to hold claim payments down and avoid rate increases for as long as possible. Since benefits above $220 per day (indexed annually) that exceed actual costs are taxable income, most newer policies are reimbursement; however a new trend is to offer an option to change a reimbursement policy into an indemnity policy for additional premium, or at least the nursing home portion of the policy. A hybrid policy (indemnity nursing home benefits and reimbursement home care benefits) can make it easier for a company to keep rates the same than a policy that is a totally indemnity policy.

Note: A few reimbursement policies allow any difference between the daily benefit you select and the room and board charge to be used to pay miscellaneous charges that are not personal items, such as drugs and medical supplies. A couple of policies even provide a specific benefit for drugs and/or supplies.

Benefit Period/Benefit Maximum

This is the amount of time (benefit period) or money (benefit maximum) the insurance company is obligated to pay benefits. This doesn't mean how long you can be covered. You might have your policy 15 years before you need to file a claim for benefits. After you file a claim, the benefit period is how long the insurance company is responsible to pay benefits. Benefit periods of one year to unlimited are on the market, although some states require benefit periods of at least two years to be offered. Common choices are three years, four years, five years, six years, or unlimited.

Most insurance companies express the maximum benefit in dollars instead of time. Benefit maximum usually means a specific number of days x the daily benefit you select. For example, a benefit maximum of 1,095 days x $100 daily benefit would be $109,500. This type of policy is usually a reimbursement policy. (See *Daily or Monthly Benefit* section.) If the charge happens to be less than your daily benefit, the remainder stays in this "pool of money" and extends your benefits. Instead of having the equivalent of a three-year benefit period, with the pool of $109,500 your benefits may last 3½ years or even longer. The insurance company won't stop paying benefits until all of the dollars are used. If you purchase inflation coverage, the daily or monthly benefit you purchased will grow each year. The overall benefit maximum usually grows as well. A few policies will allow it to grow without deducting any claim payments that were made that year. On the other hand, newer policies may sell you a dollar maximum, say $1 million, and that lifetime maximum won't grow with inflation coverage. Only the daily or monthly benefit you purchase will grow. Companies that do this are concerned about future rate increases and want to be able to plan on an absolute maximum payout for each policyholder.

After you have collected the maximum in benefits, the policy is over and you start paying out of your assets until you spend down to the qualifying level for Medicaid (welfare) in your state (Medi-Cal in California). A few states have a special program called The Partnership for Long-Term Care that allows you to shelter some of your assets and still qualify for Medicaid as a reward for purchasing a long-term care insurance policy. (See Chapter Four, **The Partnership for Long-Term Care**.)

To give you an idea of the nursing home usage, the following chart illustrates the length of stay information for patients in 1999:

Length of Stay	Percent of Nursing Home Patients
Less than 3 months	17.8%
3–6 months	10.1%
6–12 months	14.9%
1–3 yrs.	30.1%
3–5 yrs.	13.3%
5+ yrs.	13.8%

The 1999 National Nursing Home Survey, National Center for Health Statistics, U.S. Department of Health and Human Services, 6/02

The average nursing home stay is 2.4 years. Almost three-fourths of nursing home patients stayed less than three years and 42% of the patients stayed less than one year. However, 13% of the patients stayed longer than five years. Since women live longer than men, the majority of patients who need longer periods of care are women.[10] Accordingly, most insurance companies will allow couples to choose different benefit periods as a way of reducing premium; i.e. a husband might choose a three-year benefit period and a wife might choose a lifetime (unlimited) benefit period.

Most caregivers are women, so men typically are taken care of at home by a wife or daughter as long as possible before entering a nursing home.[11] When a husband buys a long-term care insurance policy for himself, it may be the wife who realizes the greatest benefit from his policy because it pays for the support she needs to keep her husband at home as long as possible.

Cynthia Coe, an insurance agent in Massachusetts, relates what she describes as "a career transforming experience":

I received a phone call from a local life insurance agent asking me to explain the benefits of a long-term care insurance policy his client had purchased from my insurance company when he lived in another state. He had recently suffered a debilitating stroke and moved back to our town to be closer to his children.

After setting an appointment with his wife, I arrived the next day to find one of the sweetest women I have ever met in tears, absolutely distraught and exhausted. The poor woman had lost 50 pounds and was absolutely frantic because Medicare was cutting back on home care for her completely disabled husband because his condition was "not improving." Her poor husband was confined to a wheel chair or hospital bed, could not take a step, and was unable to communicate with anyone, except in a strange, garbled speech that only his wife understood. She was adamant about caring for him at home, but it was patently clear that she needed more help. I contacted the company, which immediately sent out a really nice social worker who assessed the situation and authorized benefits on the spot. We were able to arrange increased care within the week.

Three or four weeks after all this, I was having a particularly horrible day. My company was insisting I do telephone solicitation. I would rather have walked over hot coals, been caged with hungry lions, or jumped out of a plane without a parachute—and I had encountered several really nasty individuals who had sworn at me and likened me to an unethical used car salesman. In other words, despite all my belief and conviction in the importance of long-term care insurance, I HAD HAD IT! I have the heart of a social worker, not a salesperson, and my fragile little ego was quivering. But, on the way home to tell my husband that I absolutely had to find another line of work,

I stopped at the bank to make a deposit, and who should be there but the wife of the client who was so disabled by the stroke. She spotted me, came rushing over, and HUGGED me with tears in her eyes and just gushed. "Thank God for you and your company, I don't know what I would have done without you." The new home care workers had given her back some semblance of a life, and she now felt she could cope with her life situation as a result of having such insurance.

Needless to say, I felt as if the Lord had given me a very strong message about the importance of the work I do. So, in spite of very regular set-backs, I still spend my days trying to spread the message about the emotional, physical, psychological and financial importance of this type of insurance—and I usually list "financial" last in this order, as the other three can eclipse everything else.

On the other hand, the wife or daughter may not have a similar caregiver, and may access benefits on a long-term care insurance policy relatively soon. The more help a family has to provide home care, the easier it is to keep a family member at home who needs long-term care. The money from a long-term care insurance policy may be the only thing that makes it possible to provide extended home health care for a loved one. In fact, a recent claims study said that in the absence of their long-term care insurance benefits, half of the people receiving home care benefits would be in a facility because they wouldn't have the support to stay home.[12]

How long a benefit period should you purchase? The answer is, as long as you can afford, without being uncomfortable with the premium. The average caregiving time in a national home care survey was five years.[13] People who take really good care of them-selves, for example, may be the very people who need long episodes of long-term care. They are less likely to suffer a major heart attack or massive stroke and instead, they just wear out! The healthier they are, the longer that can take—four years, six years, ten years!

If you purchase a longer benefit period, such as lifetime (unlim-ited), and you decide later that it's too much premium, you can always reduce your premium by reducing your benefit period, and that's fine with the insurance company. If you start out with a shorter benefit period and decide later you want to increase it, the insurance company will require you to start over with new medical questions, and you will have to pay premium for the longer benefit period at your new age. It's in your best interest to start out with the maximum benefit period you think you might want, because you can always come down. Increasing benefits later is more expensive, and if you have developed a health prob-lem, you may be ineligible for a benefit increase.

Restoration of Benefits

Some policies have benefit restoration periods that depend on being able to go a certain amount of time without using the pol-icy (i.e., a 5-year benefit period is reinstated if a patient is in a nursing home and goes home for six months at the end of four years and no claims are filed for the six-month period). The practicality of this feature is questionable as the policyholder must depend on someone else to provide care during the required period out of the nursing home.

Most restoration provisions, however, require that the patient be really better, i.e., that no care is needed for a six-month period, or at least that no expenses that would be eligible under the policy be incurred for six months. A benefit like this is good for people who have short-term problems, like mild strokes, and fully recover. Someone who needs care for an extended period of time and is unlikely to get better will not benefit as much.

> *I was enjoying a lovely dinner at the annual board meeting of the university I attended until the gentleman on my right asked me to divulge my line of work. He recoiled when he heard the words "long-term care insurance" fall from my lips. I was soon to find out why. His wife was just coming up on her fourth year in a nursing home with Alzheimer's disease. Simultaneously, the benefits of her long-term care insurance were coming to an end. The agent who sold the policy had told him a four-year benefit period would be enough, because the policy had this great restoration feature and if she used up the four years, she could get her benefits restored. Since she will never recover, this has turned out to be very bad advice.*

Some policies have separate benefit periods for home care, i.e. you could have five years for nursing home care and five years for home care, for a total of 10 years of coverage. If either side is used up, however, you can't tap into the other side to continue the benefits in the same location. In this example, if you use up the five years of home care benefits, and you still want to stay home, your remaining benefits will only be paid if you move to a nursing home.

Because of this problem, most policies today have "integrated" benefit periods. "Integrated" means that if you buy a six-year benefit period, for example, benefits will be paid however you need them—at home, in assisted living, adult day care, or in a nursing home.

Joint Policies

A new feature is catching on to make long-term care insurance policies more practical and affordable for married couples and even families. Four versions of this idea exist in current policy selections:

1) One version allows spouses to share a benefit period at a lower premium than two separate benefit periods would cost. (You and the insurance company are betting that both spouses won't need a lot of long-term care.) If one spouse dies without using all the benefits, the surviving spouse is entitled to the remainder of the benefit period at a reduced premium.

2) Another version has separate benefit periods, but for a little more premium it allows spouses to access each other's benefit period. For example, each spouse has a six-year benefit period. If one spouse uses only one year of benefits then passes away, the other spouse would have eleven years of benefits left.

3) A third version provides separate benefit periods of the same length for each spouse, then allows the couple to purchase an additional benefit equal to the primary benefit period to share first come, first served. For example, if the spouses each purchased a three-year benefit period, the insurance company would allow them to purchase a third three-year benefit period that both could access as needed.

4) The fourth version is a family policy. The applicant can select up to three immediate family members (parents, grandparents, siblings, children, stepchildren, grandchil-

dren and respective spouses) to be on the same policy. This means all share one deductible. (See **Elimination Period [Waiting Period]** in the next section and a single benefit limit.) The unlimited benefit period is not available. If the applicant dies or no longer pays the premium, ownership of the policy may be transferred to the next named family member on the policy. In this way, parents could pass any unused benefits on to children or other family members.

Elimination Period (Waiting Period)

This is the number of days that you have to pay until the insurance company pays benefits (like a deductible). Examples of choices range from 0, 20, 30, 60, 90, 100, 180, 365 or even 730 days. Some states won't allow waiting periods longer than 180 or even 100 days to be offered. Patients receiving skilled care may be able to avoid out-of-pocket costs during the elimination period because regular health insurance may pay some skilled care for people under 65 and Medicare can approve up to 100 days for skilled care for people over 65. The chances of qualifying for skilled care as long as 100 days are slim, however. (See *Why Doesn't Medicare Pay More?* on p. 15.)

The longer the elimination period, the greater the potential out-of-pocket costs. For example, someone with a 100-day waiting period who receives 30 days of skilled care reimbursed by private health insurance or Medicare, will be responsible for the 70 days of non-skilled care before the policy begins to pay. At a $180 charge per day, the out-of-pocket cost would be $12,600.

Caution: A few policies don't count days paid by Medicare or health insurance toward your waiting period. If you have a policy like the above example, you will be responsible for the full 100 days after the 30 days paid by Medicare. Ask the insurance agent to show you the section that addresses this point in the sample policy so you will have a clear understanding of how it works.

Some policies require the satisfaction of additional elimination periods if episodes of care are separated by longer than a specified time period, usually six months. For example, a patient may have a four-month nursing home stay and need to be admitted again four years later. Both admissions would require an elimination period before benefits could be paid. Most new policies require only one elimination period in a lifetime, regardless of how long it takes for you to accumulate the days of care that equal the waiting period. However, a few policies require you to accumulate the days within a certain time frame, such as six months or two years, in order for you to never have to satisfy another waiting period.

It is wise to ask how the elimination period is calculated for home health/adult day care. Some policies count only the days actual services are provided, so if the patient does not have home health care every day, it would take longer than 100 calendar days to satisfy a 100-day elimination period. Some policies count all seven days in a week toward the waiting period even though home care was only received on one day of that week. Others start counting when the physician first certifies the need for long-term care (See *Claims* on p. 89). Policies of the latter type may not require charges to be incurred during the elimination period. In other words, family members could provide the care until the elimination period is satisfied. For additional premium, a few policies allow days of care for one spouse to count toward the waiting period for both spouses.

Beware of policies that have choices of only 0 or 100 days, with no choice in between, especially if the agent is urging you to choose a 0-day waiting period, which means first day coverage and no deductible. This sounds great on the surface, but if that insurance company sells most of its policies without a deductible, it will most likely be paying out claims much faster than other insurance companies. Again, this sounds good, but it means the company will be much more apt to need rate increases to stay in business than other companies.

A new trend in long-term care insurance is to waive the elimination period for home care benefits or even for all benefits if you agree to use a care coordinator provided by the insurance company (See *Care Coordination* on p. 69). Or a policy may just not have an elimination period at all for home care benefits, regardless of whether a care coordinator is used or not - another consumer-friendly benefit that can have an adverse impact on that company's future rate stability as no deductible normally increases both the frequency and dollar payout of claims.

In addition to home care, many companies don't require the waiting period to be met prior to receiving benefits such as hospice, respite care, caregiver training, Emergency Response System, and so forth. (See *Miscellaneous Benefits* on p. 67).

Mental Conditions

If you qualify for a policy, most policies will cover mental conditions only of an organic nature, such as Alzheimer's and other dementias. Look for a written statement about coverage for "cognitive impairment," which includes Alzheimer's disease. Most policies will not cover mental conditions of a non-organic nature such as schizophrenia, manic-depressive disorders, etc. Tax-qualified policies will cover severe cognitive impairment that causes the patient to be a threat to himself or others. For example, if you have high blood pressure and you can't remember to take your medicine when you are supposed to, this could certainly make you a threat to yourself. A few new policies cover all types of mental conditions.

Waiver of Premium

In most policies, premiums are waived after a specified time, usually expressed in days of benefit payments. For example, older policies typically waived premiums after 90 days of nursing home benefits. Some policies do not require these days to be consecutive. Newer policies also waive premiums when you receive assisted living, home care or adult day care, and most policies waive premiums on the first day of benefits. The premium only comes back in most policies, if you get truly better, which means you don't incur any eligible expenses, for six months. A new trend is the "dual waiver", which means the premium is waived for both spouses when one spouse starts receiving benefits. This can be an optional benefit that requires additional premium, or it can be built into the policy at no additional charge.

Inflation Protection

The policy should have some provision to help the benefits keep pace with inflation because home care and nursing home costs are projected to grow 5.8% compounded each year according to the Centers for Medicare and Medicaid Services.[14] Here are two common inflation options offered by insurance companies:

Cost-of-Living (also called Future Purchase Option)

This method allows policyholders to buy extra coverage at certain intervals (i.e. every one to three years) equal to the percent of increase due to inflation. Typically, the amount of coverage offered is determined by changes in the Consumer Price Index and is offered as long as you haven't filed a claim in a certain period of time. Some states and some policies require those offers to continue even if you have had a claim. Some policies discontinue the offers if you turn them down four times, or even one time.

The problems with this method of inflation protection are:

1) The amount of the offer is usually determined by the overall Consumer Price Index, which is lower than the medical component of the CPI, neither of which are keeping up with actual increases in long-term care costs. CPI in 2002 was 2.4% for all items and medical CPI was 5%, according to the Bureau of Labor Statistics. A few policies offer a minimum 5% annual offer.

2) The offers are priced at your attained age, which means the age you are when you accept each offer, not the age you were when you purchased the policy.

Guaranteed Annual Increases

Other policies allow the policyholder to purchase a rider that automatically increases the daily or monthly benefit by 5%—compounded or simple—for life. A few charge a lower premium and allow the daily benefit to compound annually just until the benefit has doubled. A few policies offer other percentages besides 5%, such as 3% or 4%. (Remember that the Centers for Medicare and Medicaid Services project growth at 5.8%.) Also, some policies allow the daily or monthly benefit to grow each year, but the overall lifetime maximum doesn't grow. Whichever factor is used, policies annually increase only the benefit, not the premium with an exception: a few policies have a "step-rated compound benefit increase" which means both the benefit and the premium increase at a compounded rate of 5% annually.

Proponents of the cost-of-living method argue that since medical costs can increase faster than 5% per year, policyholders with the inflation rider may experience a shortfall at the time of a claim, which would result in increased out-of-pocket costs. However, when the cost-of-living offers are determined by the overall Consumer Price Index, these offers are even more inadequate. People who like the 5% guaranteed annual increases method best say that the periodic premium increases under the cost-of-living method are unmanageable for most budgets, and the extra benefit usually can't be purchased if there is a claim. Someone who has a five-year claim has a frozen daily benefit throughout the claim. (As noted above, some states and some policies require the future purchase offers to be made during a claim.) The 5% automatic annual increases occur even if there is a claim, and— a pleasant surprise—the premium is usually waived. (See *Waiver of Premium*, p. 59.)

The biggest problem with the cost-of-living method is that it has a lower premium when the policy is first purchased, but over the long run can cost much more than purchasing the rider that guarantees a 5% automatic annual increase. For example, a 54-year old starting out with an annual premium of $869 could be paying $31,380 per year by age 87 if she accepted offers equal to 5% compounded, or a total of $206,598 in premium over those

33 years. By comparison, she could have purchased the policy with a rider that increases the benefit 5% compounded each year for the rest of her life at an annual premium of $1,764. By age 87, she would only have paid $58,212 in premium over the 33 year period vs. $206,598 with the cost-of-living method!

If you are considering the future purchase offer method, be sure and ask the insurance agent to show you a printout of the projected premium increases over your lifetime. The insurance companies who offer this method of inflation protection are required to include that information in the proposal. If the proposal shows significantly lower premiums at older ages than I have just illustrated in this section, check to see what the benefit has grown to under the FPO method. For example, one policy's version of FPO is to allow the daily benefit to increase by 15% of the original amount every three years. So a $100 daily benefit would grow $15 every three years. By age 87, the benefit would be only $265 vs. $502 with the 5% compound rider. Premiums at age 87 are lower with this version but the obvious tradeoff is that the benefit is a little over half of what it would have been with the compound rider.

If you elect the 5% rider instead of the cost-of-living method, you may be wondering if you should choose the 5% simple (if your state allows that option) or the 5% compounded rate of growth. "Simple" means the benefit grows 5% of the original amount and doubles in 20 years. "Compounded" increases grow faster, doubling in 15 years, because the 5% increase is based on the previous year. Walter Newman, a North Carolina insurance agent, tells how this benefit really paid off at claim time:

In 1992, a locally prominent man bought a policy from me with a $100 daily benefit. After some persuasion, he agreed to *add the 5-percent compound inflation rider. He was a wealthy individual and wanted to buy a plan without inflation coverage, intending to self-insure the difference.*

Three years later he was diagnosed with Alzheimer's and was cared for at home for the next two years. When his family could no longer manage him, he was admitted to a skilled nursing facility. Thanks to the inflation coverage, he is currently receiving benefits of $141 per day, instead of the original benefit of $100 per day. The cost of his care is $5,500 a month, leaving a difference of $1,138. His family tells me his Social Security check just about makes up the difference, so all his other income and assets are available to his family. If he hadn't bought the inflation rider, the difference would have been almost $2,500!

Obviously, the younger the applicant, the better sense the 5% compounded makes, since long-term care costs are projected to triple in the next 20 years.[15] Anyone 70 and younger is well advised to consider the 5% compounded inflation method because people are living so long today. People in their 70's may want to choose 5% simple to get a lower premium. The example on page 65 shows that the growth for the first 10 years is very close to the 5% compounded rate.

Another way people age 75 or older can protect against inflation is to buy a higher benefit than the average cost of care (i.e. $200+ per day at age 78, or $350+ per day for high cost areas like New York, Massachusetts, Alaska, etc.) to build in extra benefit to accommodate future costs.

An interesting question for a 75-year-old is should she buy what the benefit will grow to in 10 years or opt for a benefit that reflects current costs with a simple or compound inflation rider? The majority of purchasers in this age range don't buy the inflation riders. At age 75, the premium is about the same for a lower benefit with the 5% compound rider vs. a benefit that reflects what the lower benefit will grow to in 10 years —say $150 with 5% compound inflation vs. $240 without the rider. (Simple inflation is about 10% less premium at age 75.) The benefits will be close between simple and compound by year 10 of the policy. If the person lives longer than age 85, the benefit gap widens — $30 a day apart by age 87, $40 apart by age 90, and so on.

But listen carefully. What about the person who bought $240 with no inflation coverage? What happens if that person lives longer than 85 years old? The benefit is stuck at $240 and does not grow at all.

> *At age 79, Spencer Jones had his foot in a cast when he bought his long-term care insurance policy from me in 1989 due to a fall in the yard. I looked at the twinkle in his eye and listened as he, his daughter and son-in-law (who were also purchasing policies in their early 50's) told me how active Mr. Jones normally was. My gut-level instinct said to me, "This man is not old." I sold him the 5% compound inflation rider.*
>
> *I just got a call that Mr. Jones is ready to file a claim for assisted living benefits at age 92! He was walking a mile a day until a few months ago when he suffered a heart attack. My instinct had served me well. He was a young 79-year-old and didn't need his policy for 14 years. Was that compound inflation rider a wise decision for him? You decide.*

It's the old "pay now or pay later" problem if you are thinking about not buying inflation coverage because it increases the premium so

The following chart shows a comparison of a $100 daily benefit with a 5% simple growth vs. a 5% compounded growth.

Year	5% Simple	5% Compounded
1	$100.00	$100.00
2	105.00	105.00
3	110.00	110.00
4	115.00	116.00
5	120.00	122.00
6	125.00	128.00
7	130.00	134.00
8	135.00	141.00
9	140.00	148.00
10	145.00	155.00
11	150.00	163.00
12	155.00	171.00
13	160.00	180.00
14	165.00	189.00
15	170.00	198.00
16	175.00	208.00
17	180.00	218.00
18	185.00	229.00
19	190.00	241.00
20	195.00	253.00
21	200.00	265.00
22	205.00	279.00
23	210.00	293.00
24	215.00	307.00
25	220.00	323.00
26	225.00	339.00
27	230.00	356.00
28	235.00	373.00
29	240.00	392.00
30	245.00	412.00
31	250.00	432.00

Pay Now or Pay Later

Age: 65, married
Daily Benefit: $150
Waiting Period: 20 days
Benefit Period: Lifetime (Unlimited)
Home Health: Same benefits as nursing home

Client #1: Daily benefit grows 5% compounded annually for life

Client #2: Either no inflation or policy has future purchase offers, but client doesn't purchase future amounts

Annual Premium: $4,286.52 x 20 years = **$85,730**

Annual Premium: $2,313.36 x 20 years = **$46,267**

ASSUMPTION: Client #2 has a long-term care need in 20 years at age 85. Daily cost in 20 years: **$450/day* or $165,000**

Client #2's deficit = $300 per day ($450 cost –$150 daily benefit purchased) X 365 days = $109,500 shortfall first year. (Shortfall grows each year as cost continues to grow with inflation.)

Client #2 "saved" $39,463 in premium over the twenty-year period, but applying the savings to the first year shortfall still leaves $70,037 coming out of Client #2's pocket and $109,500+ for years two and forward.

QUESTION: Did Client #2 Really Save?

*Annual growth rate of 5.8% according to the Centers for Medicare and Medicaid Services, 2002.

much. You can wind up on welfare immediately if your benefit is far below the cost of care when you have a claim and you can't make up the difference out of your pocket. Look at the example on page 66 before making your decision.

Miscellaneous Benefits

The better policies today have a variety of benefits in addition to those already described.

Alternate Plan of Care—If your doctor and the insurance company agree that you can be taken care of at home adequately, most policies allow money taken from your benefits to provide enhancements to your home, such as handrails, wheelchair ramps, shower stall improvements, etc., or even an emergency response system to make it easier for you to stay home. This benefit is also used to pay for new long-term care services as they are developed. This is a great feature, because without it, the insurance company would have to amend your policy to pay for new services, a process that can take a long time.

Caution: Beware of anyone who tells you the "alternate plan of care" benefit means it is not necessary to purchase home health coverage when you buy your policy. You may be able to get some home care assistance under the "alternate plan of care" provision, but it is by no means a defined benefit for home care, assisted living or adult day care. If you want home care benefits, make sure that the "home care" block is checked on the application, and that your policy specifically states that you have benefits for home care, assisted living and adult day care. (The real intent of the "alternate plan of care" provision is to find ways to provide care that is less expensive than nursing home care.)

Hospice—Most long-term care insurance policies cover hospice, which is care for terminally ill people to keep them as comfortable as possible and provide respite care to family members. Most health insurance policies also cover hospice and Medicare has a virtually unlimited benefit for hospice. Tax-qualified policies are not allowed to duplicate Medicare payments, so when would the long-term care policy pay? Medicare's inpatient respite care benefit for hospice is only five days per stay and the family may need a longer period of respite care. Medicare's home care benefit for hospice won't pay eight-hour shifts or longer except in a crisis situation. Long-term care insurance will pay eight-hour shifts indefinitely as long as benefit triggers are met and benefit maximums are not exhausted.

Respite Care—a specific benefit to give the primary caregiver a break. The break could be a few hours off to go shopping or a week or two for a vacation. This benefit is usually paid at home but the better policies pay also in a nursing home or assisted living facility to cover the 24-hour care that will be needed if the caregiver needs to be away several days. Benefit triggers (Activities of Daily Living or cognitive impairment) usually must be met to access the respite care benefit, but the elimination period often does not have to be satisfied.

Homemaker Services—a benefit that pays for personal caregiving services such as cooking, cleaning, laundry, shopping, telephoning and transportation when a benefit trigger is met. Some policies will pay homemaker services only when you are receiving other home care services, such as care provided by a home health aide, nurse or therapist.

Alternate Payer Designation (Third Party Notification)—The policyholder has the opportunity to designate someone else to get a copy of a lapse notice in case the policyholder doesn't pay the premium. Take advantage of this opportunity because this feature protects against policies lapsing if policyholders develop a mental or physical problem that makes them unable to pay the premium.

Impairment Reinstatement—If the policyholder allows the policy to lapse due to a cognitive or physical impairment, the insurance company will reinstate the policy with appropriate premium payment within a specific time period, such as five, six, or nine months. Without this provision in the policy, an insurance company is under no obligation to reinstate your policy if you miss the grace period by even one day. Tax-qualified policies are required to have a minimum reinstatement period of five months.

Bed Reservation—If you have to go to a hospital during a nursing home stay, this benefit will pay to hold your bed at the nursing home. Without this benefit, your family would have to pay or the nursing home could give the bed to someone else. Since nursing homes are 87% full nationwide,[16] most nursing homes have waiting lists. Without a bed hold payment, you would have to find another nursing home if you lost your bed to someone else and the nursing home was full. Some policies provide the bed-reservation benefit when the patient leaves the nursing home to visit family and friends, and most policies also pay to hold your bed if you have to go to the hospital while you are in an assisted living facility.

Care Coordination—This benefit pays a third party who ideally doesn't work for the insurance company or the provider of care to manage your care and report regularly to your family, although some companies require you to use care coordinators affiliated with the insurance company and even raise or lower the benefit level by whether or not you use the recommended care coordinator. The "care coordinator" would perform services like helping to determine the best place for you to receive care, i.e., at home, in an assisted living facility, adult day care or a nursing home and making sure you are getting the best care possible.

A care coordinator is especially helpful when children or other family members don't live nearby, because the care coordinator can give "care reports" regularly to the family members. Some companies want policyholders to use this benefit so much that they don't reduce the benefit maximum whenever you use it, which makes it a "free" benefit. They feel this way because they know a care coordinator will help you get the most out of your long-term care policy by using your benefits most effectively and efficiently. Some companies require the use of care coordinators before paying benefits at all, but you may have the option to hire a private care coordinator if for whatever reason you don't wish to use the free care coordinator provided by the insurance company. For example, a separate benefit for a private coordinator might be 25 X the daily benefit per year. This benefit payment would be subtracted from your lifetime maximum.

Survivor Benefit—Some policies will not require a surviving spouse to pay premiums after the death of a spouse if the death occurs after the policy has been held a specified period of time with no claims on either spouse, usually 10 years, but it could be less. For example, if the death occurs prior to the 10th year, the surviving spouse would not have a premium waiver. A few policies have a more liberal provision, however, and will waive the premium on the 10th policy anniversary of the surviving spouse. This feature is usually an option which requires additional premium, and a few companies offer both types of survivorship waiver.

Worldwide Coverage—Most long-term care policies will not pay outside the United States, but a few will pay worldwide, or in a list of specified countries, especially if you live in the U.S. at least six months of the year. Payment is usually made to you in U.S. currency and benefits may be reduced to compensate for the additional administration required to process claims with international complexities. Some policies pay in the U.S. and Canada.

Coordination with Medicare and Other Insurance—Tax-qualified policies are not allowed to make a payment if Medicare pays or if Medicare would pay in the absence of a deductible or coinsurance. Some companies interpret this provision in its strictest sense, i.e., if Medicare makes a payment on days 21-100 for nursing home care, the long-term care policy will not make a payment, even though you are responsible for a daily co-payment for those days. Most people, however, have coverage to supplement Medicare for the first 100 days—either a Medicare supplement, retiree plan or HMO. (This is further evidence that Congress intends long-term care insurance to pay for long-term conditions beyond three months, not short-term recovery conditions.)

A few policies coordinate with any other health insurance, which could include another long-term care policy but rarely does. Some companies police it another way: They won't sell you a daily or monthly benefit that, together with the policy you already have, would exceed the maximum daily or monthly benefit they offer.

Additional Benefits—Long-term care policies commonly include payment for a medical alert/emergency response system (usually $25-$50 a month), ambulance (4 trips per year) and medical equipment (30-50 times the daily benefit). Some of these expenses are picked up by Medicare and most policies will not duplicate Medicare's payment. These types of benefits are nice to have, but they shouldn't be given equal weight in the buying decision with the other benefits discussed in this chapter.

Rates vs. Ratings

Virtually all policies today lock in the rate at the time of purchase based on the age of the applicant and cannot increase premiums unless all policyholders in a certain class receive the same increase. Very few policies are "noncancellable," which means the premium can never increase. Some states will not approve a noncancellable policy because higher than anticipated demand for long-term care benefits could make it difficult for an insurance company to hold the rate. Initial pricing and the type of underwriting, liberal or conservative, play major roles in an insurance company's rate stability. "Underwriting" refers to the type of health conditions that an insurance company will accept when a person applies for coverage. Below-market rates, liberal underwriting (i.e., accepting a lot of people with major health problems), and a small asset base make future rate increases almost a certainty.

Another cause for rate increases is when an insurance company sets rates based on an assumption that a significant percentage of policies will lapse (cancel) before a claim is filed. For example, if a company assumes that 15% of policies will terminate and only 3% do, you can see that many more claims will be payable than the company originally thought.   Higher than projected claims can make a rate increase necessary. This has happened to a number of companies because long-term care insurance policyholders typically hang onto their policies. Why? Because the premium is determined by age and sometimes by health status. So it's expensive to buy a new policy at an older age, and the policyholder may be charged more or declined due to health conditions. This is why some policyholders who wish they had purchased a higher benefit just buy an additional policy to go with what they already have instead of replacing their original policy with a brand-new policy at an older age. If you think you need additional coverage or if you're just not sure, ask a long-term care insurance agent to help you make the best decision for your situation.

Do not even think of shopping for the cheapest long-term care insurance policy you can find. Some companies that started out with extremely low premium (i.e., half to two-thirds of other companies' rates) have already experienced terrific rate increases, whereas most companies have not experienced a rate increase for policies issued in the past decade, if ever. If a company is having rate increases now, what will happen to it when the baby boomers begin needing long-term care? This point can't be overemphasized. There have been cases of premiums not just doubling, but increasing 800%! If the premium is significantly less than other policies, run, don't walk, away from it.

Some legitimate premium savings can be had by paying annual premium vs. a monthly bankdraft. A few policies don't charge extra or may even reward you with a small discount for bankdraft, but annual premium is the least expensive payment with most companies. Loads of 9% for monthly and 5.5% for semi-annual are common. Rather than pay the load, many people pay annual premium out of their investments. A common

Financial Quality Ratings of Major Rating Agencies

DESCRIPTION OF RATING	STANDARD AND POOR'S*	MOODY'S	A. M. BEST	FITCH
SUPERIOR	AAA	Aaa	A++ A+	AAA
EXCELLENT	AA+ AA AA-	Aa1 Aa2 Aa3	A A-	AA+ AA AA-
VERY GOOD			B++ B+	A+ AA-
GOOD	A+ A A-	A1 A2 A3	B B-	BBB+ BBB BBB--
ADEQUATE	BBB+ BBB BBB-	Baa1 Baa2 Baa3		
FAIR			B B-	
BELOW AVERAGE	BB+ BB BB-	Ba1 Ba2 Ba3		BB+ BB BB-
MARGINAL			C++ C+	
FINANCIALLY WEAK	B+ B B-	B1 B2 B3	C C-	B+ B B-
HIGHLY VULNERABLE OR NONVIABLE	CCC+ CCC CCC-	Caa1 Caa2 Caa3 C Ca	D	CCC+ CCC CCC- CC C
UNDER STATE SUPERVISION			E	DDD
IN LIQUIDATION			F	DD

*"pi" following a rating indicates that it is based on quantitative analysis of public financial data vs. data provided by the insurance company

"w" following a rating means the rating is under watch and subject to change

Ted

strategy to find the money to pay a long-term care premium without taking it out of monthly living expenses is to convert a low-interest bearing fund such as a CD or money market account to a deferred annuity that will earn a higher interest rate tax-deferred. Most annuities allow you to withdraw 10% or so annually with no penalty or surrender charge and that makes a great funding vehicle for the annual long-term care insurance premium. Check with your accountant when you are setting up the amount to ensure that the withdrawals accommodate your tax needs as well as the long-term care insurance policy premium.

Married people get a break with spouse discounts ranging from as low as 7.5% to as high as 10%-35%. Some companies even give the discount if one spouse is declined for coverage due to a health problem or just doesn't apply for coverage in the first place. The insurance companies are betting that most married people will try to take care of each other as long as possible and not use as many claims dollars as single people without the live-in support system of a spouse.

Some of the spouse discounts extend to live-in siblings and a few are really a household discount that could include anyone living with you in a long-term situation. There are even policies that grant a 40%-50% discount, but don't get fooled by the size of the discount. Compare with a few other policies to decide if the premium is either too low or too high.

In addition to avoiding bargain basement premiums, it is not wise to consider a carrier with less than an A- rating by A. M. Best, the most well-known third-party rating service for insurance companies. Carriers with lower ratings may not have the financial strength to sustain long-term care coverage. It is also wise to ask if the carrier has assets in the billions, or if it is owned or reinsured by a company with assets that large.

"Reinsured" means that a larger company will pay claims after they reach a certain size. Some smaller companies are subsidiaries of billion-dollar companies; however, subsidiaries can always be sold. A major reason insurance companies have withdrawn from the long-term care insurance market is because they could not keep up with product design required by regulatory changes. Many smaller companies just don't have the financial flexibility to make these changes in a timely manner necessary to be competitive in the market. The chart on the previous page may help you examine ratings of companies. This gives an outline of the rating scales used by the four primary rating services. To get ratings on selected companies over the telephone at no cost, you can call Standard & Poor's at 212-438-2000, Moody's at 212-553-0377, and Fitch (formerly Duff & Phelps) at 800-853-4824. The A. M. Best rating can be obtained by visiting the reference section of your local library. Ask for the most recent Best's book, because it is published annually. Ratings are updated more frequently in the monthly magazine, *Best's Review.*

Lowering or Eliminating Long-Term Care Insurance Premium in Retirement

A few policies allow you to pay two years' annual premium when you purchase the policy in exchange for a lower lifetime rate; a 10%-25% discount for the second year forward. Or a policy may allow you to pay enough extra premium each year so that at age 65, your premium drops to half the original premium. These types of options can be meaningful for people who are trying to reduce expenses in their retirement years.

For people who don't want to pay long-term care insurance premium at all in their retirement years, there are "limited pay" policies that allow you to stop paying after 5, 10, 15 or 20 years or at age 65. A few companies even offer a single premium. States vary greatly on whether or not limited pay policies are allowed to be sold, as some insurance departments worry about limited pay policies having a potential adverse affect on rate stability. A long-term care insurance agent can tell you what is available in your state.

Rates (premiums) are the same for men and women, but are based on age. Policies are available for ages 18+, but most are sold in the 40-84 range. You're never too young to think about long-term care insurance—a 25-year-old can wind up in a coma after a car accident! If you haven't bought a policy by the time you are 40, pre-retirement ages (40's and 50's) are the best time to consider long-term care coverage, because premiums are lower and health is better at younger ages. Some people worry about buying at younger ages and experiencing rate increases that could make a policy unaffordable as they get older. A really new trend in long-term care insurance policies is to offer a limited pay option with a corresponding rate guarantee. For example, some companies offer rate guarantees from three years up to 20 years. A possibility with a policy like this is to purchase a policy that would be paid up in ten years along with a corresponding 10-year rate guarantee, a combination which provides you with a guaranteed premium.

The True Cost of Waiting

There are three solid reasons why you should ignore advice to wait until you are in your 50's or 60's to purchase a long-term care policy.

1. Anything could happen to you—see examples of younger people needing long-term care in *Long-Term Care Insurance is Not "Senior Citizen Insurance,"* on p. 124.

2. Because of Point #1, you may not be insurable. No amount of money will buy you a long-term care insurance policy after you develop a serious health condition.

Kathy Halverson's 41-year-old husband was diagnosed in 1986 with Parkinson's disease. An insurance agent in Wisconsin, he and Kathy "had it all" when it came to insurance policies— except long-term care insurance. Kathy had to learn the insurance business and take over his practice to care for him and provide for their family, especially their children's education. Her husband has since passed away, and Kathy has dedicated herself to getting the word out about how long-term care insurance can protect families. She repeatedly testifies, "We sold insurance for 31 years! We had it all . . . but not LTC . . . and after spending all our pensions, retirement, etc., to care for my husband and educate our children, we were 10 months away from seeking assistance [with Medicaid]."

3. You will pay longer, but you will pay less. The longer you wait, the more benefit you must purchase because long-term care costs are increasing so rapidly. Consider that a 30-year-old may wish to purchase a policy that

will pay about 2/3 of the cost. He could consider a $100 daily benefit for a premium of $440. If that person waited until 40 to purchase, he would have to buy a $150 daily benefit for a premium of $733 to accomplish his goal because the cost of care in 10 years will be about $220. At 50 years old, he is looking at a $250 daily benefit to pay 2/3 of the cost, for a premium of $1,682. Now multiply all three premium amounts to age 80 to see how much he would pay, depending on his purchase age. ($440 x 50 years = $22,000 vs. $733 x 40 years = $29,320 vs. $1,682 x 30 years = $50,460)

The difference is most dramatic from age 40 to age 50, but both of those ages become a moot point if he has a skiing accident at age 35 and becomes paralyzed for the rest of his life.

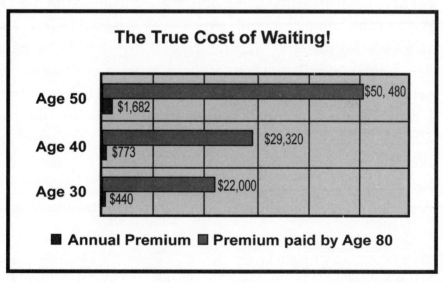

Consumer advocates advising you to wait until you're older to buy may change their advice when a younger sister or son is paralyzed from a car accident or rendered almost lifeless from a stroke or aneurysm.

Saving vs. LTC Insurance

Consider the following example of purchasing a long-term care policy versus investing in an IRA to fund long-term care. A man or woman invests $250 in an IRA at age 40 (after an initial investment of $500 to open the IRA). He or she continues to put $250 annually in the IRA until age 70½, which is the mandatory IRA distribution age. That consumer will have $26,519 ($250 each year compounded annually at 6½ percent). While that sounds like a tidy sum for a minimum investment, it will barely pay for six months of long-term care at today's cost of over $50,000, much less the projected cost of $275,000 per year in 30 years. Suppose the man or woman had decided to purchase long-term care insurance at age 40. For a little more than twice this $250 IRA investment, he or she can get coverage of $100 per day* for all benefits (home care, assisted living, adult day care and nursing home care) with a total benefit period of four years and a waiting period of only 60 days. Since this plan includes a 5% compound inflation feature, in 40 years at age 80 the daily benefit will grow to $670 per day. The annual married premium is only $545 per spouse. If neither spouse has a claim until age 80, the couple will have paid about $43,600 in premiums, and the total available benefit payout for one person will have grown to a whopping $978,200 or about $2 million for both spouses. And, don't forget that the premium stops when you are using the policy!

On the other end of the age spectrum, a 70-year-old couple may decide to save $6,415 a year, instead of spending that amount to pay the premium for a rich plan with a $150 daily benefit. (The

---

*A good plan that pays about two-thirds of the cost in most parts of the country.

other elements are the same as the plan described above for the 40-year-old.) By age 80, the couple will have saved $112,462 at 10% before taxes and investment fees, which sounds like a lot until you realize that the cost of care at that time is projected to be about $90,000 a year. Their savings at age 80 would pay for less than 1½ years of care for only one person. Had the couple bought the long-term care insurance policies, the $150 daily benefit would have grown to $233 per day by age 80, and the couple would have had an available benefit of $85,046 a year for each of them, and a potential payout of $732,192 for the next four years for two people. (If you do this calculation yourself, don't forget that the daily benefit continues to grow 5% compounded each year - $233, $244, $257, $269 and so on.)

Underwriting

Applicants for individual policies must qualify medically for long-term care coverage. Progressive conditions such as Alzheimer's, Parkinson's disease, AIDS, multiple sclerosis, muscular dystrophy, and psychiatric disorders are uninsurable. Applicants must be ambulatory to qualify for coverage, and must not need help with activities of daily living, such as bathing, dressing, toileting, transferring from bed to chair, eating or continence. Heart disease, cancer or one mild stroke can be acceptable risks after recovery periods of usually between two and five years, depending on the insurance company. Conditions such as hypertension are acceptable if controlled. Diabetes (contracted later in life, not during childhood) can be insurable if it is well under control, especially non-insulin dependent. Some companies will accept up to 60 units of insulin per day. People who take antidepressants for "situational depression" (death of a spouse, for example) usually can get a policy if their health otherwise is good.

The standard basis for underwriting is medical records from your doctor, instead of a physical exam, although some insurance companies are utilizing paramedical or face-to-face exams. A paramedical exam means a home health nurse visits you to check your blood pressure, height, weight, and to do a quick assessment of your overall physical and mental health. Some companies require a blood test for younger applicants to check for HIV. A "face-to-face" exam means that someone personally interviews you to be sure you are in good mental health. Many companies require this for applicants in their 70's and up. Underwriting commonly includes a telephone interview.

Caution: A carrier with "loose" underwriting may need future rate increases sooner than a carrier with conservative underwriting. Also, there are horror stories about carriers who do "post-claim underwriting" (i.e. medical history is thoroughly investigated **after** a claim is filed, which naturally results in a large number of denied claims.) This practice is illegal today, but be wary of a "yes/no" application with a policy issued to you in a very short period of time. It usually takes about 4–6 weeks for a policy to be issued, because the company is doing a good job of checking your mental and physical health to see if you qualify for coverage.

Some carriers will accept health problems if you pay a higher premium or will make alternative benefit offers. For example, you may be offered a four- or five-year benefit period instead of an unlimited benefit period, or a 90- or 100-day waiting period instead of a 20- or 60-day elimination period.

The most important thing about underwriting is that the younger you are, the better the chance you have to qualify for a policy. **No amount of money will purchase long-term care insurance for you once you are uninsurable due to a significant physical or mental health problem. Industry statistics show that 12 to 23 percent of people who apply at age 65 do not qualify for a policy and 20 to 31 percent at age 75.**[17] People are strongly encouraged to apply for long-term care insurance certainly by the time they reach their 40's and 50's (pre-retirement ages). (Of course, premiums are lower at younger ages and are locked in at the younger age unless there is a rate increase for an entire classification of policyholders.) On the other hand, don't assume you don't qualify for a policy without checking with some reputable insurance companies. You have nothing to lose and everything to gain to see if you can get a long-term care insurance policy.

Pre-Existing Conditions

An ideal policy will cover the policyholder from the effective date of the policy for all conditions disclosed on the application. Many policies have no restrictions at all for pre-existing conditions. A few policies have a 90- to 180-day waiting period for pre-existing conditions.

"Free-Look" Period

Policies issued today must contain a thirty-day period after policy delivery in which the policyholder may return the policy for a full return of premium if not satisfied for any reason.

Non-Forfeiture Options

For additional premium, some policies (more commonly non-tax qualified policies) may guarantee to return a specified percentage of premium to a beneficiary if the policy was not used after being in force a specified number of years. For example, a policy may guarantee to return a scheduled percentage of the premium if the policyholder terminates the policy or dies after the policy has been held at least five years. Some policies return all of the premiums if the policy is held at least 20 or more years. This feature usually costs about 30% or more in premium. The odds of using the policy and getting nothing back are very high, especially if you purchased home health care benefits. However, for even more premium, a few policies will return 100% of the premium to you, or your estate if you are deceased, after a specified number of years even if you have used the policy.

A partial daily or monthly benefit may stay in effect if the policyholder stops paying premium after five years or so. Known as a "reduced paid-up benefit," this feature has not been popular. Because the benefit is so potentially small at claim time, the policyholder is at risk to make up large balances from the very first day of care.

The policyholder must decide if these "money-back" features are worth the additional premium, or if a greater return on investment can be achieved by putting the difference in premium in a mutual fund or other type of growth investment, such as annuities, individual stocks and bonds, or life insurance, which is frequently used in wealth preservation and estate tax planning strategies.

A few tax-qualified policies have a cash-back nonforfeiture benefit but any refunded premium that was used for a tax deduction creates a taxable event upon its return.

More commonly, tax-qualified policies contain an option for a nonforfeiture benefit called a "shortened benefit period." You are not required to purchase it. If you do purchase it, the "value" will not be cash back as described above. Instead, the tax-qualified version of nonforfeiture guarantees that if you terminate your policy after three years in most states (after ten years in California), the insurance company must pay benefits equal to the amount of premium you have paid for any claim you have in the future, even though your policy is no longer in force.

For example, you paid $15,000 in premium and then decided to cancel your policy. If you had purchased this feature and you had a claim the day after you cancelled your policy, the insurance company would have to pay benefits at the daily benefit in force on the day you cancelled your policy up to $15,000. If your daily benefit were $100, the company would pay 150 days of benefits, or five months. If you had a claim 10 or 15 years from now, the company would still pay benefits of $100 per day up to $15,000. However, at future prices, this would probably pay for only a few weeks of care. This feature will cost you about 30% more in premium with most policies.

Many companies will give you the "shortened benefit period" nonforfeiture benefit, even though you didn't pay extra for it if your premium goes up past a certain predetermined point based on the age you were when you purchased the policy. For example, if you purchased your policy at age 60, the predetermined point might be 70%. So if you had a rate increase that took your premium to 71% more than your original premium, the insurance company would have to give you the "shortened benefit period" nonforfeiture benefit.

This is called "contingent nonforfeiture," because your receiving the benefit is contingent upon your premium being raised to the predetermined point that triggers the benefit. This means you could stop paying your premium and the insurance company would have to pay a claim for you at any point in the future equal to the premium you had paid in. Or, if you wanted to keep your policy in force without the additional rate increase, you could do so by accepting a reduced benefit offer that the insurance company is required to extend to you. Your benefit would be lowered, but you could keep the same premium and you would not have to pay the additional rate increase.

The National Association of Insurance Commissioners passed a new Long-Term Care Insurance Model Act in 2000, which requires all insurance companies to provide contingent nonforfeiture, because they believe it will act as a deterrent to unnecessary rate increases. Since companies don't want to give this benefit away without the additional premium it normally costs, this requirement serves as an incentive for the insurance companies to do everything possible to hold your premium down so it won't increase to the point that makes the company give you the "shortened benefit period" nonforfeiture benefit free. Each state has to pass the new NAIC model act into law, and many have done so (CA, ID, WI, MN, OK, PA). The majority of states plan to pass it because it has additional features that are expected to create a powerful deterrent to widespread rate increases in the long-term care insurance industry. In addition to requiring contingent nonforfeiture in every policy at no additional cost, highlights of the NAIC Long-Term Care Insurance Model Act of 2000 are:

▲ The 60/40 loss ratio requirement for long-term care insurance, which means that at least 60 cents of every premium dollar must go for benefits is eliminated. The NAIC thinks that's an incentive for rate increases - the higher the rate, the more money the other 40% generates for administrative costs.

▲ Rates must be actuarily certified that they aren't expected to increase.

▲ When a rate increase is approved by the state, 85 cents of each rate increase dollar must go to benefits and only 15 cents can go to administrative costs.

▲ The applicant must sign that he or she understands rates can increase.

▲ The insurance company has to disclose at time of sale the rate increase history on similar policies for the last 10 years.

▲ If a rate increase is approved by the state then turns out to be unjustified, the insurance company has to refund the money to the policyholders.

▲ If an insurance company exhibits a pattern of inappropriate rates, the insurance commissioner can prevent the company from doing business in that state for five years.

To find out if the NAIC LTC Insurance Act of 2000 has been passed in your state, contact your state's insurance department (see **Appendix B:** *Who to Call for Help*).

If your budget forces you to choose between nonforfeiture and inflation coverage, buy inflation coverage.

Assets

Individuals without assets outside a home and/or car are usually not candidates for long-term care insurance as they will quickly qualify for Medicaid. The National Association of Insurance Commissioners believes you may not be a candidate for long-term care insurance if you have an income less than $20,000 and/or assets less than $30,000, not counting your house and car. The exception to this thinking occurs when a family member (such as a child for a parent) purchases a policy to provide a higher level of care than that offered by Medicaid reimbursement and to ensure an option for home health care and other community choices such as assisted living or adult day care. Or, if nursing home care is needed as a last resort, the adult son or daughter wants the parent to have a complete choice of nursing homes. Many nursing homes have waiting lists and many admit only private-pay patients or patients with long-term care insurance as both types of patients can pay higher rates than the Medicaid reimbursement level. Since a number of nursing homes no longer accept Medicaid patients, people trying to enter a nursing home as a Medicaid patient sometimes have to go to a facility several hours away from the desired location.

Because of the poor choices on Medicaid, another exception to this rule occurs when people who are "house rich and cash poor" obtain a reverse mortgage on their home and use some of that money to purchase long-term care insurance to avoid being on Medicaid.

Some people with assets of $500,000 or more consider paying for their own long-term care. Sometimes the question is: How much of your asset base is liquid? Or will a long-term care need force you to sell property and/or investments at a loss because of poor market timing? **If you have less than $2 million in assets, it is very risky to try to self-insure your long-term care expenses.** Many financial planners advise clients with less than $5 million in assets to purchase LTC insurance.

Another reason people with significant assets buy long-term care insurance is to avoid confrontations with children over how much money is spent for long-term care. Others will purchase long-term care insurance to preserve privacy of financial records. Without a policy, private-pay nursing home patients usually have to show financial records to prove long-term payment capability. Finally, people with significant assets sometimes purchase long-term care insurance because they want money that would be spent on long-term care to go to other causes such as charities, church, their university alumni association or, their grand-children, like the gentleman who owned several McDonald's in *The Private Sector Solution* in Chapter One.

Claims

Prior to the tax-qualified policies that were introduced 1/1/97, most policies required your doctor to tell the insurance company that you needed help with at least two Activities of Daily Living (ADLs) before a claim could be paid, although a few policies only required help with one ADL. These are generally dressing, eating, transferring from bed to chair, toileting and maintaining continence. Some policies included bathing in the list. These policies have the potential to pay sooner, as bathing is usually the first ADL that people need help with. Two states added a seventh ADL to the list: Texas required "mobility" and California required "ambulating"—both just a measurement of being able to move around well. Help with ADLs can be "hands on," which means direct physical contact, but better policies also allow "stand-by" or supervisory assistance from the person who is helping you.

If you can physically perform the Activities of Daily Living but have to be told when and how to do them because you have a "cognitive impairment," the better policies issued prior to 1/1/97 will still pay your claim. Cognitive impairment is usually determined by a standardized test to determine deficiencies such as short-or long-term memory loss and general orientation (knowing one's name, place of residence, current political leaders, date, time, etc.) or bizarre hygiene habits.

The new tax-qualified policies sold after 1/1/97 changed the requirements somewhat to get a claim paid. Tax-qualified policies will pay a claim if you are expected to need help for at least 90 days with 2 or more of at least 5 Activities of Daily Living from this list:

bathing	dressing
toileting	transferring
eating	continence

This means that insurance companies can use a list of five or six ADLs, but almost all companies use the list of six. California requires insurance companies to use all six ADLs. The 90-day certification must be provided by a licensed health care practitioner (physician, registered nurse or licensed social worker). **The 90-day certification is not a waiting period.** If you have a 20-day waiting period, for example, your policy will begin paying benefits on the 21st day you need care as long as your doctor (or nurse or social worker) says that you are expected to need help with at least 2 ADLs for longer than 90 days.

The 90-day certification just assures that long-term care insurance will be preserved to pay for truly long-term conditions. Short-term conditions like fractures and mild strokes usually require skilled care such as physical, speech or occupational therapy. The previous sections *Why Doesn't Private Insurance Pay More?* on p. 14 and *Why Doesn't Medicare Pay More?* on p. 15, explain that conventional health insurance and Medicare pay only for skilled care and will therefore cover most short-term conditions, also called "sub-acute" or "post-acute" care.

The new policies also pay if you can do all of the Activities of Daily Living, but you need help due to a severe cognitive impairment. This means that you are cognitively impaired to the point of being a threat to yourself or others. For example, if you can't remember how to take your medicine appropriately and you have high blood pressure, you are probably a threat to yourself since by not taking your medicine when you are supposed to could cause you to have a stroke.

Non-tax-qualified policies are still being offered by some insurance companies, even though almost 90% of individual long-term care insurance policies purchased in 2002 were tax-qualified policies.[18] These policies do not require the 90-day certification, and may require help with only one Activity of Daily Living to get a claim paid. Instead of needing help with Activities of Daily Living or being cognitively impaired, some non-tax-qualified policies will also pay a claim if your doctor says you need care that is "medically necessary," which means that you need care for some type of illness or injury. Most policies like this allow only nursing home benefits to be paid if you need medically necessary care, but a few policies will allow home care to be paid as well. For example, you may be able to perform all of the Activities of Daily Living and you may not be cognitively impaired, but you can't completely take care of yourself because you have crippling arthritis in your back. If your policy pays "homemaker" benefits such as cooking, cleaning, laundry, etc., and pays for medically necessary care under the home health benefit, it could pay for homemaker services because your arthritis makes it medically necessary for you to have help. This "medically necessary" benefit trigger is not in the new tax-qualified policies.

Needing help with Activities of Daily Living, cognitive impairment or needing help because it's medically necessary are all called "benefit triggers," because satisfying one of these requirements is necessary to get the policy to pay benefits.

Tax-Qualified or Non-Tax Qualified

Some people say that the new tax-qualified policies are more restrictive than policies sold before 1/1/97 because of the required 90-day certification and because the medically necessary benefit trigger is no longer allowed. While this is true, there is a very good reason for the tightening up of the access to benefits.

A few years before this law was passed, long-term care policies began growing more liberal. Some policies would pay for any type of care at home or in a nursing home if help was needed with only one Activity of Daily Living, and the list included bathing. A growing number of policies also had the medical necessity benefit trigger. That made it easier to collect benefits, especially when it applied to home health care. A couple of policies were introduced that would pay nursing home care at the "policyholder's discretion"—that means you say you want to go to a nursing home and the insurance company pays your claim! Another policy that became extremely popular paid benefits if you just needed help with two "Instrumental Activities of Daily Living," such as cooking, cleaning, laundry, grocery shopping, telephoning for doctor's appointments, and the like. This brings to mind the old phrase, "If it sounds too good to be true, it usually is."

Why did this happen? The free enterprise system allows insurance companies the opportunity to sell more policies by offering policies with liberal benefit access. The combination of easy access to benefits, low premiums and liberal underwriting (which means that policies are issued commonly to people with significant health problems) means these companies could be more competitive in the marketplace and sell more policies. But these features that sound so good now mean bad news for the consumer in the long run in the form of future rate increases.

Congress saw this trend and stepped in. If the benefits are too easy to obtain, and if the policies are sold to people who have a high likelihood of using the coverage in a short period of time, the policies will pay out more than the collected premiums will support. This means that in the next 10–15 years when the claims activity is high, the long-term care insurance market could "crash" due to large rate increases that many consumers could not afford to pay. And, of course, smaller insurance companies can be hit harder and need bigger rate increases than larger, more financially solvent companies, and that's if they are even able to stay in business.

The taxation issue often is presented as the center of the controversy on whether to purchase a tax-qualified or non-tax qualified policy, i.e., will the IRS ever rule that benefits from a non-tax-qualified policy are taxable income?

Insurance companies are required to provide Form 1099-LTC to anyone who receives benefits from any type of long-term care insurance policy, tax-qualified or non-tax-qualified. The policyholder is required to report benefits paid from any type of long-term care insurance policy to the IRS on Form 8853, Medical Savings Accounts and Long-Term Care Insurance Contracts. The IRS matches up these 1099s with individual tax filings and sends letters requesting an explanation from people who failed to report benefits received from long-term care insurance policies.

Some insurance companies that actively promote non-tax-qualified policies promise to convert your policy to a tax-qualified policy if the IRS makes such a ruling. Read the fine print. Beware of advisors who explain nonchalantly that it's no big deal because the cost of your care is a deductible medical expense that will offset the taxable income. Not so! IRS Form 1040: Schedule A—Itemized Deductions plainly states in the block marked "Medical and Dental Expenses": *Caution: Do not include expenses reimbursed or paid by others.* Any amount reimbursed by a non-tax-qualified policy cannot be deducted as a medical expense.

Is the tax question the real issue or was Congress trying to use the tax liability as a velvet hammer to swing the market to tax-qualified policies with more reasonable benefit triggers? Even today, some people think the average ten percent additional premium charged for non-tax qualified may be inadequate to support the volume of short-term claims payable by these policies.[19] The measures Congress took in the 1996 health care reform legislation will function as *consumer protection measures* to ensure that long-term care insurance is there for us when we need it by restoring long-term care insurance to its original purpose, and that is to pay for long-term conditions. For this reason, there's an excellent chance that improved tax deductions for long-term care insurance premiums will apply only to tax-qualified policies.

Getting a Claim Paid

Regardless of which type of policy you buy, the better insurance companies have streamlined claims filing procedures. Most allow you to call an 800 number and notify the company that the need for long-term care has arisen. At that point the claims representative will assist you with the necessary paperwork and help you obtain the 90-day certification from the appropriate medical practitioner. Most companies will even pay for a care coordinator, which is someone to evaluate your needs on a local level to ensure that you get the appropriate level of care in the best setting for your condition, i.e., home care, adult day care, assisted living or nursing home care.

When claims are paid, the benefit checks are usually sent to you, but some insurance companies will pay the provider of care if you like, especially if the provider files the claim for you. If this is your choice, it's a good idea to get a family member or someone else you trust to audit the bills and claim payments every month to be sure you are being billed correctly for the services you receive.

Ask the insurance agent or company for references from satisfied policyholders who have been through the claims filing process. You can also ask the department of insurance in your state if any complaints have been filed about the insurance company. (See **Appendix B** for the address and telephone number of your state's insurance department.)

Policy Improvements

Ask your agent how the insurance company has treated existing policyholders when new policies or policy improvements to existing policies have been introduced. Were the existing policyholders offered the new policy or improvements for a period of time (90 days perhaps) without medical questions? Was premium charged at current age, or age when the policy was first purchased? The better companies don't treat existing policyholders like brand new applicants when new policies or policy improvements are offered.

Note: Policies purchased prior to 1991 may have benefit restrictions that need to be analyzed carefully to see if you need to upgrade or replace your policy with a new one. Some examples of restrictions in these older policies are:

▲ a "prior hospitalization" requirement before benefits for nursing home can be paid

▲ a "prior nursing home" requirement before benefits for home health care can be paid (if home care benefits are important to you)

▲ a requirement for skilled care before non-skilled care can be paid

▲ a lower benefit for non-skilled nursing home care than skilled care

▲ an exclusion for Alzheimer's disease and other organic mental disorders

▲ a 50% home health care benefit if care is required to be provided by a home health agency; home health care aides average $18 an hour ·when provided through a home health agency [20]

▲ no inflation coverage

Caution: Upgrading a policy that was issued before 1/1/97 may cause you to lose the "grandfathered" status that allows it to be a tax-qualified policy. You may be better off keeping the old policy and purchasing a new one on top of it, especially if you are trying to add inflation coverage. Your insurance agent can advise you on the best thing to do. Whatever you do, never cancel an existing policy until a new one is in effect.

Your Customized Benefit Selection Process

To simplify the benefit selection process, you just need to remember that there are six major choices that impact a premium. Here is each choice and a recommendation.

1) Daily or Monthly Benefit—Look at the average cost in your area and buy a daily or monthly benefit as high as you can afford—even $20-$30 more than the average cost in your area if you can afford it. Inflation is strong, and you'll probably need the extra benefit at claim time. (The national average cost for semi-private room and board is $143 per day. "High cost areas" like Alaska and New York City can easily cost $320 per day for semi-private room and board.)[21] A private room usually costs $10-$20 more per day than a semi-private.

If you are planning on self-insuring some of the cost, don't forget to account for the average of 20% or so for additional charges like drugs and miscellaneous supplies that are billed in addition to the room and board rate. Adding an additional 20% to the national average would bump it from $143 to $171 and the "high-cost area" from $320 to $385. Prescription drugs represent the biggest chunk of that, so if you have other coverage for prescription drugs you won't need to budget as much as 20% extra.

Some insurance agents may be able to provide you with a local cost survey, or you can call some providers listed in the Yellow Pages: assisted living facilities, home health agencies, adult day care centers and nursing homes. Your local Agency on Aging also may have this information. You can get that number by calling your state's Agency on Aging office. (See **Appendix B**, *Who to Call for Help*.) Another excellent resource for average cost information for home health care agencies and nursing homes is the MetLife Mature Market Institute at www.maturemarketinstitute.com.

Cost surveys normally will reflect just the room and board rate for nursing home care, not the additional charges for drugs and supplies. Most reimbursement policies will pay no more than the room and board charge and you are on your own for these miscellaneous charges. An indemnity policy that pays the selected daily or monthly benefit regardless of charge makes it possible to build in extra benefit to cover the extra charges. Most policies are reimbursement, because the theory is that people will use insurance more wisely if there is some cost sharing and a wiser use of benefits will help hold rates down in the future.

Here's an example of how to calculate a daily or monthly benefit for yourself: if you are considering a reimbursement policy and you are willing to pay about 20% of the long-term care cost, yet have no coverage for prescription drugs, you could consider a daily benefit of $150, if the average cost in your area for semi-private room and board is $140 - $150.

Some people purchase lower daily benefits, however, because they decide to put some of their income toward the cost of care, especially if they do not have a spouse and do not need their income to maintain a home. For every $1,000 of income you are willing to contribute to the cost of your care, you could reduce the initial daily benefit you purchase by $20-$30.

For an example of premium impact, the premium difference between a $140 daily benefit and a $100 daily benefit is, interestingly, about 40%.

2) Waiting Period (Elimination Period)—Most people will choose a waiting period (deductible) of 100 days or less. If you have over $1 million in assets (not counting your house and car), you can look at waiting periods of greater than 100 days. (Some states allow insurance companies to offer waiting periods as long as 180, 365 or even 730 days.) If you have assets less than $100,000, definitely choose a shorter waiting period like 20 or 30 days. If you have assets greater than $100,000 most companies offer waiting periods of 60 days, 90 days or 100 days. (The premium difference between 20 and 100 days with most companies is about 20%, so you have to contrast that with self-insuring the cost for an additional 80 days—not just at today's costs but at future costs.) Look at policies that require only one waiting period in a lifetime.

Assets * *Does not include house and car	Suggested Waiting Period (in days)		
	20–30	60–90	100+
Under $100,000	X		
$100,000–$500,000	X	X	
Over $500,000			X

A few policies do not require formal charges during the waiting period. If you are considering that type of policy, the question becomes "How long can I *wait* before benefits begin vs. how long can I *pay*"—in other words, how long could you manage with help from informal caregivers, like family and friends before benefits start?

3) Benefit Period/Benefit Maximum—Choose at least two years and longer if you can afford it, but don't ever sacrifice inflation coverage for a longer benefit period. If you live in a "Partnership" state (Connecticut, New York, Indiana, California) See **The Partnership for Long-Term Care** on p. 140 for guidance.

The average benefit period purchased in 2000 was five years, and one-third of the policyholders purchased the lifetime (unlimited) benefit period. A recent claims study showed that a five year benefit will pay benefits for the full duration of expected care for about 85 percent of people who need long-term care. [22]

Average premium differences:

lifetime vs. 6 years = 20%
lifetime vs. 5 years = 30%
lifetime vs. 3 years = 50%
6 years vs. 3 years = 32%
5 years vs. 3 years = 23%

4) Inflation Protection—The method that makes your benefit grow 5% compounded every year for the rest of your life is *nonnegotiable* if you are age 70 or under. If you are in your early 70's, you can choose the method that makes your benefit grow 5% of the original amount (5% simple) for the rest of your life, if your state allows that option. (Tip: At age 75, the premium difference between compound and simple is about 8%-10%.) If your state doesn't allow a simple inflation option, purchase the 5% compound. If you are in the upper 70's or older, you can purchase an extra benefit—perhaps an extra $30-$50 per day—to build in immediate inflation protection. The exception? If you think you will live longer than 10 years like my client, Mr. Jones, you should seriously consider either the simple or compound inflation option.

5) Home Health and Community Coverage—If you have someone to live with who can be a primary caregiver, you can select this coverage if it is optional on the policy you are considering. Some policies include it and it's not an option. If you do not have a primary caregiver and home health care benefits are required, the policy may allow you to lower your premium by choosing a reduced percentage such as 50%. If you are younger (30's–50's) and you don't know if you will have a primary care giver, buy it if you can afford it so you will have maximum choice when you need care.

Note: If you have no one to live with, you may be better off buying a "Facility Only" policy with "cadillac" benefit levels, such as private room coverage, 5% compound inflation, lifetime benefit period, and the like. Not everyone is a candidate for home health benefits. One of my clients is a retired schoolteacher with little family. She absolutely did not want to stay home If she needed extensive help. We used her premium dollars to purchase the best assisted living/nursing home policy she could afford. She now resides in a beautiful assisted living facility after suffering a stroke about a year ago. Bill Comfort, Jr., an agent in St. Louis, had a similar story:

After a lengthy discussion of all the wonderful long-term care insurance policy features that would allow for her to stay in her own home, a new client of mine looked at me and said, "If I ever need this kind of help, I don't want to stay in my own home."

I couldn't believe it. Doesn't everyone want to stay in their own home as long as possible? No. My client is a single woman with no family in town. She knew that if she needed on-going long-term care that it would be time to move—part of life. We found a policy with the best assisted living and nursing facility benefits she could get.

The premium difference between a comprehensive policy with home care benefits and a facility-only policy that covers assisted living and nursing home care is 30%-40%.

6) Non-Forfeiture—This benefit is something you can do without. It increases your premium significantly with very little value in return. The extra 30% or so you would spend for this option is better spent on purchasing the 5% inflation rider or if you are 75 or older, at least a higher daily benefit to combat inflation or a longer benefit period if you've already taken care of inflation.

The Bare-Bones/Best Value Policy for the Premium Conscious

Summary: If premium is your main consideration, the most bare-bones policy with the best premium value for the dollar is a policy that pays:

▲ assisted living and nursing home only, sometimes called a "Facility Only" policy
▲ a 20-or 30-day waiting period
▲ a two or three-year benefit period
▲ the appropriate inflation choice for your age (See "Inflation Protection" p. 59).

You can delete the home care as long as assisted living is covered. **Do not delete the inflation coverage.** If your benefit is too small at claim time and you can't make up the difference, you could wind up on Medicaid immediately (or whatever type of public assistance/welfare benefit is available at the time).

Some Parting Advice

Many companies are competing for your premium dollar, so don't fall prey to marketing strategies that may cause unnecessary rate increases in the future. Companies that offer very low premiums compared to most of the other companies, sell policies to people with significant health problems, and make it very easy to obtain benefits (see *Claims* p. 89) are at a higher than average risk for rate increases—particularly if the company is small. (There are companies selling long-term care insurance with $100 million in assets and there are companies with $100 billion and more in assets.)

You can also call your insurance department to ask about earlier rate increase activity as well as any complaints that have been filed against the insurance company. (See **Appendix B** for the contact information for your state's insurance department.)

Chapter 3

Long-Term Care:
The New Employee Benefit

〰〰〰〰〰〰〰〰〰〰〰〰〰〰〰〰〰〰〰〰〰〰〰〰

With the emergence of four-generation families, the future is
going to be filled with double-decker sandwiched generations.
As a result, the average 21st-century American will actually
spend more years caring for parents than children.[1]

—*Dr. Ken Dychtwald,* **AgePower**

Over 5,000 employers in the United States offered long-term care insurance to their employees in 2002.[2] This number is expected to explode in the next century, when elder care is projected to replace child care as the #1 dependent care issue in the United States by 2005, when 1 out of 3 workers will be more concerned with caring for a parent than a child.[3] If that sounds like *Future Shock* and something that can't possibly come true in our lifetime, think again. A recent study said each year 23 percent of Americans provide assistance to ill, disabled or aging persons. An earlier study said the number of households in the United States providing elder care tripled between 1988 and 1996—in other words, in less than a decade![4]

The fuse to encourage employers to offer long-term care insurance was lit by 1996 health care reform. Benefits from policies issued 1/1/97 and later are tax-free to employees whether the employee or the employer pays the premium. Premium contributions are now a business expense to employers and are not classified as taxable income to employees. With employer-sponsored plans having tripled in the last few years,[5] the new laws should propel the number of employers on the fence about long-term care insurance to make it available to huge numbers of Americans in the very near future.

If legislation is the fuse, employee demand is the bomb, and it is exploding.

▲ Two-thirds of the employees who participated in a 1999 National Council on Aging/John Hancock Survey reported they would like long-term care insurance to be offered at their workplaces.[6]

▲ Long-term care insurance was the single benefit most desired by employees in the William M. Mercer, Inc. 1998 Survey on Employee Benefit Preferences.[7]

▲ 73% of employees surveyed in a MetLife study are concerned about providing for their own or their spouse's long-term care needs.[8]

Employers are responding to the outcry. Although only 15 percent of employers currently offer long-term care coverage in a recent survey, the great news is that 48% of the group not offering group LTC insurance may offer it in the future.[9]

What is driving this intense and urgent demand from employees? Quite simply, it's the caregiving needs in their personal lives that threaten to eclipse their professional lives.

Consider that 5.75 million Americans are in the "sandwich generation" of caring for both children and parents,[10] and out of that is hatching caregiving demands unlike our society has ever known. Forty-two percent of employees surveyed in 1998 expect to assume elder-care duties by 2003[11] and a 1998 national public opinion poll showed that more than half of Americans say it is likely they will be responsible for the care of an elderly parent or relative by 2008.[12] There are approximately 7 million Americans involved in long-distance caregiving.[13]

And finally, two-thirds of employees who responded to the 1999 National Council on Aging/John Hancock Survey agree that LTC is the greatest threat to their standard of living in retirement.[14]

As baby boomers are watching the phenomenal emotional and financial price exacted on parents and grandparents who haven't planned ahead, the result is a generation that is demanding a better way. Existing health insurance and Medicare don't pay for long-term care, and the dependent care benefit that allows employees to set aside $5,000 tax-free annually for elder or child care is just a drop in a bottomless bucket with long-term care averaging $60,000 a year on up. So employees in all size companies are searching for answers through long-term care insurance.

Surprisingly, the largest growth is in small firms. By the end of 1999, two-thirds of the companies offering long-term care insurance plans had less than 500 employees.[15] This is probably happening for two reasons:

▲ small companies feel the productivity loss caused by caregiving needs more dramatically than large employers; and

▲ small business owners can react to a problem and make quicker decisions than large companies.

This trend will be stimulated as more people who are self-employed or who work for a company with 50 or less employees understand that long-term care insurance can be paid for with pre-tax dollars through the new Medical Savings Accounts (See p. 24 in **Long-Term Care and Your Financial Security**).

There are several kinds of long-term care insurance plans are available today.

A growing number of insurance companies are offering their individual long-term care insurance product to small employers, all the way down to a minimum of three applications in a group. While employees have to be in reasonably good health to be eligible, the company usually provides a payroll deduction discount of 10%–15%. This is especially great if the coverage also is offered to parents and in-laws. An employee who terminates employment can keep the policy and usually the group discount as well.

Group long-term care insurance offered through larger employers typically allows the employee to get coverage without checking the employee's health. (A few plans treat the spouse the same way.) This "guaranteed issue" coverage for the employee normally is available only to large employers, but at least one insurance company offers it to employers as small as 200 employees. At least six other companies offer a similar version for companies with 100 employees down to as small as 15 employees (and as small as 10 if the employer pays 100% of the premium) with only two or three health questions, such as "Have you needed help with activities of daily living (bathing, dressing, eating, toileting, continence, transferring from bed to chair) in the last 12 months?" and "Have you missed more than five consecutive days of work in the last six months?" Assuming the employee is actively at work and the answer to the questions is "No," the employee is approved for a policy. A couple of these small group plans will even provide a small policy to employees who are declined for health reasons.[16]

Plans for larger employers usually offer coverage to employees, spouses, parents, in-laws, and some plans even offer coverage to grandparents. The good news is that for family members, the medical underwriting may be less restrictive than for individual long-term care policies. In most companies the employee's portion of the premium is automatically deducted from his or her paycheck via payroll deduction. Parents and in-laws may be billed directly. If the employee terminates employment or retires, the policy is portable and the employee may keep the coverage, usually at the same premium. Coverage is generally available from age 18 to age 79, and some have no maximum age limit.

Employees are buying long-term care insurance for two reasons: to help with the escalating need for elder care, and for their own long-term care needs. Let's address the need for elder care first.

Productivity Insurance

The National Alliance for Caregiving/AARP study referenced earlier reports that three-fourths of households in America that contained a caregiver in the last twelve months are still providing care. That's about 11,000,000 caregivers and two-thirds of these caregivers are employed full or part-time.[17] About 13% of the workforce today provide care,[18] and as noted on p. 107, 42% expect to have caregiving responsibilities by 2003. These numbers do not even count the number of caregivers who are providing care for the 40% of Americans needing long-term care who are working-age adults, ages 18-64.[19] How will productivity be affected by these staggering long-term care needs?

The National Alliance for Caregiving/AARP study portrayed the following list of sacrifices made by employed caregivers who provided help with two or more Activities of Daily Living for 40 or more hours a week.[20]

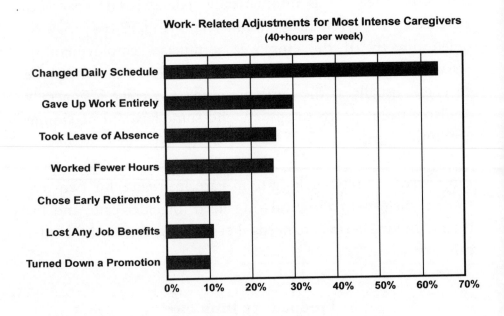

Work- Related Adjustments for Most Intense Caregivers
(40+hours per week)

Of *all* caregivers, 54% had to make changes at work to accommodate caregiving, but 64% of the most intense caregivers (40+

hours per week) had to make changes to their daily work schedule, 30% had to give up work entirely, 15% took early retirement and 26% had to take a leave of absence.[21]

Caregivers providing care for more than two years are only half as likely to be in the workforce as those who are providing care for fewer years, sometimes because the recipient gets progressively sicker and requires more care over time, or sometimes because either the caregiver or the employer is no longer comfortable with having to make workplace accommodations.[22] The Conference Board, a well-known employee benefits "think tank," estimates replacement costs to be 75% of the annual salary of the employee who quits.[23]

Born in 1919 and married at 15 to Everett Corker, Margie Evelyn Bowles Corker devoted her life to motherhood. She raised her children, Justine and Bill, with strength of character, teaching them to respect others and to aspire to high values and the reflective behavior. When Terri and Perry put in their surprise appearance 20 years after Justine, she hadn't changed— they got the same "schoolin'" as their older brother and sister. Statistically, they beat the odds—not one black sheep out of a flock of four. Margie wondered when Terri, the younger of the twins, turned toward music, and she really worried when Terri left home to tour with a popular singer.

Her fears were groundless. Terri's straight-arrow upbringing didn't fit with life on the road where booze and drugs were the roadmap. When lung cancer took Everett in a few short months in 1983, West Virginia didn't seem as confining, but Terri knew the music couldn't happen there. A few years after his death, she made the move to Nashville, with Margie in tow, who was already using a crutch due to the instability caused by degenerating arthritis. Her mother refused to drive in the big city, and the role reversal began.

Renting an apartment with her mother, Terri couldn't afford the footloose, hand-to-mouth existence of many Nashville musicians, nor did she want to live that way. She advanced in her day job to Operations Manager with an industrial supply firm and worked the songwriter venues nights and weekends. After several years of dues-paying, some of her original songs were recorded and things looked promising. Then Margie's health began to fail rapidly. Terri gave up a weekly songwriter night she had hosted for two years and began to pass paying music "gigs" to other musicians. Her first CD coincided with a blur of breast cancer, surgeries due to severe arthritis, pneumonia, congestive heart failure and an endless stream of multiple medications. The CD bypassed the back seat and went into the trunk of her life. Personal relationships came and went as Terri's first priority was to Margie. She wrote three new songs instead of 10 the following year. Terri saved furiously, knowing what was ahead, even though she had to pay a sitter three hours a day to help Margie with her meals. She never returned to work after a four-month leave of absence from her job in 1998 while Margie underwent extensive radiation treatments.

After Margie's death in January 2000, the eight year circus finally ended. Five months after the funeral, Terri is still looking for the identity she feels she has lost through it all. She doesn't regret the time with her mother in any way—she's just trying to assess where she is at age 42 with her career, her personal life, and what's left after the many years of caregiving that brought

her to this point. Her motto "The only routine is there is none"
no longer applies. Have the years of caregiving stolen her dream
for a music career?

Even long-distance caregivers who don't do the most intense caregiving and live more than an hour away from their older family members devote an average of 35 hours a month, equal to nearly one work week, to providing or arranging housekeeping, meals and other services for these aging family members, says a National Council on Aging study. Fifteen percent of these "long-distance caregivers" report taking unpaid leave from work, and have been helping out an average 5.1 years.[24]

The really astounding bird's-eye view is that among all caregivers, not just intense or long-distance, 21% have provided care for five to nine years, and 10% for 10 years or more.[25]

Caregiving Periods

Seven in 10 caregivers provide care to just one person, but 23% take care of two people, and eight percent care for three or more people![26]

Caregivers' Responsibilities

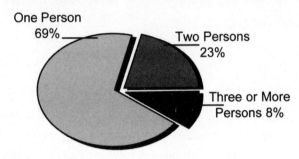

One Person
69%

Two Persons
23%

Three or More
Persons 8%

Caregiving responsibilities have a number of hidden impacts on job performance and overall company expenses, including:[27]

▲ workday interruptions to handle emergencies and phone calls

▲ absenteeism

▲ increased employee stress often resulting in health-related problems

▲ increased necessity for time off and leaves from work

▲ decreased willingness to relocate or travel for work

▲ decisions to cut back to part-time or leave the work force altogether

▲ decrease in motivation and morale due to pressures outside the workplace

▲ decline in productivity

▲ replacement costs ("employees who cut back or leave positions in order to care for elders average between 5 and 17 percent depending on the company")

The annual price tag for employers is somewhere around $30 billion,[28] although the Alzheimer's Association just issued a new survey that puts costs to employers at $61 billion for Alzheimer's alone![29] This list just adds up to one big word for the employee: Stress.

Since most people under 65 must work, long-term care insurance can provide a wonderful solution to employees with elder care needs. LTC insurance provides financial assistance, which in turn reduces stress levels by allowing the employee to keep his or her job, and by giving the employee peace of mind knowing that the parent or in-law is receiving high quality care while the employee is at work.

What if you can't afford to pay your parent's premium by yourself? JoAnn Canning, a New York City-based long-term care specialist, reports in the January 4, 1993 issue of *National Underwriter* that "when children enter into a 'multiple support' agreement (under which they agree to provide funds for the parent so that the parent can be claimed as a dependent for income tax purposes) they can also join in purchasing an LTC insurance policy for the parent."

This way, the LTC insurance policy can relieve both children's and parents' anxiety by making sure that many choices for care exist when needed, i.e., alternatives to nursing home care, which is usually the only option when the patient is on Medicaid. The LTC insurance policy also acts to safeguard the children's inheritance instead of spending the parents' savings on long-term care expenses. Many attorneys recommend LTC insurance policies for this reason.

Thanks to the recent health care reform legislation, a portion of the premium based on the parent's age is counted as a medical expense and becomes a potential tax deduction for the child paying the premium, as long as the parent is a dependent. (This just means the child or children must provide greater than 50% of the parent's support.) In the case of multiple support agreements as explained above, one child each year can take the tax deduction as long as that child contributed at least 10% of the parent's support for that tax year.

The wave of the future is companies like Lancaster Labs in Lancaster, Pennsylvania, which offers on-site adult day care at a reasonable cost to employees of $35 per day, in addition to child care.[30] Long-term care insurance will pay for adult day care. How many insurance policies will pay for child care?

Robert Ridgley, chairman of Northwest Natural Gas, a Portland, Oregon, utility, is another example of an employer who recognizes how serious long-term care is for his employees. His company surveyed 1,350 workers about child-care needs, only to find that "We had as many or more people spending a significant amount of time and emotional capital on elder care."[31]

Lifestyle Insurance

Numbers like this affect all segments of society, but the fastest growing segment of corporate America—small business—has a huge stake in this problem. Many Americans look forward to getting their children at least in high school or even through college, and then experiencing "The American Dream"—starting the business they've always dreamed of. Starting a business usually means long hours—60+ hours a week is not unusual for the entrepreneur. Suddenly, a spouse, parent, or in-law has an accident or a stroke, and caregiving becomes the #1 priority. The dream never happens.

Bev Fulkerson is 42. On the surface, her life seems to be going well. She just got a promotion to state director of a new suicide prevention grant for a crisis intervention center in Nashville, Tennessee. Without talking with her, you wouldn't know how deeply she appreciates being back in the workforce with a meaningful job. Her appreciation is tinged with sadness, however, because it means she isn't running her own private practice as an addictions/mental health counselor for adolescents, a business she tried to start six months ago.

Two years ago, her energetic 72-year-old mother, known for her pep, spunk and tremendous sense of humor, entered a Louisville, Kentucky, hospital for a routine heart bypass. Her father's similar surgery a year earlier had kept him in the hospital a mere five days. The day of the surgery, Bev accepted a new job as director of a counseling center just outside of Nashville that catered to adolescents. After 16 years in the field, she was ecstatic.

Her mother came home 12 1/2 months later.

Allergic to the medications used during surgery, her recovery time stretched past two months. Just as she was being transferred to the rehabilitation wing, she couldn't shake the feeling that something was wrong, that the wound wasn't healing properly. She had a staph infection, a phrase that strikes terror to anyone in the medical profession, especially the people who handle the billing and the legal functions. Did the hospital cause *it? Will the exorbitant bill be paid in full? (Mrs. Fulkerson's bill went over $2 million.)*

It was five more months before the actual rehabilitation treatment could begin and another three before she was transferred to an independent skilled nursing facility in Louisville. She was there 3 1/2 months before coming home, unable to walk or even turn herself in bed. She began eight months of home health care which ended in mid-April, 2000. Today her youthful looks have dissipated, she has lost 70 pounds, and her sense of humor is a dim light in the distance. In the midst of the hospital stay, Bev was successful at getting an anti-depressant prescribed for her mother only after four months of insisting and a meeting with the hospital administrator, a feat which deeply underscores the need for family advocacy even when someone is in a medical facility. Bev was lucky. Her younger brother in Louisville took a three- month family leave when the problems began and has been extremely supportive during the entire episode. Bev was able to keep her job by commuting to Louisville, two hours away, every weekend and usually at least once during the week for two years.

Last December, when it looked like Mrs. Fulkerson might actually come out of it, Bev decided to go for her big dream, which was to start her own private practice as an adolescent counselor. By January, she was ready to go. Then her father discovered a lump in his groin, and was diagnosed with lymphoma. Her mother couldn't be left alone during the weeks of extensive testing, so for Bev, the nightmare began all over again.

The good news is that the lymphoma appears to be dormant so no ongoing treatment is necessary and Bev is free to return to the workforce. The bad news is that financially she no longer has the resources to start her own practice. In her words, "The dream of having a private practice went out the back window. Anything I wanted to do or needed to do for myself is put on the back burner."

The following caregiver wasn't so fortunate.

Linda, a 48-year-old supervisor at a bank and a divorced mother of two children in college, had planned a very different life for herself. Five years ago she was anticipating her youngest child's departure for college and looking forward to a new personal chapter in her life—a chapter that included more time for herself, a chance to study art history and perhaps even a second career. Instead, her mother, previously an independent and active widow in her early 70's, was diagnosed with Alzheimer's disease. Since then, Linda's dreams have ceased to exist. Her mother has lived with her three years, with Linda footing the bill for adult day care so she can continue working. The strain on her budget is unbelievable, especially when combined with the cost of drugs and a few other medical services not covered by Medicare.

Linda also had never imagined how difficult things would be as a result of no personal time. She misses her shopping trips, movies with her friends and is frustrated by her inability to attend parent functions at her children's colleges. But the hardest part is the isolation she feels. She doesn't want people at work to think she's down all the time.

The caregiving responsibilities Linda has undertaken will continue to increase, especially now that her mom has started wandering at all hours.

The above caregiving story is an excerpt from the National Family Caregivers Association (NFCA)/Fortis Report, members of which are primarily involved in intense caregiving situations. Nearly half were employed and three-fourths of them worked more than 30 hours per week. The average length of time these working caregivers have been providing care is 7.9 years and 28% have been at it longer than 10 years. Half of the remaining caregivers expect to be providing care more than ten years!

The most reported emotion is a sense of isolation, even among the employed, because, like Linda, they probably feel as though they have to be "up" while on the job.

Three out of five of these caregivers reported they were depressed as a result of their caregiving activities, a number that is six times the national average for clinical depression. Younger caregivers in their 30's and 40's especially reported depression and particularly those who provided care more than 40 hours a week, which almost half do.

The caregivers in the NCFA report were a mixture, with half of them caring for a spouse, a fourth for a parent, 20% for a child and remaining caregivers took care of a sibling or friend. Of all of them, children caring for parents have the highest depression and lowest feelings of inner strength. The three greatest difficulties the adult children named were role reversal, isolation, and loss of leisure time.[32]

Take a look at the chart on the next page from *USA Today* that illustrates the sacrifices made by adults age 35–54 who have provided long-term care for family or friends.[33]

The 1999 National Council on Aging/John Hancock survey reported that more than one-quarter of respondents providing financial assistance for a friend or relative has used their retirement savings and 12% used money set aside for a child's education. Nineteen percent gave up a job to provide care, while another 19% took a second job.[34]

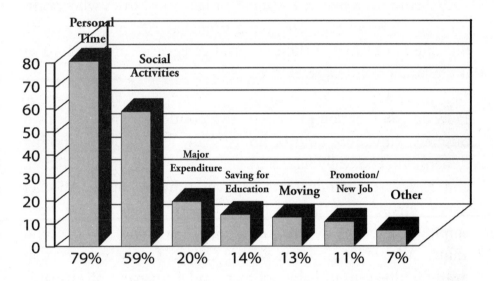

It's easy to see from these numbers that caregivers often suffer significant drops in income as a result of a caregiving situation. In a follow-up study of 55 of the most intense caregivers from the study referenced above, Metropolitan Life Insurance Company was able to quantify an average total lost wealth amount of $659,139 due to the intense caregiving situation ($566,443 lost wages, which caused an average of $25,494 in lost Social Security benefits since they couldn't work as much and earn as much, and for those eligible, losses in pension benefits averaging $67,202). The average caregiving time of these 55 intense caregivers was eight years, but one-third had provided care for ten or more years.[35]

What sacrifices were made in both time and money in these families? How did each individual family member suffer? How welcome would a home health aide providing at least 40 hours of care per week have been?

The typical caregiver in the National Alliance for Caregiving/ AARP study is a married woman in her mid-forties who works full-time. The average caregiving time was 18 hours per week, but one out of five of these "typical caregivers" provided 40 or more hours of care a week.[36]

How do you function in an executive position or grow your own business with those kind of hours? Now let's throw in another dimension. The really hard part comes when caring for children and parents or grandparents happens simultaneously. Another major survey said that at least 20% of caregivers are both employed and have children under age 18 at home.[37] The second annual Allstate "Retirement Reality Check" survey reported that nearly ten percent of baby boomers and 19 percent of Hispanic baby boomers expect to be sandwiched by responsibilities for both parents and children during retirement.[38]

Because the predominant number of caregivers are women, caregiving may turn out to be the biggest threat to the women's movement in the next century. Even today, the average 21st Century American is projected to spend more years taking care of aging family members than raising children.[39]

Here is an example of what the incredible pressure from both ends looks like:

Jenny is an example of multigenerational caregiving. Jenny and her husband provide support for her 88-year-old mother and her husband's 89-year-old mother, and their 28-year-old daughter just moved back home with her three children ages 6 and under. Jenny's name was on a prayer request list.[40]

Families can't do it alone. They have to have help, and long-term care insurance may be the main key to the help they need, in addition to lots of prayers! The AARP study says "prayer is the most common way of coping with the stresses and strains of caregiving—almost three in four caregivers (74%) use this method."[41] Future long-term care insurance policies may earn the name "lifestyle insurance," because the policy may be the only thing that allows an adult child to continue a career or even keep a marriage from falling apart from the strain of a caregiving need of a very long duration.

Well-known columnist Terry Savage from the *Chicago Sun-Times* wrote about buying long-term care insurance on her parents in the June/July 2000 issue of *Mirabella* magazine:

> *When I bought a policy for each of my parents as a holiday gift a few years ago, the reaction was predictable. My father smiled and thanked me . . . and then went out for a jog. My mother's reaction was a little more emotional: "After your grandmother, you promised you'd never . . ." The words trailed off as we both remembered. Then I smiled at her and reminded her that this policy would pay for someone to come into her home and give needed care. We'd never have to face the issue of a nursing home (I hope and pray). And if we do, I know I've ensured her the best of care. That's why I also bought a policy for myself.*

Long-term care happens not to an individual. It happens to the entire family, and this popular columnist sees this clearly.

Long-Term Care Insurance Is Not "Senior Citizen Insurance"

Long-Term Care and Your Financial Security explained there is a 1 out of 2 chance of needing either home health care or nursing home care at some point in your life.[42] The two-edged sword of long-term care is that it can be needed at any age. As noted on p. 110, 40% of Americans needing long-term care today are working age adults ages 18-64![43] Only about 10% of nursing home patients are under 65,[44] so most of these younger people needing long-term care are being cared for in the community, at a very large sacrifice for family members. Consider these actual cases:

▲   a 29-year-old had a massive stroke a month before her wedding day. Her fiance continues to care for her 11 years later—her mind is fine, but she communicates with her eyes and is confined to a wheelchair. They live with her parents.[45]

▲   a 25-year-old Cookeville, Tennessee, man who slammed into the side of a dump truck that pulled out in front of his motorcycle was discharged from a nursing home seven months later after an extended coma, then spent the next three years relearning every skill he was born with—his wife's life stopped with his as she stayed by his side throughout.[46]

▲   a 49-year-old Nashville woman still raising her 11-year-old son, is bed-ridden in her 11th year of Lou Gehrig's disease. Her muscles and body virtually petrified, she taps out Morse Code through sensors attached by Velcro to her fingertips, which signal a laptop computer to write and speak her thoughts through a synthesized voice.[47]

And consider the nursing home stories of younger people:

▲ a 50-year-old man who is in a nursing home from a May, 1999 stroke that incapacitated his left arm, the only independent functioning part of his body left from a bout with polio as a child.[48]

▲ an Illinois woman lying comatose in a nursing home after suffering a stroke during childbirth in her late 30's.[49]

▲ a 26-year-old in a coma after an automobile accident in which he was forced off the road by the driver of the car he was passing who was angry because he forgot to dim his headlights.[49]

A quick reminder: Conventional group health insurance does not cover long-term care because it covers mainly skilled care in a nursing home or at home, and almost all long-term care is not skilled. People who just need help with bathing, getting in and out of bed, taking medicine, toileting, eating, etc. do not receive payment for this type of help from conventional health insurance. A perfect example of someone who needs this type of help and who is not helped by traditional health insurance is someone who is paralyzed from an accident or stroke. Once the patient settles into a chronic, maintenance state and just needs help with basic activities of daily living, payment for caregiving stops under regular health insurance.

Many younger people think disability income insurance takes care of them. Disability income coverage just provides money with which to pay bills (mortgage, utilities, food, etc.) and does not provide an extra $3,000-$6,000 a month to pay for long-term care expenses.

A Health Insurance Association of America survey reports that the average age of employees who have purchased long-term care insurance is 46.[50] Younger people are more likely to see long-term care insurance as just another part of their plan for retirement. The money accumulated in pension plans, 401K, investments, annuities, real estate, etc., is in jeopardy if long-term care is needed. The 40-year-old today is facing long-term care expenses of almost $600,000 per year in forty years if present trends continue with an annual growth rate of 5.8%.[51]

Tips for Benefit Choices in Group Plans

Group long-term care insurance plans are similar to individual policies, but there are a few specific areas you should check before deciding on a plan:

Inflation Coverage—You may be offered a plan with or without inflation coverage. **BUY INFLATION COVERAGE.** There are different types of inflation coverage. For example, you may be offered a plan with low premiums now and a chance to buy additional coverage in the future. Usually, if you have a claim, these offers are withdrawn. If you are offered the opportunity to buy a plan that guarantees your daily or monthly benefit will grow automatically each year as long as you hold the policy, take it. The premium will be more than the other kind in the beginning, but you will pay much less over the long haul and your benefit has a much better chance of keeping up with the rising cost of long-term care. Also, if you have a claim, your benefit will continue to grow and in most plans, your premium will stop. Select the automatic increase option that grows compounded (not simple) each year and only the benefit should increase annually, not the premium.

Home Health Care—Many group plans offer benefits that cover long-term care outside of the nursing home, such as home health care, adult day care, foster home care, etc. as an option. You are well advised to take it because even today, nursing home care only makes up less than 15% of the long-term care picture.[46] It is expected that since nursing home beds are less than 90% occupied today, that research will provide more and more ways to provide future long-term care in the community.[53] Most people would rather be cared for at home as long as possible, anyway. If you have a choice between a home care benefit that pays less than the nursing home benefit (i.e., 50%) and one that pays equal to the nursing home benefit, choose the one that is equal (the best choice), or at least 75%-80%, since home care costs can equal and even exceed nursing home costs.

Non-forfeiture/Return of Premium Benefits—Some group plans include a return of premium at death benefit and you have no choice but to accept it. Others offer this benefit as an option or they offer the shortened benefit period option we discussed in Chapter Two, **Features of a Good Long-Term Care Insurance Policy.** If extra premium is charged for this privilege, analyze carefully if the extra premium is a wise expenditure. The odds are great that you will use the coverage, never get any money back, and you will have paid the extra premium for nothing. You might be better off putting the extra premium in your 401K or other retirement fund or a mutual fund, etc., or use it to buy a higher level of benefit: an increased dollar amount of coverage, or better inflation or home care benefits.

Also, some new group plans don't offer a lifetime (unlimited) benefit period or shorter waiting periods like 20, 30 or 60 days unless you specifically request them.

Here is a summary of why employees are buying long-term care insurance:

1) To take care of their own long-term care needs, as the need can occur at any age.

2) To help with elder care needs so they can continue working while taking care of aging family members.

3) To take advantage of lower premiums for themselves at younger ages and underwriting concessions for the employee, in particular since the employee usually gets covered with no health questions, and for any available underwriting breaks for family members who may find it more difficult to qualify medically for individual LTC policies.

4) To help the private sector fund the long-term care crisis, because the more people who wind up in nursing homes on Medicaid (welfare), the higher our taxes will be to help the government pay the bill. (Sweden has a national long-term care program and a tax rate of over 50%!)[54]

You may be able to enroll in a group or association long-term care plan by mail, but you and your spouse should attend any meetings held by your employer or association as well so you will get a first-hand explanation of long-term care issues and the products being offered. Your parents and in-laws are usually welcome at these educational meetings.

The Federal Long-Term Care Insurance Program
(The Long Term Care Security Act of 2000)

The largest employer-sponsored long-term care insurance program, estimated at 20 million people, was launched in March of 2002 with limited benefits, and during Open Season (July 1 – December 31, 2002) with full benefits and abbreviated underwriting for active employees and spouses. The Office of Personnel Management (OPM) selected John Hancock and MetLife to offer The Federal Long Term Care Insurance Program (FLTCIP) and those two companies formed a new company, Long Term Care Partners (LTCP). Long-Term Care Partners is exclusively dedicated to serving the long-term care insurance needs of the Federal Family.

Even though Open Season has ended, the FLTCIP is still available with full underwriting to all eligible classifications of the Federal Family. A good rule of thumb is to realize that it is offered to anyone who is eligible for the Federal Employees Health Benefits Program – they don't have to enrolled in the FEHB, just be eligible for it, and they have to be eligible at the time they apply for FLTCIP. (This means it's not enough to just have FEHB because they could have FEHB due to a continuation of coverage provision and no longer be eligible for it.) Two exceptions: 1) Tennessee Valley Authority employees are not eligible for FEHB but **are** eligible for FLTCIP and 2) Some District of Columbia employees and retirees are eligible for FEHB, but **are not** eligible for FLTCIP.

Eligibility

Actives:

▲ Federal Civilian and Postal Employees (must be in pay status).

   ▲ Temporary employees have to complete one year of continuous current employment. Non-appropriated fund employees are not eligible to apply. (These are people who work on military bases in the PBX exchange or commissaries who are paid out of funds not appropriated from Congress.)

▲ Members of the Uniformed Services, including National Guard (must be on active duty at least 30 days)

   ▲ Selected Reserve but not the Individual Ready Reserve – Selected Reserve includes Drilling Reservists and Guardsmembers assigned to Reserve Component Units; Individual Mobilization Augmentees who are Reservists assigned to Reserve component billets in Active Component units, performing duty in a pay or nonpay status; Active Guard and Reserve members who are full-time Reserve members on full-time National Guard duty or active duty in support of the National Guard or Reserves

Annuitants (Retirees)

▲ as long as they are receiving regular payments from their annuity (The "five-year rule" doesn't apply – this means there is no requirement to have had the coverage for a designated length of time as an employee in order to be able to carry it into retirement.)

Qualified Relatives (even if employee, annuitant, member or retired member of Uniformed Services does not apply or applies and is declined)

▲   Current spouses, including surviving spouses of a member or retired member of the uniformed services as long as they are receiving a survivor annuity. Receipt of Dependency and Indemnity Compensation (DIC) from the Dept. of Veterans Affairs qualifies as a survivor annuity. (Former spouses are not eligible even if eligible for FEHB and/or receiving a survivor annuity.)

▲   Parents, parents-in-law and stepparents (those of annuitants and retired members of the Uniformed Services are not eligible)

▲   Parents-in-law include parents of a deceased spouse, as long as the employee or member of the Uniformed Services has not remarried

▲   Stepparent must be currently married to the employee's parent or was married to the parent at the time of the parent's death

▲   Adult children 18 and up (includes adopted and stepchildren, but not foster children) but spouses of adult children are not eligible unless they fall into another eligible group

Applicants must be age 18 and up. There is no age maximum.

Benefits

You may want to review Chapter Two, **Features of a Good Long-Term Care Insurance Policy**, for additional information on definitions of any of the following.

Two plans are offered: Comprehensive and Facilities-Only

<u>Daily Benefits</u> – $50 - $300, in $25 increments

There is an option on the Comprehensive plan to have benefits available on a weekly basis for home health care at 7 X Daily Benefit for an average additional premium 6% (varies by age). 100% of the Daily Benefit applies to nursing home, assisted living, hospice (facility and home), bed reservations, caregiver training, respite services (facility and home). **For facility benefits (nursing home, assisted living and hospice), the plan covers drugs, incontinence supplies, dietary supplements, personal medical equipment and laundry services.**

<u>Waiting Period</u> – 30 or 90 days of eligible charges

The waiting period is met by actual dates of service and days do not need to be consecutive. The waiting period does not have to be met to receive benefits for hospice care, respite care and caregiving training. The waiting period can never repeat.

<u>Benefit Period/Benefit Max</u> -- 3 or 5 years or lifetime (pool of money)

The three or five year benefit period is a "pool of money", which means it is the daily benefit x 1095 days or 1,825 days. For any day the charge is less than the daily benefit, the difference stays in the pool and can extend the benefit longer than the three or five years. The lifetime benefit is unlimited and averages 35% more premium than the five year benefit period. Care coordination services continue after benefit maximum is exhausted (see below for definition of care coordination).

Home Health/Adult Day Care– 75% of daily benefit (optional weekly benefit)

Home health care services do not have to be provided by a home health agency. The plan will pay for licensed professionals (RNs, LPNs, professional therapists – physical, respiratory, speech or occupational) who are "freelancing", as long as they are operating within the scope of their license.

Informal care: If approved by an LTC Partners care coordinator, the plan will pay for a non-licensed caregiver who did not live with the insured at time of claim; however the person could move in after benefit eligibility is established. This benefit can include a homemaker not provided through a home health agency. Evidence of services must be submitted (caregiver name, social security number, number of hours, along with a charge for each service). For family members (parents, grandparents, siblings, adult children and respective spouses) this benefit is limited to a lifetime benefit of 365 days.

Home health care is optional. A Facilities-only plan, which covers assisted living, hospice and nursing facilities, averages 30% lower premium than a Comprehensive plan.

Assisted Living – 100% of Daily Benefit

<u>Access to Benefits</u> – Tax-Qualified definition (includes standby assistance), as the FLTCIP is a tax-qualified plan (See p. 92 for this definition). LTC Partners also has to agree in addition to the health care practitioner, and LTC Partners has to approve a written plan of care established by a licensed health care practitioner **or** an LTC Partners' care coordinator. Benefit eligibility is reassessed at least once every 12 months but no more frequently than every 30 days. In the event of a dispute, the policyholder is entitled to an independent third-party review.

<u>Inflation Options</u> – Automatic Compound Inflation or Future Purchase Option

Automatic Compound Inflation Option: The Daily Benefit and the remaining lifetime maximum less any claims paid out that year will increase 5% compounded annually.

Future Purchase Option: Beginning 1/1/04, the Daily Benefit will increase based on the medical Consumer Price Index and every two years on Jan. 1st with no underwriting, unless receiving benefits or unless the insured has declined three times. (Underwriting will apply after the insured has rejected a FPO three times and wishes to resume receiving offers.) Notification will go out in the fall, and the insured has to submit a written rejection to stop it. (Coverage must have been in effect 12 months to get the first increase.) Increases due to the FPO are priced at attained age and premiums in place at that time, so with this option, premiums will increase every two years and will eventually surpass the ACI premium. With each FPO notice will come an offer to switch to the Automatic Compound Option. The premium for ACI will be at the insured's age on the date of the switch, and the switch won't be allowed if the insured is receiving benefits.

Some people who need an initial low premium due to pressing current financial obligations (i.e. college tuition for children) buy the Future Purchase Option to keep their premiums low in the first few years with the intention of switching to the Automatic Compound Inflation option as soon as possible in order to stabilize their premium. This can be a good strategy as long as they understand the risk that they won't be able to switch if they start receiving benefits.

<u>Waiver of Premium</u> – First day of the month following the date eligibility for benefits is established and the waiting period is met, unless that date happens to be on the first day of a month, in which case it would be the same day.

The premium waiver applies to hospice even though there is no waiting period for hospice benefits. Premium resumes on the first of the month following the month in which the insured is no longer eligible for benefits. Premium that has been paid is refunded for any time period paid after death or after the waiver of premium starts.

<u>Pre-Existing Conditions</u> – No exclusion for pre-existing conditions

<u>Reimbursement/Indemnity</u> – Reimbursement, including informal care

<u>Coordination of Benefits</u> – This plan will be secondary to Medicare, group medical benefits and any other employer-sponsored long-term care insurance plan.

The FLTCIP is secondary to any benefits for long-term care services received under any plans established by the Federal or a state government. It does not coordinate with individual or association long-term care insurance policies. The Coordination of Benefits provision doesn't apply to international benefits (See below). The FLTCIP will not pay for care in a government facility, including a Dept. of Defense or Dept. of Veterans Affairs facility.

Nonforfeiture – Contingent nonforfeiture is built into the policy at no extra charge.

The shortened benefit period for additional premium is not an option.

Rates – Rate increases must be approved by The Office of Personnel Management (OPM).

There are no spouse or preferred discounts as OPM spread the discounts equally in order to provide equal treatment for all. Premiums can be viewed by using the premium calculator on the LTC Partners website: www.LTCFEDS.com

Portability – The policy is portable at no increase in premium if the policyholder is no longer a member of the Federal family.

If the group policy ends for any reason, OPM will replace it with another group policy with substantially same coverage and premium based on issue age under the old group policy. (Note: The claims reserve for this program does not belong to the insurance company or companies who administer the plan, nor is it available for any other lines of business or to creditors of the insurance company. If OPM selects another insurance company, the fund will move to the new carrier.)

Additional Benefits

Alternate plan of care: In the Facilities-only plan, this benefit can mean an alternate facility, but nothing outside of a facility. In the Comprehensive plan, it can mean home modifications, durable medical equipment and emergency response system. APOC benefits are subject to the waiting period and count toward the lifetime maximum. All APOC benefits must be authorized by the LTC Partners' care coordinator.

Bed reservations: 30 days per calendar year (includes assisted living and hospice facilities)

Caregiver training: The lifetime maximum is equal to 7 X 100% of the Daily Benefit. The waiting period does not apply and Caregiver Training doesn't count toward the waiting period. The Caregiver Training benefit is paid in addition to the daily or weekly maximum so it doesn't figure into the daily or weekly benefit calculation.

Respite services: 30 X 100% of the Daily Benefit per calendar year. In the Facilities-only plan, the benefit is available in an assisted living facility, hospice facility or in a nursing home. The Comprehensive plan includes respite care by a formal or informal caregiver at home or in adult day care.

Care coordination: Free (does not reduce the lifetime maximum) and is required as the LTC Partners' care coordinator, who is a registered nurse, is the person who approves benefit eligibility in addition to the insured's health care practitioner. The care coordinators also develop a plan of care and assist with altering it as needs change, monitor ongoing benefit eligibility and provide access to discounts for long-term care services, when available. Care coordination is available at $59 per year to qualified relatives (single or couple), whether or not they are enrolled in the FLTCIP. This "service package" is also offered to any member of the Federal Family who is declined for a policy in the underwriting process.

Exclusions – No exclusion for mental disorders. No exclusion for war, except the benefit period may be shortened if the war is determined to be a Catastrophic Event as this could undermine the financial stability of the Federal Program (unlikely as Federal Program reserves grow).

International Benefits – 80% of the Maximum Lifetime Benefit is available for international coverage and payment is made at 80% of the domestic benefit amount. For those who choose a lifetime benefit period, the international Maximum Lifetime Benefit is 10 years (3,650 days) x 80% of the Daily Benefit. If the policyholder returns to the United States, the benefits return to the full amounts.

(The rationale for the 80% compensates for the additional cost to cover higher claims expenses with provider verification and unknown utilization in another country, both of which protect the financial stability of the plan and guard against rate increases.)

The Office of Personnel Management is committed to both premium and benefit oversight of this plan to ensure rate stability and benefit modernization (i.e. robotic care could be covered if that becomes an approved form of caregiving!) Additional information is available on the LTC Partners website at www.LTCFEDS.com or by calling (1-800-582-3337) (TTY: 1-800-843-3557) during the following times for a customer service representative:

Monday through Friday from 8:00 am EST to 8:00 pm EST
Saturday from 9:00 am EST to 5:00 pm EST
Closed on Sunday and all Federal holidays

An automated voice response system is available 24 hours a day, 7 days a week.

Whether you review the Federal Long-Term Care Insurance Program or private group or individual long-term care policies— **DON'T WAIT** to purchase a policy for yourself and anyone you even think you may wind up taking care of. **Caregivers whose family members have long-term care insurance are twice as likely to stay in the workforce as those whose family members don't have long-term care insurance.**[55] American families desperately need to prepare today for a long-term care need that could strike at any time.

Chapter 4

The Partnership for Long-Term Care

╲╲╲╲╲╲╲╲╲╲╲╲╲╲╲╲╲╲╲╲╲╲╲╲╲╲╲╲╲╲╲

T he Partnership for Long-Term Care is a public/private alliance between state governments and insurance companies that was originally funded with $14 million in grants from the nation's largest health care philanthropy, the Robert Wood Johnson Foundation. The program is operational in Connecticut, New York, Indiana, California and approved in Iowa. Variations of the Partnership have been approved in Illinois, Massachusetts and Washington, but the main Partnership activity continues to reside in the original four states.

The idea of the partnership is to provide a way for the Medicaid program to work together with private long-term care insurance to help those people who are caught in the middle: they can't afford to pay the cost of the care or even the cost of a long-term care insurance policy with unlimited benefits, yet their assets are too high to qualify for Medicaid to pay their long-term care expenses. Many middle-income workers and retirees also find themselves in this position.

Participating insurance companies in the Partnership recognize the needs of these middle-income Americans by providing LTC insurance policies that have built-in consumer protection benefit standards, and participating states cooperate by allowing these policyholders to access Medicaid without spending down their assets almost to poverty level if the insurance benefits run out. Without the Partnership, people have three choices to pay for long-term care:

1) Pay for care out of assets and income, which can lead to financial ruin if long-term care costs wipe out savings.

2) Transfer assets to qualify for Medicaid either to children or other family members or to a trust—either way means losing control of the money and losing financial independence.

3) Buy a standard long-term care insurance policy which works—unless the policy runs out of benefits or the benefit isn't enough to cover the cost of care. This can happen because you bought what you could afford, and it turns out not to be enough when you need it. (For example, you couldn't afford the premium for inflation coverage, you could only afford a one- or two-year benefit period, or you bought a daily or monthly benefit significantly lower than the cost of care in your area and you couldn't make up the difference at claim time.)

A fourth option is available with the Partnership for Long-Term Care. Now consumers can purchase a state-approved LTC insurance policy that provides asset protection after the benefits run out. Here's how it works in all of the above-mentioned states except New York.

▲ You purchase a special Partnership policy from an insurance agent. For every dollar in benefits paid by the policy, you can shelter a dollar in assets. For example, let's say you buy a two-year benefit period because that's what you can afford. If this policy pays, say, $60,000 in benefits, and if the Medicaid asset eligibility in your state requires you to spend down to $2,000, in this example you would be able to qualify for Medicaid when your assets reach $62,000, not $2,000. In other words, you get to keep, or "shelter" $60,000 of your assets and still get Medicaid to start paying your long-term care expenses after your policy runs out.

▲   In New York, Partnership policies must cover three years of nursing home benefits or six years of home care (or a combination of both), and once the benefits are exhausted, the policyholder can qualify for Medicaid regardless of the amount of assets.

While New York offers unlimited asset protection, this desirable feature only happens after you have used up the benefits of the policy. A danger is that if you purchase a daily benefit that is inadequate for your needs, you could use up your assets paying the difference between your policy's benefit and the cost of care before your benefits are used up.

For example, in 2003 New York requires new Partnership policy purchasers to purchase a minimum of $163 for the daily nursing home benefit. The New York City metropolitan area averages $330[1], not counting the miscellaneous charges for drugs and medical supplies. If you only buy the minimum, you could easily wind up paying $160 per day or more out of your pocket, which amounts to over $175,000 over the three-year benefit period for nursing home care. Based on the 1999 map below, it's easy to guess that the cost of care, while lower in other parts of New York, can still easily run as high as $200 per day. (Use the information at the end of this chapter to contact the New York State Partnership for Long-Term Care in spring of 2003 for new cost figures.)

Estimated 1999 Daily Average NYS Nursing Home Rates By Region*

$179

$157

$195

$209

$144 $170

$251

*Data based on a sample of New York State nursing home rates.

NOTE: Average nursing home rates for each region are shown. Some daily rates may be significantly higher than the regional averages. It is recommended that nursing homes be contacted directly to determine actual costs.

▲ Indiana provides a combination of these two models. The combo plan provides the dollar-for-dollar asset protection just as it does now for all of the states except New York, but if the policyholder purchases a benefit maximum that will pay about four years of benefits, the policy will provide total asset protection like the New York model. Since $178,679 represents about four years of benefits at current costs, purchasing a policy that would pay out that much in benefits would qualify you for the total asset protection feature in Indiana. (The $178,679 is the 2003 amount and will increase each year to account for inflation.) An insurance agent who is approved to sell Partnership policies can help you identify the best combination of benefits for your needs. The Indiana Partnership maintains a list of agents who have had special Partnership training. Call the Indiana Partnership telephone number or access the website listed at the end of this chapter for a directory of approved agents.

In all states, your income goes to pay for the cost of care once you qualify for Medicaid. So the Partnership program protects assets, not income. But income is important for three reasons:

1) If your income is greater than your long-term care costs, you won't qualify for Medicaid and wouldn't benefit from a Partnership policy. People in this situation can consider a standard long-term care insurance policy—perhaps with an unlimited benefit maximum.

2) Income can guide you to a benefit selection. For example, the average cost of care in Indiana is $116 per day. Indiana residents may be able to purchase a policy for $100 a day and pay the difference out of income. (In higher cost areas like New York, Connecticut or California, you would probably be purchasing policies in the $250+/day range. The average cost of care in Connecticut, for example, is $232.) Just be careful—if

your care costs more than the insurance policy pays in benefits, you will be responsible for paying the additional costs, and don't forget that drugs and medical supplies are usually billed on top of the room and board charge. Consider carefully how much you can afford to pay out of your income and insure yourself adequately. The Partnership policies include an inflation benefit for appropriate ages so that inflation doesn't erode your benefit.

3) Since you are responsible for paying your premiums, your discretionary income must be sufficient to pay your long-term care premiums and keep your policy in force, although there is a premium waiver if you have a claim. Individuals with income less than $20,000 or couples with incomes less than $40,000 may not have enough discretionary income to purchase long-term care insurance as premium payments may significantly impact their standard of living. If you fall into these income categories, and if you have assets less than $50,000, not counting your house and car, you probably will qualify for Medicaid in a short period of time, and LTC insurance of any type—standard or Partnership—may not be an appropriate purchase for you.

For many people, the Partnership LTC policies offer a wonderful alternative to transferring assets and relying on the government (Medicaid) to pay for their long-term care expenses. In addition to the legal pitfalls (See **The Medicaid Benefit for Long-Term Care**, p. 151), there are significant problems with transferring assets, such as:

▲   Children can lose the money due to divorce or law-
    suits. Remember, it doesn't take bad people to do bad
    things. Children may be tempted to spend the money
    in a financial crisis by subconsciously thinking they
    will inherit it any way, so why not use it now when they
    really need it? Then when you need long-term care, the
    money simply isn't there anymore.

▲   We tend to judge ourselves by what we have, either
    consciously or unconsciously. Once we have turned
    our assets over to someone else, either a child or a
    trust, we have lost control of them. We may not enjoy
    the feeling of not being able to access our assets ever
    again.

▲   Transferring assets and using government money
    means using our own money as taxpayers. In New
    York, for example, a significant portion of each
    county's tax goes to the Medicaid program, in addition
    to state tax. County contributions are necessary to sup-
    port the Medicaid program in New York which is run-
    ning about $32 billion annually.[2] A really shocking
    equation that most New Yorkers don't realize is that
    two out of every ten Medicaid recipients spend $8 out
    of every $10 of Medicaid benefits. The two recipients
    spending most of the money are spending it for long-
    term care. Seventy-five percent of the remaining eight
    recipients who are left with the $2 are *children*.[3]

Let's take this picture national: One-third of the
Medicaid budget in the United States is being spent on
long-term care.[4] Two-thirds of nursing home patients

are on Medicaid.[5] The impact of people who have transferred assets to qualify for Medicaid is hurting all of us as taxpayers.

Transferring assets has been a safety net in the past to prevent losing a lifetime of hard-earned savings, but it hasn't been a *dignified* safety net, due to losing control of assets and thereby losing financial independence. Long-term care insurance provides the dignified safety net, and particularly the Partnership policies that now make that possible for middle-income Americans.

A few points you may be wondering about with the Partnership policies:

> **Benefit Choices**—Benefit choices are the same as for non-Partnership policies, in that there is a daily or monthly benefit, an elimination (waiting) period, a home health care/adult day care benefit level, an inflation feature, and a benefit period/lifetime maximum. You may be surprised to learn that many California and Connecticut Partnership policyholders purchase a lifetime (unlimited) benefit period. They do this because they really don't intend to access Medicaid, but if for any reason their assets are lowered for reasons beyond their control; i.e. a stock market plunge, they have asset protection provided by their Partnership policy. This is true because at any time benefits paid out equal your assets plus the amount Medicaid (MediCal in California) allows the healthy spouse to keep, policyholders are allowed to access Medicaid and shelter their assets. For example, if a policy had paid

out $250,000, the person receiving care could apply for Medicaid when the couple's assets are spent down to $340,660, which is equal to the $250,000 in benefits plus $90,660, the 2003 asset maximum for the healthy spouse. (Indiana and New York have total asset protection after benefits paid equal $178,679 for Indiana and after the three year benefit period for New York is exhausted.)

Portability—If you move to another state, the Partnership policy will pay, and the benefits will accumulate toward your asset protection threshold. However, to qualify for Medicaid and take advantage of the asset protection offered by the Partnership policies when your benefits run out, you must move back to the state in which you bought your Partnership policy and re-establish residence. Future legislation may make it possible for Partnership states to reciprocate the asset protection feature with each other, and Indiana and Connecticut are very close to accomplishing reciprocity.

Underwriting—You still must qualify for the Partnership policy medically just as you would for a standard long-term care insurance policy. The younger you are, the better the chance to qualify for a policy, and the lower the premiums. Pre-retirement ages (40's and 50's) are strongly encouraged to apply. In fact, two-thirds of all Indiana Partnership policy purchasers as of 9/30/02 were under age 65 at time of purchase, and the age range of current policyholders is 19-90!"[6]

Arbitration—In some states, the Partnership policies have stronger mechanisms for claims appeals than standard long-term care policies. In those states, a rigorous consumer protection appeal process is in place for any Partnership policyholder who disagrees with a benefit determination.

Policy Continuance—If for any reason the Partnership program is discontinued either nationally or in its particular state, all policies will be honored and appropriate benefits paid by the insurance company that issued the policy.

Due to a change in the 1993 budget bill, Partnership states other than Connecticut, New York, Indiana, California and Iowa can offer asset protection only during the policyholder's lifetime. At death, the state is required to seek estate recovery for Medicaid's payment. This unfortunate legislation slowed development of Partnership programs in other states, but Illinois and Washington tried to push ahead by allowing certain transfers during a person's lifetime as a reward for purchasing a Partnership policy. These programs met with little success without the full strength of the original Partnership concept and are no longer in existence. Massachusetts offers another variation: Medicaid guidelines have to be met as usual so there is no up-front asset protection, but the house is not subject to estate recovery if the policyholder enters a nursing home with a long-term care insurance policy with a minimum daily benefit of $125 and a minimum two-year benefit period.

Interested in finding out about your state's position on the Partnership program? Just call the National Partnership office listed below. If you wish to lobby to get the Partnership in your state, contact your congressional representatives and senators. Even if your state isn't participating in the program at this time, your phone call as an interested person can stimulate your state's legislators to become a participant. For example, Rep. John Peterson (R) of Pennsylvania introduced the Pennsylvania Long-Term Care Partnership Bill 721 in 2002 to restore the Partnership to its original form.

State and National Partnership Offices	
California 800-227-3445 www.dhs.cahwnet.gov/cpltc/	Iowa 515-281-6867
Connecticut 860-418-6319 www.opm.state.ct.us/pdpd4/ ltc/home.htm	New York 518-473-8083 www.nyspltc.org
Indiana 800-452-4800 (in IN only) www.in.gov/idoi/shiip/lt_part- nership.html	National Partnership Office 301-405-2532

Chapter 5

The Medicaid Benefit for Long-Term Care

~~~~~~

M edicaid is the public welfare program for the indigent jointly funded by federal, state and, in some states, local governments. Medicaid's huge growth in recent years is for "aged and disabled" recipients. These people make up just over a fourth of the people entitled to Medicaid benefits, but they consume almost two-thirds of the benefit dollars. The Congressional Budget Office estimates that over half of the $16 billion in federal Medicaid growth between 2001 and 2002 was due to spending on the elderly and disabled.[1] A third of Medicaid funds were for long-term care in Fiscal Year 2001.[2]

The Problem

The aging population combined with the escalating cost of long-term care and loopholes in Medicaid eligibility laws have encouraged a growing number of older Americans to transfer assets to capture public funding for long-term care expenses. However, shrinking tax dollars caused by the severe decline in the ratio of workers to Social Security beneficiaries, due to the aging population, have caused dire financial straits for the Medicaid program just as it has for Medicare. (A May 2002 government survey reports that 39 states had Medicaid shortfalls in

FY 2001 and 28 states were anticipating shortfalls in FY 2002.)[3] There have been several attempts to actually criminalize asset transfers either for the person who is seeking Medicaid benefits or for the advisor who paved the way. These attempts to date have been unsuccessful, but many legislators believe the issue is too important to let it drop. The purpose of legislation of this nature is to restore Medicaid's original purpose—to help poor people.

Medicaid long-term care benefits are intended for people with low income and very low assets. This means that an applicant has to meet both income and asset criteria to qualify for Medicaid benefits. Since the majority of Medicaid's long-term care benefits are for nursing home patients, this chapter will explain the eligibility qualification process for nursing home benefits.[4]

Income Eligibility Criteria

States are able to choose one of two methods to determine income eligibility:

1) The most drastic method allows the nursing home spouse to have income up to three times the Supplemental Security Income (SSI) amount, or $1,656 for 2003. Because that amount is so low compared to the cost of nursing home care ($3,500-$5,000 a month nationwide), the 1993 budget bill made a way to help people with low assets and income that exceeds this low monthly allowance but is not enough to pay privately.

These people can assign their income to a "Miller trust," also called a "qualified income trust," which is a special irrevocable trust designed just for the purpose of helping someone in a cap state whose assets qualify for Medicaid, but income is greater than the cap but not enough to pay privately.

Here's how it works: The individual is allowed to keep a personal-needs allowance, usually $30 a month. All of the remaining income can be assigned to the trust or just the amount that exceeds the cap plus a little extra just to be safe.

For example, if someone has $1,800 a month in income, which exceeds the $1,656 cap by $144, it would be wise to put at least $175 into the Miller trust in case of income fluctuations due to interest rates, etc. The individual's income still goes to the nursing home every month, but it will be a combination of the income retained by the individual and a monthly payment from the Miller trust, unless the individual assigned all of his or her income to the trust. In that case, the trust will make a single payment to the nursing home each month. Medicaid then makes up the difference between the individual's income and the Medicaid rate for the nursing home, which varies by facility.

The state is entitled to any excess income that has accumulated in the trust at the death of the applicant to pay Medicaid back for nursing home expenses Medicaid paid while the person was alive.

The 19 states that work this way are called "income cap" states and they are: Alabama, Alaska, Arizona, Arkansas, Colorado, Delaware, Florida, Idaho, Iowa, Louisiana,

Mississippi, Nevada, New Mexico, Oklahoma, Oregon, South Carolina, South Dakota, Texas, and Wyoming.

2) The remaining states allow the applicant to have income up to the cost of care, usually the Medicaid rate for the nursing home. This amount—about $2,500-$3,500 for most states, but can run as high as $8,583 a month or so for "high cost areas" like metropolitan New York City-varies by facility but there is a maximum for each state. The Medicaid rate is lower than the private pay rate in most states, but a few states allow applicants to have income up to the private pay cost of nursing home care. Check with your Medicaid department for your specific state information. (See **Who to Call for Help** on page 250.)

How is income determined? First, "the name on the check" rule applies. Social Security or pension income is easily attributable. Trust or investment income that is directed jointly to a married couple is divided 50/50. Starting with the gross monthly income for the Medicaid applicant, all individuals are allowed to keep a "personal needs" allowance—about $1 a day, or $30 a month in most states—but it can be as high as $81.75 a month, as in Arizona. In non-cap states, there are a few allowable deductions to get the income down to the Medicaid qualifying level.

▲ health insurance premium, such as a Medicare supplement or retiree health premium

▲ any medical expense not reimbursed by Medicaid or any other source (for example, a particular prescription that Medicaid doesn't cover)

▲ income needed for the spouse at home, subject to a range established by Medicaid ($1,493* minimum— $2,266 maximum per month)

For example, Mr. Jones has $2,000 a month of his own income. After subtracting $30 for the personal needs allowance, $100 for a Medicare supplement premium, and $50 for his monthly prescriptions that aren't paid by any other source, he is left with $1,820. Mrs. Jones has $800 a month of her own Social Security income and a small pension. This means that Mr. Jones can transfer $693 of his income to her to bring her up to $1,493,* the minimum monthly Medicaid allowance for the spouse at home. This gets his income down to $1,107, which easily qualifies him for Medicaid to pay his nursing home bill.

His income of $1,107 then goes to the nursing home. Let's say that the Medicaid rate for that nursing home is $100 per day, or $3,000 a month. Medicaid will then make up the difference between his income and the Medicaid rate and will pay the nursing home $1,893 a month on his behalf ($3,000-$1,107).

You're wondering how the spouse at home can receive more than the minimum monthly income allowance. Some states just use the maximum and allow the spouse at home to keep that much income if the couple has that much income between them. The states that allow the maximum income allowance for the spouse at home are Alaska, Arizona, California, Georgia, Hawaii, Illinois, Iowa, Kentucky, Louisiana, Mississippi, Nebraska, New York, North Dakota, Oklahoma, Texas, Wyoming, the District of Columbia and Wisconsin is $1,935.

*This amount changes each July.

Other states require the spouse at home to justify the need for more income than the minimum of $1,493 per month. The justification process is based on whether or not there are "shelter costs" such as rent, a mortgage payment, homeowners insurance, property taxes, a condominium maintenance fee, utilities, etc. If these shelter costs exceed a monthly amount called the "excess shelter allowance" ($448 for 2003*), the spouse at home can keep additional income. Here's how it works:

The difference between the total shelter costs ($900 a month, for example) and the Excess Shelter Allowance ($448) is added to the $1,493 and this becomes the monthly allowance for the spouse in this example:

$ 900	Total monthly "shelter" costs
– $ 448	Excess Shelter Allowance
$ 452	Additional spousal income allowable
+ $1,493	Minimum monthly spousal income allowance
$1,945	Total monthly spousal income allowance

Some states are allowing couples to retain more resources to generate the above allowable monthly income. This is called the "asset first" or "resource first" rule. This means a couple could retain enough assets to generate the community spouse's income shortfall by the investment income for the retained assets. Using this method may not make it possible to pass resources on to heirs if the spouse meets or exceeds life expectancy as all of the money would be paid out during the spouse's lifetime.

*This amount changes each July.

Conversely, some states, like Ohio and New York, practice the "income first" rule, which means the state won't allow a couple to retain resources to generate income for the spouse until the nursing home spouse has shifted all possible income to the spouse at home.[5] Then if the spouse's income is still below the minimum, the state will allow additional income from retained resources. The "income first" rule keeps the amount of resources retained for this purpose as small as possible. The Supreme Court ruled that states can choose whether to use the "income first" rule or the "resource first" rule. *(Wisconsin Dept. of Health and Family Services v. Blumer,* Supreme Court of the United States, 00-952, February 20, 2002)

Asset Eligibility Criteria

Applicants for Medicaid also have to meet stringent asset criteria as well as income criteria. Generally, people with "countable" assets of about $2,000 ($3,000-$4,000 if both spouses need nursing home care) can qualify. (This amount varies slightly by state.) Assets do not include the house and car if you have a spouse still living in the house and using the car. The house and car still won't count for a single person if that person has a reasonable hope of getting better and going home. If the single person is not likely to return home, usually for six months, then the state can require the house to be sold.

"Countable assets" include anything that is available as a resource to you. In other words, anything that you can take money out of, even if you have to pay surrender charges (for example, an annuity that is only a couple of years old) or sell at a loss (for example, stock or property outside your primary residence). Here's a partial list of assets that count:

▲ cash (checking and savings accounts)

▲ certificates of deposit (CDs)

▲ money market accounts

▲ mutual funds

▲ stocks

▲ bonds

▲ deferred annuities

▲ property outside the home*

▲ cash value in life insurance for policies with a face value of $1,500 or more

▲ revocable trust (a living trust, for example)

▲ burial trusts beyond a minimum amount, unless they are irrevocable**

▲ retirement accounts like 401(k), Keoghs, SEPS, IRA plans, etc.

The rule of thumb is, if you can access the principal, it counts as an asset for Medicaid purposes.

If you are married, you can't just put everything in your spouse's name. When you apply for Medicaid to pay nursing home expenses, all countable assets (See list above) are considered, regardless of whose name the assets are in—husband's or wife's—and includes a spouse's retirement account with rare exception. This is true even if you and your spouse have a prenuptial agree-

---

*Some states won't count property outside the home as an asset if rented, but those states usually count the rental income toward the income eligibility requirements. Also, income-producing property outside the home, such as a business location or a working ranch or farm, usually is not counted.

**Varies by state.

ment. Many states will not honor a divorce agreement if the state believes the purpose of the divorce is solely to establish Medicaid eligibility for long-term care.

The minimum asset amount for the spouse at home is $18,132 for 2003, which means if one-half of the assets is less than the minimum, the spouse at home is allowed to keep the minimum.

Total assets are divided equally between you and your spouse. The spouse applying for Medicaid spends his or her half down to the state's asset requirement (usually $2,000) and the spouse at home can keep a maximum of $90,660 for 2003. In most states, the only way the spouse at home receives the maximum is if one-half of the assets is equal to or exceeds the maximum. Otherwise, the spouse at home receives 50% of the assets.

Here's how it works:

Example #1:	$200,000 in countable assets: One-half is $100,000, which exceeds the maximum. The spouse at home keeps $90,660.
Example #2:	$80,000 in countable assets: One-half is $40,000, which does not equal or exceed the maximum. The spouse at home keeps $40,000.
Example #3:	$20,000 in countable assets. One-half is $10,000, which is less than the minimum. The spouse at home keeps $18,132.

Some states are more liberal and allow the spouse at home to keep the maximum of $90,660 as long as the couple has that much in assets. Those states are Alaska, California, Colorado, Florida, Georgia, Hawaii, Illinois, Kentucky, Louisiana, Maine, Massachusetts, Mississippi, North Dakota, Vermont, Washington, Wyoming, and the District of Columbia. A few other states have minimums in between:

Alabama	$25,000	New York	$74,820
Delaware	$25,000	Oklahoma	$25,000
Iowa	$24,000	South Carolina	$66,480
Minnesota	$25,247	South Dakota	$20,000
New Mexico	$31,290	Wisconsin	$50,000

In those states, the spouse at home is allowed to keep the amount shown as long as the couple has that much in assets.

Transferring Assets—The Myth

Surely the simple solution to all this is to just give assets to children or place them in a trust—perhaps for a favorite charity. That way the nursing home doesn't get your hard-earned assets, and you get something back for all those years of paying taxes. The really important thing is to get the house out of your name, so Medicaid and/or the nursing home can't get it.

Between the 1993 budget bill (OBRA '93) and the 1996 and 1997 health care reform, Congress thinks these are very bad ideas. Here's why:

When someone in a nursing home applies for Medicaid to pay nursing home expenses, Medicaid "looks back" 36 months (30 months in California) to see if a transfer has occurred, for example, to children.* The look-back period is 60 months for transfers to an irrevocable trust; that is, a trust set up so that the applicant cannot receive any income or principal from it. If a transfer has occurred during that time, the applicant is ineligible for Medicaid benefits for the number of months equal to the amount of the transfer divided by the state's average monthly cost of nursing home care. The Medicaid office in your state can tell you your state's average cost of care. (See **Who to Call for Help,** p. 250.) Prior to 10/1/93, the longest an applicant would have to wait for Medicaid benefits after a transfer was 30 months, but OBRA '93 eliminated the cap. Now the "period of ineligibility", also called a "penalty period", for Medicaid benefits depends on the amount of the transfer.

For example, a $300,000 transfer divided by a $3,500 average monthly cost for nursing home care equals 85.7 months (seven years) of ineligibility.

Transfers can be outright gifts or done in more subtle ways:

▲ Transferring $11,000 per year ($22,000 if you are married) to your children and grandchildren to stay within the federal gift-tax exclusion.

▲ Setting up a joint checking account with a son or daughter, then removing the parent's name from the account.

▲ Putting a home in the name of a son or daughter or other family member or friend.

*If the application is made before being admitted to a nursing home, the look-back period is counted back from the date of nursing home admission, not from the date of application.

▲   Transferring assets into an immediate annuity, which changes the assets into income. Medicaid compares the amount of the annuity with your life expectancy. Any projected payout that exceeds life expectancy is treated as a transfer and will trigger a period of ineligibility. Some people get around that by purchasing a "balloon annuity" that has a small payout each year and then pays the remaining money in a lump sum in the last year of life expectancy. (Since the life expectancy tables have nothing to do with the health of the annuitant, the idea is that he or she will probably be deceased by the time the last payment is made.) Keeping the payout small until then preserves principal to maximize the lump-sum payout to the beneficiary. Some states like Indiana have outlawed the balloon annuities. Indiana also stopped "Medicaid planning" practices of converting assets into savings bonds and buying rental property then giving it away to children without a penalty.[6]

▲   Transferring assets into an immediate annuity and producing a monthly income for the spouse at home, also known as "the community spouse." Note: a February 28, 2000, Ohio case ruled such a transfer was improper and denied Medicaid benefits for the appropriate penalty period.[7] Minnesota law changed July 1, 2002 and no longer permits a community spouse to convert assets above the community spouse's maximum ($90,660 in 2003) into an unavailable stream of income with an immediate annuity, if the annuitization occurs after the other spouse has been admitted to a nursing home.[8]

▲ Transferring assets into a trust to fund a college education for a grandchild.

▲ Setting up a trust that will benefit a charity after your death, so you can receive the income while you are alive.

▲ Setting up a trust that will benefit a charity with regular income before your death, then the principal will go to a family member when you die.

▲ Donating to a "pooled-income fund"—similar to a mutual fund operated by a charity for smaller investors to reap the tax benefits of charitable giving without having to invest large amounts.

All of these methods can count as a transfer of assets and trigger a penalty period, which means a period of ineligibility for Medicaid benefits. The motive of the transfer has no bearing on this process.

Since the penalty period begins on the date of the transfer, there are professionals (attorneys, accountants, financial planners, etc.) who have helped people make transfers around the look-back period (i.e., 37 months before applying for Medicaid or 61 months if trusts are used). The advisor might suggest keeping enough assets to pay privately during the lookback period, in case the person needs nursing home care before the lookback period has expired. Then the person could apply for Medicaid after the lookback period had expired. This is sometimes called the "half-a-loaf" theory—transfer half of your assets and keep half of your assets to pay privately during the 36 or 60 month lookback period. However, a New Jersey appeals court would not allow a son to do this on behalf of his mother so he could keep part of her estate. The mother had given the son a power of attorney and authorized him to apply for Medicaid on her behalf, but the power of attorney didn't authorize him to make gifts on her behalf. (*In the Matter of Keri*, N.J. Super. Ct., App. Div., No. A-5949-01T5, Dec. 19, 2002)

A precedent-setting proposal was introduced in 2002 by the state of Connecticut that would weaken the "half-a-loaf" technique. If approved by the federal government, the period of ineligibility would begin on the date of application for Medicaid, assuming the application is otherwise approved. The state's goal is to discourage the transfer of assets to qualify for Medicaid and to promote personal responsibility by encouraging the purchase of long-term care insurance.

Note: Setting up a special trust for a disabled dependent can be accomplished in certain instances if you designate that the principal will revert to the state at the death of the disabled dependent. You should seek advice from an elder law attorney for help with this and any type of trust. Visit the National Academy of Elder Law Attorneys at www.naela.org for a list of elder law attorneys in your area.

Estate Recovery

People who qualify for Medicaid by transferring assets successfully around the lookback period or whose assets are tied up in their home which is a non-countable asset face yet another huge hurdle. OBRA '93 requires states to recover from the estate of anyone who receives Medicaid benefits at the death of the second spouse. Some states like North Dakota, California

Why Transferring Assets Can Be a Bad Idea

Divorce	Half your assets go to buy your favorite son-in-law or daughter-in-law a red BMW!
Financial Difficulties	Every family has financial down times. Your daughter is thinking "I'm going to inherit the money anyway . . ."
Mis-Use of Funds	It looked like the best stock pick of the century.
Lawsuit	Your son is sued and your assets—now his assets as far as the court is concerned—are attached.
College Financial Aid	Your grandson no longer qualifies for financial aid because you shifted your assets to his father.
Cost-Basis	You paid $10 a share for the stock you just gave your daughter. It is now worth $100 a share. She sells the stock and owes tax on the gain of $90 per share . . . the tax bill may be more than a lifetime of long-term care insurance premium for you!
Early Death of Adult Child	The unthinkable happens—your son or daughter predeceases you. Your assets are now in the hands of the in-laws.
Adverse Tax Consequences	Interest earned on the transferred assets are taxable income to your children and amounts above $11,000 transferred in any one calendar year use up part of your lifetime estate and gift tax exemption ($1,000,000 in 2003). Some states have separate gift taxes from federal gift taxes.

A good long-term care insurance policy can mean you don't have to worry about these problems!

and Minnesota include recovery from the spouse's estate of any assets that the Medicaid recipient at the time of death conveyed to the spouse "through joint tenancy, tenancy in common, survivorship, life estate, living trust, or other arrangement" (*North Dakota Dept. of Human Services v. Thompson,* December 22, 1998).[9] Another North Dakota case said all assets in which the Medicaid recipient once held an interest are subject to estate recovery, even if those assets had not been formally conveyed.[10]

Effective January 24, 2000, the U.S. Health Care Financing Administration (the organization that oversees Medicare and Medicaid) ruled that a state has the option to recover Medicaid expenditures from the surviving beneficiary of an annuity that was owned by a Medicaid nursing home patient.[11] However, recovery cannot be made as long as a surviving spouse or minor or disabled child is alive.

The recovery process also includes in most states the right to place a lien on your home in the amount of Medicaid payments made on your behalf for your care. When the property is sold or title is transferred, the lien must be paid. States have the right to place a lien on even a "life estate," which is simply a legal interest you keep in your home after you have transferred the deed to someone else. And if you give your house away outright, you lose the capital gains exclusion.

Your children (or to whomever you give the house) could take advantage of the capital gains exclusion, but only if they live in the house at least two of the last five years before the house is sold. Giving your house to your kids and continuing to live in it can mean your children wind up paying a steep capital gains tax when the house is sold if they don't adhere to the capital gains exclusion rules of living in the house the appropriate time before its sale.

"More than half the states place liens on homes to protect their interest," according to *Kiplinger's Personal Finance Magazine.*[12] The lien is not enforceable, however, until the death of the second spouse, even if he or she does not live in the house, and Medicaid must notify your family in advance that a lien is being placed. Nevada places liens on the homes of the surviving spouses of deceased Medicaid beneficiaries. While the lien isn't enforced until the surviving spouse dies, he or she can't sell the home and use the money for other purposes without paying off the lien first.[13]

Liens also cannot be enforced if:

▲ There is a child under age 21, or who is blind or disabled, whether or not the child lives in the house.

▲ There is a brother or sister with a joint ownership for the year immediately prior to the nursing home admission, but only if he or she lived in the house continuously since that date.

▲ There is a non-disabled adult child who had lived in the house two or more years prior to the parent's admission to a nursing home, and who had provided care that delayed admission, but the child must have lived in the house continuously since then.

An excellent publication, entitled *Questions and Answers on Medicaid Estate Recovery for Long-Term Care Under OBRA '93,* is available free from AARP by writing the Public Policy Institute, 601 "E" Street, NW, Washington, DC 20049, or you can access it online at http://research.aarp.org.

The Bigger Problem—The Criminal Side Revisited

A variety of legislative attempts to criminalize asset transfers for the sole purpose of qualifying for Medicaid has put a huge chill on the practice of "Medicaid planning," the process of impoverishing oneself on paper to qualify for Medicaid's nursing home benefit. The Balanced Budget Act of 1997 had this to say about Medicaid planning:

Whoever . . . for a fee knowingly and willfully counsels or assists an individual to dispose of assets (including by any transfer in trust) in order for an individual to become eligible for medical assistance (Medicaid), if disposing of the assets results in the imposition of a period of ineligibility for such assistance . . . shall . . . be guilty of a criminal offense.

Due to the efforts primarily of the New York State Bar Association, this legislation was declared unenforceable in 1998 by [then] Attorney General Janet Reno. A little publicized comment in her letter on the subject to [then] Speaker of the House Newt Gingrich was that she would be glad to help Congress write something that would be enforceable. An injunction against the law was granted later in the year by New York Judge Thomas McElvoy in September 1998, who also ruled that it was unconstitutional. Attorney General Reno then filed a notice of appeal on December 18, 1998, which was the necessary step to protect the Justice Department's right to appeal the injunction. Prior to the Balanced Budget Act's attempt, the Health Insurance

Accountability and Portability Act of 1996 made it a criminal offense, effective January 1, 1997, for the person who transfers the assets, not the person's legal or financial advisor. That law quickly earned the name, "The Granny Goes to Jail Law." The National Association of Elder Law Attorneys raised a huge outcry and lobbied furiously to get it repealed, saying it just wasn't fair to send Grandma to jail, and the law should be dismissed. Congress agreed only partially with their case and eliminated the part about Grandma going to jail and replaced it with the above language in the Balanced Budget Act that seeks to punish the professional who charges a fee to help someone transfer assets to qualify for Medicaid.

The present status is that the Justice Department withdrew the December 1998 notice of appeal mentioned above in March 1999. However, these attempts show an increasing interest to restrict access to Medicaid to the truly needy.

Why does such a strong interest exist to close the loopholes for Medicaid planning?

Because there aren't enough tax dollars to pay for a national long-term care plan, and that's the direction this program is taking when you consider that Medicaid pays 47.5% of nursing home costs and two-thirds of all nursing home patients are Medicaid recipients.[14, 15] 44 cents of every Federal income tax dollar in the U.S. goes to pay for entitlements (mainly, Social Security, Medicare and Medicaid), and this is only a prelude *before* the baby boomers start applying for Medicaid nursing home benefits![16] In view of these facts, it is reasonable to expect that legislative activity to curtail Medicaid planning will continue.

The Biggest Problem

All of the above are problems, but the biggest problem is that by giving your assets away, you lose access to them, and you lose the one thing that matters most—**your independence and control.** That's why you gave the assets away to start with—to keep from losing them to a nursing home—and now for one or more of the above reasons, you've lost them anyway.

Here's what it means to be a Medicaid patient in most states:

▲   You can't get into strictly private-pay facilities that don't accept Medicaid patients.

▲   Medicaid pays very little for home health care, so being on Medicaid in most states means being in a nursing home. All states have obtained permission (waivers) to use Medicaid dollars for home and community-based services.[17] The demand for the home and community-based services has exceeded what is available and has resulted in waiting lists in most states.[18] The reality is that priority must given to the people who require nursing home care, and this makes dollars for home care scarce. In fact, a national claimant survey showed that in 1999, the Medicaid waiver program was paying an average of $485 per month for home care, whereas the average monthly benefit from long-term care insurance was $1,527.[19] *Medicaid does not pay the room and board charge in assisted living facilities,*[20] and that's the bulk of the charge.

▲   Medicaid pays less than private-pay rates in most states, so the waiting lists are long for Medicaid patients.

▲   You have to go wherever there is a bed, which could be hours away from your family.

▲   If the facility doesn't accept Medicaid and you run out of your own money, you can be required to move to a facility that accepts Medicaid, and that's a hard situation for families to deal with.*

▲   Nursing homes that operate with predominantly Medicaid patients don't have as much funding as private-pay facilities to upgrade services, furnishings, etc.

▲   You simply don't have as many choices as a private-pay patient—a private room, for example, is not allowed—because as a Medicaid patient, you aren't paying the bill.

As Joan Gruber, a Dallas financial planner who works mainly with families of the elderly, says, "No one would voluntarily set themselves up for Medicaid if they understood what it's like."[21] And a spokesperson for the American Association of Homes and Services for the Aging (which represents nonprofit nursing homes) says, "The more money you have, the more options you will have in terms of paying for care at home or for assisted living. I would never recommend that someone who has money get rid of it to go on Medicaid."[22]

---

*On March 25, 1999, President Clinton signed into law the Nursing Home Resident Protection Act of 1999 which means that nursing homes that voluntarily drop out of Medicaid can refuse to admit new Medicaid patients, but they can't force Medicaid patients already in residence to leave. This does not, however, prevent nursing homes from dropping out of Medicaid altogether and being totally private-pay facilities. To prevent surprises, this law requires private-pay facilities to notify patients upon admission that they will have to leave if they run out of their own money and need to apply for Medicaid.

Long-Term Care Insurance—A Better Way

The message sent by the federal government is clear: Medicaid is a program for poor people and is not to be used by middle- and upper-income Americans. Many reliable publications such as Suze Orman's **The 9 Steps to Financial Freedom** (Three Rivers Press, 2000), Dave Ramsey's **Financial Peace Revisited** (Viking Penguin, 2003) and *Fortune* magazine encourage people to buy long-term care insurance instead of relying on Medicaid. Well-known financial advisor Jane Bryant Quinn says that Medicaid planning is unethical in *The Washington Post*, June 3, 2001.[23]

Growing numbers of middle- and upper-middle-class people don't like these rules. They're willing to take care of themselves as long as they maintain their health. If a nursing home looms, however, they decide to quit being responsible. They look for ways of leaving their money to their children, while forcing the taxpayer to provide their care.

Ultimately, the transfer may prove to be ineffective if there are no Medicaid beds available when you need one. Even today, some communities have year-long waiting lists for Medicaid beds!

The primary reason people are purchasing long-term care insurance policies is to maintain choice, and consequently, **independence.**[24] (See **Long-Term Care and Your Financial Security.**)

If you are the type of person who enjoys being in control, a long-term care insurance policy may be the only thing that makes it possible for you to stay in control by guaranteeing that you will have purchasing power—and consequently decision-making power—when you need long-term care, which means choices other than a nursing home—home health care, adult day care, and the beautiful private-pay assisted living facilities that represent the fastest growing form of long-term care.

If a nursing home patient thinks he or she will qualify for Medicaid eventually, it is recommended that an application be made to Medicaid upon admission to the nursing home so a financial assessment can be made at that time. Applicants who wait until assets are spent down to the qualifying level of $2,000 must furnish financial information back to the admission date, and that is not always easy to do.

If you are interested in applying for Medicaid to pay your nursing home expenses, contact your local Medicaid office, which is usually listed in the state government section in the blue pages of your telephone book or see **Who to Call for Help** on p. 250 for state Medicaid offices.

Since the Medicaid qualification process can be complex, some people ask an elder law attorney to help them with the Medicaid application. Contact the National Academy of Elder Law Attorneys for an elder law attorney in your area who specializes in Medicaid (www.naela.org).

Chapter 6

Alternatives for Financing Long-Term Care

∿∿∿∿∿∿∿∿∿∿∿∿∿∿∿∿∿∿∿∿∿∿∿∿

Other ways people consider financing long-term care are through accelerated death riders to life insurance policies, viatical or life settlements, life/long-term care policies, annuity/long-term care policies, reverse mortgages and critical illness policies. An overview of each of these six options is presented as additional information for the long-term care planning process.

Accelerated Death Benefits

An alternative to purchasing a long-term care insurance policy as described in the preceding section is to purchase a life insurance policy that will provide cash advances against all or a portion of the death benefit to pay for long-term care expenses while the insured is still living. Because the death benefit can be paid out early, this form of long-term care payment as a part of a life insurance policy is commonly referred to as an accelerated death benefit, but you also may hear it referred to as a "living needs" benefit or "rider." Early versions only paid if the policyholder suffered from a terminal illness, and that is still the most common triggering event. At least 20% of these policies make the benefit available for chronically ill people as well. Many of these pay only for permanent confinement in a nursing home, but some pay also for home and community-based care, like assisted living, and a handful pay only for home care.[1]

The accelerated death benefit is an alternative to traditional LTC insurance policies for some people because this provision can be added to a life insurance policy for little or no cost. It also can help someone who cannot qualify for a traditional LTC policy at an older age if the benefit was included in the policyholder's life insurance at time of purchase, as is the case with many younger purchasers of life insurance today.

Typically, monthly benefits for long-term care will equal 2% of the face value of the policy for nursing home care and 1% for home health care. For example, if the face value of the policy is $150,000, the nursing home benefit would be $3,000 a month and the home care benefit would be $1,500. Some policies do not reduce the payout for home care.

Newer policies tend to be reimbursement policies, which means they will pay actual charges up to the available benefit equal to 2% of face value. Older policies were commonly indemnity plans, which paid out the 2% amount, regardless of charge. The Health Insurance Portability and Accountability Act of 1996 (HIPAA) is primarily responsible for this change (See *Tax Incentives for Long-Term Care Insurance* on p. 19 for a list of provisions). Benefit payments in excess of $220 per day in 2003 (or the monthly equivalent) that exceed the actual cost of care will be taxed as income, so most long-term care insurance policies of all types stick with paying the actual charges to help the policyholder avoid a precarious tax situation.

The pitfalls? Even at 2% of the face value for all benefits, the monthly benefit payments are likely to be lower and durations of coverage shorter than under freestanding LTC insurance products, because many people do not have life insurance policies with large face amounts. So if the life insurance policy has a face value of $100,000, the monthly benefit would be $2,000. In metropolitan areas, that benefit amount would only pick up about half the cost of either a nursing home or daily eight-hour shifts of home health care. If the policy advanced the entire face amount, in this example, the benefit duration would be only about four years.

Other pitfalls are that some policies still pay a lower benefit for home health care. An especially serious problem is that inflation may not be addressed. Also, if the primary need is for life insurance, utilizing the death benefit for long-term care expenses defeats the purpose of the insurance by leaving the survivors with little or no death benefit after the insured is deceased. However, the Health Insurance Portability and Accountability Act of 1996 provided much needed clarification that accelerated death benefits will be treated as if they were the proceeds payable on account of death—that is, income-tax free—if the benefits meet the criteria of HIPAA. Non-qualified versions are being sold, however, so check carefully to see if the sales brochures, sample policies, etc., have notification on the front that the policy is tax-qualified. Policies that are intended to be tax-qualified are supposed to be clearly marked.

Since the cost to add an accelerated death benefit option to a life insurance policy is minimal with most policies, younger people may consider the rider a very good purchasing decision, similar to purchasing the right to buy a discounted freestanding LTC insurance policy at older ages when purchasing a disability income policy. Many employers have an accelerated death benefit provision in their group life insurance plans.

Traditional Viatical Settlements

Taking its name from "viaticum"— the supplies needed to perform last rites that were routinely sent into battle with Roman soldiers (who commonly weren't expected to return)—a traditional viatical settlement allows a terminally ill individual to "sell" a life insurance policy to a third party. The core idea is that the proceeds from the sale of the policy would provide "financial supplies" for the final journey of death. The reality is that the third party (the viatical company) pays the terminally ill person a percentage of the death benefit and becomes the owner and beneficiary of the life insurance policy and takes over the premium payments. The terminally ill person gets funds to live on during the very costly time before death, and the third party receives the full death benefit after the person dies.

"Terminally ill" for a viatical company can be anyone with a life expectancy of five years or less, but typically is 2–3 years.

The amount paid for the policy is based on the life expectancy of the insured and is influenced by other factors such as:

▲ **The Capitalization of the Viatical Company**—Most viatical companies do not bear the risk of the viatical arrangement of paying out a discounted death benefit and waiting until the person dies to collect the entire death amount. Rather, most viaticals are brokers that bring together investors and terminally ill people. At least one insurance company acts as a viatical settlement provider and bears the risk of buying life insurance policies.

▲ **Case Diversification of the Viatical Company**—The viatical business started with AIDS patients. Viatical companies that have continued to purchase mainly the life insurance policies of AIDS patients are not doing well because technology has drastically extended the lives of AIDS patients. A successful viatical company has a good mix of terminal conditions, like cancer and heart-related conditions, as well as late-stage conditions, such as Alzheimer's.

▲ **Rating of the Insurance Company**—Viatical companies make a lower payment if the insurance company has a rating of B+ or lower according to the A.M. Best company, the largest third-party rating service for insurance companies. Why? Because if the lower-rated company goes out of business, the viatical company gets stuck with a policy on which it probably can't collect.

▲ **Waiver of Premium Status**—If the premium of the policy is waived due to a provision that waives the premium because the policyholder is disabled, the viatical company will have more money available since it won't have to assume premium payments.

▲ **Investor Mix**—Investors who are short-term, high-return speculative investors demand a higher interest rate for their investment dollars which will lower the amount available to pay out in discounted death benefits.

Viatical companies buy all kinds of life insurance policies: term, whole life, universal life, and group life. A viatical settlement can be a "knight in shining armor" for an employee who is too sick to work and must convert the group life policy to an individual policy in order to keep it. The premium for a converted policy can be steep, and many employees aren't prepared to pay a high premium. A viatical company can purchase the policy and pick up the premium.

The Viatical Settlement Process

The terminally ill person submits an application. The viatical company confirms the insurance policy with the insurance company and obtains medical records to determine the life expectancy of the applicant. There is no application fee.

If the viatical company decides to purchase the policy, the minimum payment to the insured based on life expectancy may follow this table which represents minimum guidelines suggested by the National Association of Insurance Commissioners:

Life Expectancy of Insured	% of Net Death Benefit* Paid
1–6 months	80%
6–12 months	70%
12–18 months	65%
18–24 months	60%
24 +	50%

* Payment is based on net death benefit, not face value of the policy. Net death benefit means the actual benefit payable at death, which may have been reduced by policy loans or withdrawals.

These percentages can be higher based on criteria listed at the beginning of this section and can be 5% lower than these guidelines if the insurance company is rated B+ or lower. In 1999, a "reasonableness standard" was added as an alternative to the table of minimum payments. Your insurance department can explain further about this alternative as criteria is jointly developed using data supplied annually by viatical settlement providers and reasonableness criteria provided by the National Association of Insurance Commissioners.

A large viatical company reports that forty percent of applications are approved. Sixty percent are declined because life expectancy is beyond five years, which means the payment offer is usually low and not attractive to the applicant.

There is a 15-day rescission period, which means the applicant can change his or her mind for any reason and resume ownership of the policy. One viatical company's practice is to reinstate the original beneficiary if the original owner dies within the 15-day rescission period, although there is no requirement for the viatical company to do so.

Policies of all sizes are viaticated. One company's range is $5,000–$6,000,000, with an average of $102,000 in death benefit.

Most states (including most of the larger ones) have adopted viatical settlement legislation, so most of the population in the United States is covered by consumer protection regulation for viatical settlements.

The Health Insurance Portability and Accountability Act of 1996 (HIPAA) enables viatical settlements to be tax-free for terminal

individuals with a two-year or less life expectancy or for chronically ill individuals. Note: It is the health care practitioner (physician, nurse, or social worker) that determines the tax status. The
viatical company may think life expectancy is three years, but if
the health care practitioner thinks two, then the discounted death
benefit paid out will be tax-free because the IRS goes by the
health care practitioner's certification. Also, the IRS doesn't look
back. If the individual exceeds life expectancy, the IRS won't chal-
lenge the tax-free benefit status.

To receive the settlement tax-free, however, the viator must do
business with a viatical company that is licensed in the states that
require licensing or adheres to the NAIC guidelines for payment
(described on the preceding page) in those states that do not
require licensing. The NAIC also has specific consumer disclo-
sure requirements, so that viators understand all of the ramifica-
tions of the viatical settlement.

Several states, such as California and New York, have also made
viatical funds free of state income taxes.

Viatical Settlements vs. Accelerated Death Benefits

▲   The ability to accelerate the death benefit, that is, to collect a portion of the death benefit while still living for
chronically ill individuals, not just terminally ill, is only
available on a small percentage of life insurance policies in
force. (A little over three million policies had been sold
with a chronically-ill trigger benefit as of the end of 1997,
the majority of which will only accelerate the death benefit if you are permanently confined to a nursing home.
Less than 7% of these will pay for home and community

care.)² Viatical companies, on the other hand, can purchase policies from any insurance company.

▲   The accelerated death benefit (ADB) policy may only
    pay out a portion, then apply a loan interest rate to the
    remaining death benefit, which means the beneficiaries
    won't get the entire remaining death benefit.

▲   Even though the health care reform legislation of 1996
    allows the "terminally ill" requirement for an ADB to
    be up to 24 months, most ADB policies are six to 12
    months, much shorter than a viatical settlement which
    runs up to five years.

▲   An ADB policy can lapse if premiums are not paid. The
    viatical settlement is a one-time procedure and all the
    money due the applicant is paid out all at one time. The
    terminally or chronically ill person no longer has to worry
    about paying premium and keeping a policy in force.

Some ADB policies may have a payout that is less than 50% of
the death benefit, and a little over half of them are capped at
50%. The payout on a traditional viatical settlement is usually
50%-80% but typically is higher than an ADB policy that is
capped at 50%. There is no maximum age at which a viatical settlement can occur. In fact, viatical arrangements are now available to individuals aged 70+ with no medical underwriting (See
next section, *Life Settlements*)

Viatical Settlements vs. Long-Term Care Insurance

▲   For people without long-term care insurance, a viatical
    settlement can provide a solution to immediate cash

needs. A small portion of the settlement could also be used to purchase a long-term care policy for the surviving partner.

▲ Viatical settlements represent a great alternative to Medicaid planning for the person who is unable to qualify for long-term care insurance due to problems with health or affordability.

▲ LTC insurance stretches the money out vs. paying the full cost of long-term care services with a lump-sum viatical settlement, which can disappear quickly, especially with the temptation to spend it on things other than the cost of care.

▲ Long-term care insurance can preserve the death benefit of the life insurance policy for family members.

▲ A long-term care insurance policy with an unlimited benefit period can pay benefits tax-free for an unlimited time period vs. a lump-sum viatical settlement that will run out.

Life Settlements

In addition to traditional viatical settlements as outlined above to help people who are chronically or terminally ill, a broad expansion of this idea, entitled a "life settlement," is available **for older people who are not ill**. These are just people who no longer need a death benefit because the original reason they bought life insurance doesn't exist anymore (for example, college tuition, change in estate size, sale of a business or divorce) or perhaps they can't afford the premium after retirement, a classic problem with term life insurance.

Today any male age 70 or older or any female age 74 or older who has life insurance (group, individual, term, whole life, universal life) can sell their policies to a life settlement company for their present value, an opportunity that can be a significant estate planning tool. Policies of almost any size can be purchased, from $5,000-$35,000,000, for example. This includes the policies held in irrevocable life insurance trusts, buy-sell agreements, and "key-man" policies. The proceeds from the policy sale are unrestricted, and high net worth individuals have the ability to use the funds for such options as:

▲   making cash gifts to family members
▲   purchasing a minority interest in a closely held business to reduce estate taxes
▲   facilitate the transfer of a business to the next generation
▲   funding the purchase of permanent life insurance that will insure a spouse to cover estate taxes
▲   paying long-term care expenses for someone who is uninsurable
▲   funding the purchase of long-term care insurance for a spouse
▲   making charitable gifts and funding planned giving techniques
▲   purchasing a business
▲   paying down debt
▲   investing the proceeds

As you can see, disposition of the funds is up to the imagination and simply represents a way to use life insurance while living. A few life settlement companies will even purchase a life insurance policy from someone as young as 65 if the life expectancy is in the 12 year range, which may be the case with certain health conditions.

Here is an example of using proceeds from a life settlement for long-term care:

> *An 80-year old gentleman, with some health concerns, had a $400,000 universal life insurance policy that had very little cash value. Making the premium payments was becoming a financial burden, and they were also concerned about long-term care for each of them. Unfortunately, he did not qualify for long-term care insurance because of his health problems. A life settlement gave him $175,000. The sale of this policy not only relieved this couple of the monthly premium payments but the life settlement funds enabled the client to purchase a long-term care policy for his wife, and also provided funds for his own long-term care needs.[3] Lifetime settlement payments incur tax liability to the original policyholder in two ways. First, the difference between the settlement payment and the cash surrender value is taxed as a capital gain. The difference between the total premiums paid (the tax basis) and the cash surrender value is taxed as ordinary income.[4]*

You should discuss your individual tax situation with a professional tax advisor.

Single Premium Life/Long-Term Care Policies

A growing number of consumers have expressed interest in a long-term care funding method in which a single premium is paid—i.e., a lump sum deposit—and that premium is guaranteed not to change. In standard LTC policies, there are very few companies with a one-time premium guaranteed not to change, and relatively few that have a limited payment option, such as 10-pay or 20-pay or "pay to age 65". Most policies require premiums to be paid for life, just like health insurance, and the premium can be increased in the future if it is increased on an entire classification of policyholders.

Increasingly, the consumer interested in the lump sum, paid-up approach says, "I want to pay one time, and if I don't use the policy, I want my money to be passed on to my [children, grandchildren, church, charity, etc]." The policy is then considered "paid-up" and no future deposits are required. Typically, this type of consumer may be thinking self-insurance is the best option vs. gambling that many years of insurance premiums may not pay off if care is never needed.

If this is the way you are feeling, you'll be glad to know this "almost too good to be true" type of funding method is actually available in a specially designed life insurance policy to help pay for long-term care expenses. Here's how it works:

Issue ages for single individuals generally begin about 30, and joint policies for two people (e.g., mother and daughter, as well as spouses) can be written, if the average age of the two people falls within certain parameters. Age 80 is typically the maximum issue age, although there is no age limit for the benefit payments once a policy is issued. Money can be used to make the single premium deposit with cash, CDs, money market accounts, non-qualified and qualified annuities, or IRAs and Keogh plans. You may also be able to move the cash value from another life insurance policy into this one with no adverse tax consequences. Issue ages can vary based on the source of the premium (i.e., older issue ages of 59½ may be required for transfers from qualified annuities, IRAs and Keoghs).

The idea of this policy is that whatever amount you deposit purchases a death benefit like any other life insurance policy. What's new and different is that at least double the amount of your deposit becomes immediately available to you for long-term care. If you need the benefit for long-term care almost immediately, the policy could pay as much as four years of benefits for you at 2% per month of the long-term care amount or two years at 4% per month. The longer you have the policy without filing a claim, the more accumulation and the longer your benefit period. While minimum deposits can be in the $10,000–$20,000 range, a meaningful benefit based on today's costs requires somewhere in the $100,000 range for a 60-year-old couple. A $100,000 deposit provides a monthly benefit for about four years of approximately $5,000 each, a meaningful amount if both spouses need long-term care. Smaller deposits, such as $50,000 or less, can be made if you are willing to self-insure a significant part of your long-term care expense. For added flexibility there usually is a certain amount of money available each year that can be accessed without surrender penalties. (Surrender penalties are graded downward each year until they disappear after 10 years or so.) Withdrawals from gain are subject to income tax. If you elect not to take withdrawals, the money will grow tax deferred, which means it will grow faster than in savings accounts, CDs, money market funds, or similar taxable accounts. This growth is designed to help with inflation.

The pitfalls? If care is needed in the early years of the policy, the insured can expect a benefit period of about four years, instead of longer benefit periods, such as lifetime, which means unlimited. However, newer versions of this policy provide an option to allow the policy to pay benefits for an unlimited number of years if you pay the extra premium for that option, or intervals in between such as five, seven, eight or ten years.

Other pitfalls? Inflation coverage can be tricky. One popular version prior to 2002 allowed you to purchase a 5% increase in the prior year's amount each year without checking your health. You would be continually putting money into the policy each year that you accept the offer; however, the offer stopped when it was declined once. The newer version allows you to buy a 5% compound inflation rider that starts immediately on the entire benefit and never stops growing as long as you have the policy.

Another company allows you to purchase a rider that extends your benefit period to either eight years or unlimited by creating an additional monthly benefit that won't be available until the base plan is used up. This extension of benefits rider also includes an inflation rider that *increases only that additional monthly benefit 5% compounded, not the base plan.* The reasoning is that the base plan grows through the dividends. However, dividend growth can be small and at claim time, one must exhaust the base benefit before being able to access the extended benefit that has grown at 5% compounded annually since the date the policy was purchased. A good way to handle this problem is to choose the highest acceleration option for the base benefit. For example, you can choose to have the base benefit paid monthly at 4%, which means it would be exhausted in two years, at which time you can access the portion that has been growing at 5% compounded annually. If you want the base policy to pay out at a more meaningful benefit, you can overfund the policy when you first buy it. Your insurance agent can work with you to make the benefits meet your expectations at claim time.

Premium for these optional riders may be included in the lump-sum deposit, or paid separately and ongoing even if you made a lump-sum deposit, depending on the insurance company offering the product. If the premium for the rider is ongoing, the good news is that the premium is guaranteed not to ever go up, so it is a budgetable expense.

Effect of the 1996 Health Insurance Portability and Accountability Act (HIPAA)

This legislation allows benefit payments to be totally tax-free as long as benefits do not exceed the greater of $220 per day in 2003 or actual costs. The separate premium for options as described above that extend the benefit period and/or increase the inflation coverage may be taken from the cash value of the policy and if it is, a portion may be taxable income to you. (If you are under age 59½, that amount is normally also subject to a 10% federal surtax.) This premium for the options is the only part of the premium that will be treated as a medical expense and eligible for a tax deduction if medical expenses exceed 7.5% of your adjusted gross income.

With the main portion of the policy, however, you get the best of both worlds—tax-deferred growth and tax-free benefits—which many people think far outweighs having just the premium for the extra inflation/benefit period extension rider as a potential tax deduction or as taxable income. People who are thinking about self-insuring especially like this policy because if long-term care is never needed, the money goes tax-free to your beneficiary as it is paid out in the form of a death benefit. Or, if for any reason you decide to cancel the policy, the guaranteed surrender value is never less than the single premium you paid, less any long-term care benefit payments, of course. If you need long-term care, however, there is a multiplier that makes the money available to pay long-term care benefits worth much more than the face value of the policy.

If you don't want to make a lump-sum payment, newer versions of this product are available with annual and 10-pay premiums as well.

Long-Term Care Insurance and Estate Planning

One company that sells this type of policy has a suggestion to help you with estate planning: Make your adult child owner and beneficiary of a 10-pay policy with you as the insured. Give the child the premium each year through the $11,000 annual gift tax exclusion. Your accomplishments are four-fold:

▲ You accomplish the $11,000 annual gift to decrease the size of your taxable estate.

▲ The policy is not includable in your estate because you are neither the owner nor the beneficiary.

▲ Your long-term care needs are taken care of if you fund the policy adequately:

▲ Your child will receive a significant death benefit if you never need long-term care.

Moreover, many estate planners recommend aggressive gifting, but many people are just not comfortable with gifting assets without a source to pay long-term care costs. Therefore, long-term care insurance, particularly the "nothing to lose, everything to gain" policy described in this section, can play a vital role in constructing and preserving a carefully crafted estate plan that requires aggressive gifting.

For example, those of you who have large estate tax problems could make the benefits of this policy payable to an irrevocable trust with your children as beneficiary, and just pay the long-term care costs yourself, which will further reduce your taxable estate. However, the benefits of the policy going into the irrevocable trust execute a large, tax-free gift to your children.

An article in an estate planning magazine summarized the advantages of the single-premium life insurance policy, which the authors referred to as "deposit-based long-term care insurance."[5] The article said by moving emergency funds that would otherwise be invaded for a long-term care need into a deposit-based long-term care insurance policy, you would:

1) preserve your principal;
2) have immediate access to the funds;
3) earn a modest return;
4) create a death benefit; and
5) most importantly, in the event of a long-term care need, multiply the value of these emergency funds by 200+ percent, depending on your age when you are issued a policy.

Your tax advisor can tell you if any of these ideas are helpful for your situation.

Long-Term Care Annuities

A long-term care **deferred** annuity can play a huge role in helping people who cannot qualify for long-term care insurance due to age or health problems. This annuity is available to age 85 and there are seven, very broad health questions that will not be difficult for most people to satisfy. The questions deal with major conditions like dementia, Parkinson's disease, multiple sclerosis, Lou Gehrig's disease, and whether or not you are dependent on a walker or wheelchair or are bedridden. Being in a nursing home in the past two years would disqualify you, but having a couple of weeks of home health care in that same time frame would not.

This concept uses an annuity with two funds. One fund, which is for long-term care expenses, grows at a higher interest rate, 4.55% as of January, 2003, with a five-year rate guarantee, then current interest thereafter. (A 4.55% rate is equal to 6.5% in a taxable fund for someone in a combined 30% tax bracket.) The other fund, which is just the regular cash fund in an annuity, grows at the guaranteed rate of 3%. The five-year jumpstart on the long-term care fund ensures a higher amount available for long-term care. At the end of the fifth year, you decide if you want the strategy of growing the LTC fund at a higher rate to continue, or if you want to equalize the growth rate between the two funds. (The funds are automatically equalized around your 90th birthday.)

The purpose of the separate LTC fund is to allow you immediate access to the money for services from a licensed home health care agency, adult day care center, assisted living facility or nursing home care. Otherwise, early withdrawals from an annuity mean limitations on the amount you can withdraw, usually 10%, without penalty.

Benefits begin after only a 7-day waiting period when your doctor verifies that you either need help with at least two of six Activities of Daily Living (bathing, continence, dressing, eating, toileting and transferring) or you are cognitively impaired. The benefit is reimbursement, not indemnity, which means it will pay no more than actual expenses up to the monthly limit for a minimum of 36 months (18 months if a joint policy and both annuitants are receiving care at the same time). There is a lifetime rider available if you are willing to pay the additional premium.

Here's an example of how LTC withdrawals will be calculated:

$100,000   (LTC fund balance at time of claim)
÷   34.5   (factor to ensure a minimum of 36 months of coverage)
  $2,898   per month available benefit for actual expenses

Money withdrawn from the LTC fund reduces the cash fund proportionally. For example, a $3,000 withdrawal from the LTC fund means a $1,500 withdrawal from the cash fund. Conversely, a $1,500 withdrawal from the cash fund means a $3,000 withdrawal from the LTC fund.

If you do not use up all of the money on long-term care, the amount remaining in the cash fund will be passed to your beneficiary outside of probate at your death, or the surviving annuitant (second-to-die) if it is a joint contract.

This product is a deferred annuity, which many people prefer over low-interest bearing accounts like CDs and money market funds because of the tax-deferred earnings. Having this product in place with money that you keep for an emergency anyway could give you the flexibility to have a longer waiting period on a traditional LTC policy. Some companies offer longer waiting periods in those states that allow it of 180 days, 365 days or even 730 days.

Since it is a deferred annuity, you are taxed on the gain as withdrawals are made.

Now for a pitfall. This product was introduced as a non-tax-qualified long-term care policy. That means you are at risk of being taxed on the money that is dispersed from the LTC fund if the IRS rules against non-qualified policies. Beware of anyone telling you that you can deduct all of your LTC expenses as medical expenses at tax time so it really doesn't matter. **This is a reimbursement policy,** which means it will only make a payment from the LTC fund when a claim for an actual service or charge is presented, so it is directly reimbursing long-term care expenses. There's a very good chance the IRS would disqualify your deduction for medical expenses, because IRS Form 1040, Schedule A—Itemized Deductions plainly says *"Caution: Do not include expenses reimbursed or paid by others."*

This book in no way intends to give tax advice, so please see your personal tax advisor for an opinion on how this policy would apply to you.

If the product were changed to satisfy the benefit criteria of a tax-qualified policy (i.e., mainly that benefits are available when your doctor or a registered nurse or licensed social worker certifies that you are expected to be unable to perform at least two Activities of Daily Living for at least 90 days, or that you have a severe cognitive impairment), this product could present a very interesting option for long-term care financing, especially for people with significant health problems. It also has added flexibility in that the 10% allowable annual withdrawals from the cash fund give you money to use for associated costs with long-term care that are not covered as an eligible long-term care expense, such as prescription drugs and miscellaneous supplies.

Other advantages over other annuities that allow withdrawals for long-term care expenses are that they may allow withdrawals only for nursing home expenses after an extended stay such as six months, and the LTC fund may not have as high a growth rate as in this new LTC annuity. If you consider switching from another annuity to this one, exchanges are possible from single annuitant to single annuitant but not from single annuitant to the joint policy. However, a single annuitant contract can provide joint coverage with a rider that covers an additional insured.

A final caution on this product, as with the life insurance products discussed in this section, is to make sure you put enough money into it to accommodate inflation needs. Project the average cost for care in your area at a 5.8% compounded annual growth rate for the time frame in which you think you may need to access the LTC fund, which will be largely determined by your age (10, 15, 20 years, etc.).

A long-term care **immediate** annuity is available even to people already receiving long-term care, for example, a nursing home patient. This concept involves making a single premium which is converted into a monthly income guaranteed for the life of the policyholder. You can even select an annual rate for the payment to increase anywhere from 1%–10% to provide for inflation.

Why would anyone want to do this and what makes this type of annuity different than a regular immediate annuity? Here's the main reason: A regular annuity is not medically underwritten and the same life expectancy tables are applied to everyone, regardless of medical condition. So an 82-year-old male desiring a monthly benefit of $3,500 would normally have to pay about $300,000 in a single premium. However, if he had advanced Parkinson's disease, this special long-term care annuity would require only $134,000 to obtain the same $3,500 monthly benefit. You can even structure the annuity so that your beneficiary will receive a portion of the money if you die earlier than the insurance company thought you would. For example, a 91-year-old male with a severe stroke impairment who desired a $5,000 monthly benefit with a 75% refund if he dies sooner than his life expectancy would have to deposit $145,500 instead of $282,770 in a regular annuity. Of course, you should seek advice from a professional tax advisor about the tax consequences before pursuing an option of this nature.

Reverse Mortgages

Since the majority of older Americans own their homes and have paid off their mortgages, many people find themselves "cash poor" and "house rich." Because of these characteristics, a certain amount of activity is occurring in the marketplace to help people tap the value of the home without giving it up as long as they live in it. Converting the equity of the home into cash can be accomplished either through sale plans or loan plans. The sale plans, which involve selling the home then leasing it back as long as the seller is able to live in it, are not popular for tax reasons. It's possible that the IRS will not view the plan as a bona fide sale if the house is not sold at fair market price, or if the buyer is receiving favorable treatment, or if the buyer does not assume full ownership until the death of the seller. If the IRS does not view the plan as a bona fide sale, the one-time capital gains exclusion is not available to the seller. In other words, people sometimes try to give their kids a bargain, and the IRS doesn't look favorably at special deals for children or any other buyers.

Home equity conversion loans in the form of reverse mortgages are available, in which no repayment of the loan is generally required until the borrower dies, sells the home, or permanently moves. Started by the federal government in 1988 to help older Americans on fixed incomes, the program allows homeowners over 62 to convert part of the equity in their homes into tax-free income without having to sell the home, give up the title, or take on a new monthly mortgage payment. You must be a single-family homeowner, which can include a condominium or townhouse as long as the development meets FHA guidelines. Other eligible residences are manufactured homes and 1- to 4-family owner-occupied dwellings. Others who are not on a fixed income also see the benefits of "cashing in" on the equity in their home for additional investments. There are no income qualifications and limited credit qualifications, because unlike an equity loan from a bank, a reverse mortgage requires no monthly payments.

The monies available to the homeowner are tax free and don't count as income for Social Security eligibility purposes. The balance due grows as monies are disbursed to the homeowner. The funds can be disbursed in several ways. Cash available can be taken in monthly payments over a period of years, a lifetime, or as a line of credit you can draw down as needed over a number of years. You can even receive a combination of regular monthly payments and a line of credit. You still own the home. It can be sold at any time (for example, if you decide to move) and when sold, any balance due on the reverse mortgage is paid and the remaining equity goes to you or in the case of your death, to your estate. Equity remaining depends on how long you remain in the home and the value of the home at the time of sale.

The reverse mortgage market is poised to grow substantially as the baby boomers move into their retirement years. As of this writing, there are three products available but that will increase to meet various demands of clients. Presently the most widely used product is FHA's Home Equity Conversion Mortgage (HECM). The Federal National Mortgage Association, known as "Fannie Mae," offers a product called the Home Keeper. Fannie Mae doesn't make direct loans. It buys loans from lenders, packages them and resells them to investors. Financial Freedom, headquartered in Irvine, California, offers the Financial Freedom Cash Account loan, a private reverse mortgage product.

The older you are and the more valuable your home, the more you can borrow. Each program has a "lending limit" and the amount available to the client depends on age, and in some programs, on the number of borrowers (but all have to be over 62). It also depends on the value of the home, the amount of built-up home equity, and the interest rates at the time. Generally, a borrower in his or her early 60's could get about 38% of the home's equity, a 75-year-old could get about 58%, and someone in his or her 80's could get about 60% of the home's value.

There are also equity share reverse mortgages that allow you to receive a greater cash benefit in exchange for a portion of your home's future value. The potential amount shared is limited by an overall interest rate cap.

Generally there is no cash out-of-pocket when you get a reverse mortgage. The proceeds of the reverse mortgage will be used to pay off an outstanding first mortgage or any other debt on the home. The associated fees such as the origination fee, the mortgage insurance fee, an appraisal fee and other standard closing costs may be financed as part of the reverse mortgage. You are just responsible for keeping up payments for your homeowner's insurance and property taxes, and to maintain the condition of your home.

Fannie Mae is utilized more frequently by older, single people than by married people, and the Financial Freedom product is geared to higher valued homes.

If you take the money in monthly payments but live so long that the payments exceed the home's value, you or your heirs do not have to pay back any amount larger than the worth of your home. All reverse mortgages offered today have built-in consumer protection features that prevent you or your heirs from owing more than the value of your home at the time the loan comes due - even if your home declines in value. This risk is assumed by the lender. After you die, your children (or other heirs) can keep the home if they like—they just have to pay the balance in full. They can pay off the reverse mortgage using their own money or they can sell your house. If they sell your house for more than is owed, they can keep the difference. Some people (or their children) purchase a life insurance policy on the homeowner when they get the reverse mortgage so the children can use the death benefit to pay off the mortgage and keep the house.

The interest rates on reverse mortgages are adjustable. Interest adds to the balance that will be owed when the property is sold. FHA offers either an annual or monthly adjustable interest rate and Fannie Mae has only a monthly adjustable. FHA's rate is the weekly average of the one-year Treasury Bill plus a margin of 1.5% for the monthly adjustable or 2.1% for the annual. For example, on December 31, 2002 the one-year T-Bill was 1.36%, so the annual rate was 3.46% and the monthly rate was 2.86%. Fannie Mae's rate is the weekly average of the one-month CD rate plus a margin of 3.4%. The one-month CD rate on January 31, 2003 was 1.09%, so the rate for a Fannie Mae reverse mortgage was 4.49%. Monthly adjustments to this interest rate will not affect monthly payments, unless you have chosen to take your money as a line of credit. Otherwise, fluctuating interest rates will only affect how much money is owed when you die, move out of your home, or sell your home.

Most of the cash from the various plans has been used for home modifications, home repairs, to weatherize homes, to make homes accessible for the handicapped, for supplemental retirement income, and some of the money is being used to fund long-term care services.

Rather than pay for long-term care services directly, much more "mileage" can be obtained from the money by purchasing long-term care insurance if you are insurable. You can purchase a long-term care insurance policy outright by paying a monthly, semi-annual or annual premium. Some borrowers take the reverse mortgage as a line of credit, then use the interest growth each year to pay their long-term care insurance premiums. Or, a lump-sum obtained from a reverse mortgage can be used to purchase a single-pay long-term care insurance plan that is available in some states or an annuity, which can then be set up to pay the LTC insurance premiums for the rest of the insured's life. Or, the lump sum can be used to purchase a life insurance or annuity long-term care policy as described on pp. 185-196 that pays LTC expenses with a guaranteed premium.

When implemented by HUD, The American Homeownership and Economic Opportunity Act of 2000 will waive the upfront fee for the mortgage insurance premium for older Americans who use the money from a reverse mortgage for long-term care insurance premium. The value of the waiver is 2% of the lending limit, which varies by state. (For example, a lending limit of $132,000 in Colorado on a $200,000 residence results in a waiver of $2,640.)

For a list of lenders who offer reverse mortgages in your state, call the National Reverse Mortgage Lenders Association at 866-264-4466 or visit the website at www.reversemortgage.org and click on "Find a Lender".

To make sure families understand the program, FHA requires a free individual information meeting with a HUD-approved housing agency separate from the lender so you can learn about the program objectively and decide if it's right for you. You can get the name of a local counseling agency or qualified telephone counselor from a reverse mortgage lender or by calling AARP

(800-424-3410), Fannie Mae's Homepath service (800-732-6643) or HUD's Housing Counseling Clearinghouse (888-466-3487).

Your State Agency on Aging also has information on organizations to contact if you are interested in obtaining a reverse mortgage. An AARP bulletin contained a warning from Andrew Cuomo, the Department of Housing and Urban Development (HUD) secretary. Mr. Cuomo cautioned against salespeople contacting you to do a reverse mortgage and charging hefty fees for information and forms that HUD offers free. He said the legal limit for counseling and referral services is $50, and you should not be charged more than that. If you suspect a scam, you can check out the organization that contacted you by calling HUD directly toll-free at 1-888-466-3487, and HUD will investigate at no charge to you.

Critical Illness Insurance

Critical illness policies were introduced in the United States in the mid-1990's and pay a lump-sum upon diagnosis of one of a dozen or so conditions including Alzheimer's (for people who need help with three or more activities of daily living and require permanent daily supervision as diagnosed by a board-certified neurologist), multiple sclerosis, heart attack, stroke when effects of the neurological injury last for at least 30 days, life threatening cancer (malignant and growing uncontrollably outside its original location) major organ transplant, paralysis, kidney failure requiring dialysis, blindness, deafness, and perhaps severe burns. Some policies even pay if you need help with three or more activities of daily living for at least 90 days, even if you don't have Alzheimer's. Some policies have a return of premium benefit, which means the premium will be returned to a beneficiary less any benefits paid out if the policyholder dies without receiving all of the benefits.

A partial benefit, perhaps 25%, is paid for conditions such as malignant cancer in one location, heart angioplasty and heart bypass surgery.

You may be charged a higher premium if one or more of your immediate family members (parents and siblings) have had any of these conditions.

Common issue ages are 20-64 but you can keep the policy as long as you live. However, benefits usually reduce to 50% at age 65 or five years after the effective date if you were older than 60 when you purchased the policy.

The lump-sum benefit can be anywhere from $25,000 to $1,000,000, depending on how much you purchase when you buy the policy. One company recommends 3-5 times annual salary for employed people plus any outstanding mortgage balance.

Critical illness policies can be standalone or some are sold as a rider on a life insurance policy or annuity. If sold in the workplace, there may be only a few medical questions in order to qualify.

The lump-sum benefit of a critical illness policy can be used to cover the miscellaneous expenses connected to a major illness such as:

▲ insurance deductibles and co-pays

▲ travel expenses such as meals, lodging and airfare to seek additional medical treatment

▲ experimental treatment and/or drugs

▲ treatment outside of a managed care network

▲ child care or elder care

▲ salary replacement for time away from work

▲ household help like cooking, cleaning and laundry

▲ home modifications

▲ mortgage payments and other debts

The point is, the lump-sum benefit of a critical illness policy is a cash benefit that can be used for anything.

Critical Illness Insurance vs. Long-Term Care Insurance

Can critical illness coverage be an alternative payment option for long-term care? Possibly, especially if you are not able to qualify for long-term care insurance and you are able to get a critical illness policy through your employer with simplified underwriting, which means just a few medical questions.

What are the pitfalls?

1) Access to benefits is tougher as even Alzheimer's patients would have to need help with at least three activities of daily living. Long-term care insurance policies require help with only two ADL's and there is no ADL requirement for an Alzheimer's patient.

2) The critical illness benefit is a lump-sum cash benefit which can bring a strong temptation to spend it for things other than long-term care services.

3) A lump-sum cash benefit may be difficult to budget so that it lasts throughout a long-term condition – you might remember from Chapter One that the average lifespan of an Alzheimer's patient is eight years but can be 3 – 20.[6]

4) Benefits reduce at age 65, and a long-term care insurance policy is sometimes most needed at older ages.

5) $1,000,000 benefit is projected to pay about three years of care in 30 years,[7] and that may not be enough long-term care coverage for someone purchasing a critical illness policy at age 50 or younger.

On the positive side, critical illness insurance can be relatively inexpensive at younger ages, especially if it is a rider on a life insurance policy, and the benefit would be invaluable if long-term care is needed at a young age. At any age, critical illness makes a good supplement to long-term care insurance as the money can be used for any need.

In summary, one funding method for long-term care does not fit all. Since this is America, it's safe to say that we will continue to see much product innovation and variety throughout this century as our country struggles to find a way to pay for long-term care with private funding as much as possible and prevent unprecedented taxation—the inevitable result if the baby boomers wind up on any kind of public assistance for long-term care.

People Who Do Not Qualify for LTC Insurance

People with significant health issues may not be able to qualify for a long-term care policy. Here are some suggestions:

▲   Apply with another insurance company. Seek a company that doesn't just say "yes" or "no." There are companies that will sell you a policy for extra premium or will issue you a policy with an alternative benefit offer—perhaps a three-year or five-year benefit period instead of lifetime, or a 100-day waiting period instead of 20 or 60 days.

The majority of long-term care claims are less than three years so a policy with a shorter benefit period may work out fine for you.[8] However long your policy will pay is that much time for you to be a private-pay patient, which will increase your choices and independence.

▲   The new long-term care annuities discussed in this section may be an especially good option for you since some of them ask only a few medical questions, and one will provide benefits even if you already need long-term care.

▲   A viatical or life settlement as discussed in this section may be an option for you if you have any type of life insurance.

▲   A reverse mortgage as discussed in this section may be an option if you have your home paid off or almost paid off.

▲   You may be able to get a critical illness policy that only asks a few medical questions, especially if it is offered through your employer.

▲   There are annuities on the market that have no surrender charges if the withdrawal is used for nursing home expenses.

▲   Seek the advice of a good elder-law attorney and your State Agency on Aging. Contact the National Academy of Elder Law Attorneys, 1604 North Country Club Road, Tucson, Arizona 85716 or go to www.naela.org for a national registry of elder-law attorneys.

Where Do I Go from Here?

To choose the best long-term care insurance policy, call an insurance agent you can trust. Call as soon as you can to take advantage of rates based on your current age and your good health. Health is our most precious asset. Once health problems occur, it can be impossible to get a good insurance policy, especially a long-term care policy.

For decades, most of us have lived in denial regarding the physical, emotional and financial trauma, that often characterizes LTC. We refuse to talk openly about the possibility of someday needing protracted medical care. Instead, we say, I'll never have a stroke or develop Alzheimer's disease. Even if I do, the Veteran's Administration or Medicare or my Elk's Lodge or children will take care of me. After all, we reason, I'm sure that after working and paying taxes for 40 years, I'm at least entitled to some kind of care.

Tragically, the ultimate consequence of that denial is often both traumatic and unnecessary to the individual, their spouse and family, and their community. *

So, go to the telephone and call for help today. Do it now, for yourself, but mostly for your family.

* "Jousting with Dragons: A Manifesto" by Martin K. Bayne

Appendix A:
Senior Benefits

Medicare Benefits

~~~~~~

Medicare, a federal program, is the cornerstone of the older American's health care benefits and is available to all Americans at age 65. Some people think Medicare is sufficient to handle their health care financing needs, but as this chapter will show the program has some very big gaps—gaps that can leave you with huge bills if you are not prepared. The largest gap is long-term care, according to LifePlans, Inc., one of the nation's leading research firms for long-term care issues.[1]

Enrolling for Medicare

Most Americans are automatically enrolled for Medicare when they reach age 65. Your Medicare card shows you the effective date of your coverage. The program is administered by the Centers for Medicare and Medicaid Services (CMS) of the U.S. Department of Health and Human Services. The Social Security Administration provides information about the program and handles enrollment. You should contact your local Social Security office for information at least three months before you turn 65. You can also call the Social Security toll-free number 1-800-772-1213 any business day from 7 a.m. to 7 p.m. EST if you have questions about Medicare eligibility or need enrollment information.

Two Parts of Medicare

Medicare has two separate parts. **Part A** covers inpatient-type care—inpatient hospitalization, skilled nursing facility stays, psychiatric hospitalization, as well as hospice care and home health care. **Part B** covers medical services—physician services, related medical services and supplies, outpatient hospital treatment, X-rays and laboratory tests, ambulance services, physical, occupational and speech therapy, mental health services and Pap smears.

Part A is financed through part of the Social Security (FICA) tax paid by all workers and their employers. You do not have to pay a monthly premium for Medicare Part A if you or your spouse are entitled to benefits under either the Social Security or Railroad Retirement systems, or have worked a sufficient period of time in federal, state or local government employment to be insured. If you do not meet the qualifications for premium-free Part A benefits, you may purchase the coverage if you are at least age 65 and meet certain requirements. The Part A premium for 2003 is $316 per month if you have less than 29 quarters of Social Security coverage. It is $174 per month for 30–39 quarters.

Part B is optional and is offered to all beneficiaries when they become entitled to premium-free Part A. It may also be purchased by most people age 65 or over who do not qualify for premium-free Part A coverage. (Note: If you purchase Part A, you must purchase Part B as well.) The Part B premium in 2003 is $58.70 each month and is deducted from your Social Security or Railroad Retirement check.

You are automatically enrolled in Part B when you become entitled to Part A unless you state that you don't want it. Although you do not have to purchase Part B, it is an excellent buy because the federal government pays 75% of the program costs.[2] Your Medicare card will show the coverage you have—Hospital Insurance (Part A), Medical Insurance (Part B) or both—and the date your coverage started. If you have only one part of Medicare, you can get information about getting the other part from your local Social Security office.

If you are still covered under an employer's health insurance plan after you are 65 or because you or your spouse is still working, you should accept Part A Medicare but elect to postpone enrolling for Part B until you are no longer covered through the group. You will save the Part B premium of $58.70 a month. Once you retire or your group insurance terminates (whichever comes first), you have eight months to enroll in Part B without a penalty. Contact your Social Security office as soon as you know your group coverage is going to end to obtain the necessary forms: 1) for the employer to certify that you have had group coverage and 2) for you to complete indicating that you now want Part B. If you are not covered by an employer's health plan, you should enroll in Part B during your initial enrollment period, which is the seven-month period beginning three months before you are first able to get Medicare. For most people, this means three months before the 65th birthday. If you don't accept Part B during that seven month period, you will have to wait until the next general enrollment period to enroll (January 1 through March 31 of each year). Your premium will be 10% higher for each year you wait, and the coverage won't begin until the following July. For more detailed information about how Medicare works with other benefits such as group plans, VA benefits, TRICARE (formerly CHAMPUS), or any other plan, ask your Social Security office for a copy of *Medicare and Other Health Benefits: Who Pays First?* This booklet is published by the Health Care Financing Administration, U.S. Department of Health and Human Services.

Individuals younger than 65 can get Medicare solely on the basis of permanent kidney failure or after two years of receiving Social Security Disability benefits. To get a free copy of *Medicare Coverage of Kidney Dialysis and Kidney Transplant Services,* write to Medicare Publications, Center for Medicare & Medicaid Services, 7500 Security Blvd., Baltimore, MD 21244-1850, or visit the official Medicare website at www.medicare.gov. If you have questions about specific Medicare requirements or benefit features, be sure to consult *Medicare and You,* which is available from any Social Security Administration office, by calling 1-800-MEDICARE (800-633-4227) or by writing to Medicare Publications at the address above you can also visit the official Medicare website at www.medicare.gov.

The Medicare Gaps

When Medicare was created, Congress determined that the patient should share in paying for the cost of the care he or she received. The underlying concept is simple: If the patient shares in the costs of care, he or she will be more likely to use the benefits wisely. So, the program was designed with deductible and coinsurance amounts the patient must pay.

In the first years of the Medicare program, these deductible and coinsurance charges were moderate amounts. But after more than three decades of annual increases, these charges can add up to a major expense. For example:

▲ You must pay the first $840 of your bill when you are hospitalized.

▲ You must pay $105 each day for days 21 through 100 in a skilled nursing facility.

▲ You must pay the first $100 of the Medicare-approved amounts for doctor services, medical supplies and equipment, outpatient services and ambulance.

▲ You must pay 20% of the cost of your bills for doctor services, medical supplies and equipment, outpatient services and ambulance.

▲ You must pay charges above the Medicare-approved amount billed by doctors who do not accept Medicare assignment (up to a 115% cap—see p. 217).

▲ In addition to your 20% co-payment, you must pay all costs for physical or occupational therapy provided by independent therapists (outside a nursing home or hospital) in excess of Medicare's maximum annual allowance. The annual allowance is limited to $1,500 but may change 7/1/03 and physical therapy includes speech therapy.

These expenses can add up quickly, and this is only a representative sample of some of the most common Medicare gaps. In addition to financial gaps caused by the deductible and coinsurance amounts, there are also gaps caused by coverage limitations and administrative considerations.

Medicare-Approved Charges

One of the most misunderstood aspects of Medicare is the way doctor charges are determined.

All of your doctor's charges may not be considered eligible for the 80% Medicare Part B reimbursement. Medicare payment is based on the Medicare-approved amounts, not the actual charges billed by the physician or medical supplier. The Medicare-approved amount is based on a national fee schedule. This schedule assigns a value to each physician service based on the specific service performed, his or her medical practice costs, malpractice insurance costs and a geographical factor. Each time you go to the physician, the amount Medicare will recognize for that service will be taken from the national fee schedule. Medicare will generally pay 80% of that amount. (Example: The doctor charges $100. Medicare may approve $70 and pay 80%, which means that Medicare would actually pay $56.)

Doctors who take assignment on a Medicare claim agree to accept the Medicare-approved amount as payment in full. They are paid directly by Medicare, and you pay them any deductible or coinsurance amount due. Ask your doctor if he or she accepts Medicare assignment.

Many physicians and suppliers accept assignment on a case-by-case basis. If your physician or supplier does not accept assignment, you are responsible for the bill, and Medicare will reimburse you. However, physicians who do not accept assignment of a Medicare claim are reimbursed at a lower level and are limited by law as to the amount they can charge you for covered services. The most a non-participating physician can charge you for services covered by Medicare is 115% of the fee schedule amount. (Some states also have special laws that limit how much physicians can charge—Connecticut, Massachusetts, Minnesota, New York, Ohio, Pennsylvania, Rhode Island and Vermont. Check with your state's insurance department or office on aging for more information. See **Who to Call for Help**, p. 250.)

Regardless of whether physicians accept assignment, they are required to file your Medicare claims for you. If they accept assignment, Medicare pays the physician and sends you a notice, called a Medicare Summary Notice (MSN), to let you know how much was paid. If the doctor does not accept assignment, Medicare pays you and you pay the doctor the amount Medicare paid plus all permissible charges, which may include your $100 calendar year deductible for Part B, your 20% co-payment, and any charge above the Medicare-approved amount up to the 115% cap. Only Medicare-approved amounts count toward the $100 Part B deductible, not the actual charges billed by the physician or medical supplier.

You may contact the insurance company that administers the Medicare Part B program in your area for a list of the doctors in your area who take assignment. However, it's still a good idea to check with the doctor when you make an appointment because the doctor may have stopped taking assignment since the list was printed. After January 1, 1998, patients may enter into private contracts with doctors who do not participate in Medicare at least two years after the private contract is signed as long as the claim is not filed with Medicare or with Medicare supplemental insurance. **In this situation, you agree to be responsible for all charges and no limits apply to the amount you can be charged by the doctor for his or her services.**

Be Informed

As shown above, Medicare does not pay the entire cost for all services covered by the program. You or your Medicare supplemental insurance must pay certain deductible and coinsurance amounts and charges in excess of Medicare's approved amount. When you are enrolled in Medicare and Medicare supplement insurance, you will receive complete details on the limitations and exclusions of Medicare. Be sure to read that information carefully. As with any insurance plan, understanding your benefit provisions up front helps you avoid many financial and administrative problems when you file claims. **So, carefully read your Medicare and Medicare supplemental insurance literature.**

Appeals

If you don't agree with how Medicare handles a claim or if you think more should have been paid, you have the right to appeal the claim. Best results are obtained if you send a letter from your doctor with your appeal. Just ask the doctor to write a letter that further justifies the services performed. Many times an appeal results in an additional payment. Send the appeal to the Medicare carrier listed on your Medicare Summary Notice.

2003 Medicare Benefits

Medicare Part A

HEALTH CARE FACILITY SERVICES

Medicare pays:

Inpatient Hospital Services, Semi-Private Room and Board, Miscellaneous Hospital Services and Supplies, Drugs, X-Rays, Lab Tests

All but $840 during 1st 60 days of a benefit period.*

All but $210 a day for 61st through 90th day of a benefit period.*

All but $420 a day for 91st through 150th day of a benefit period* (while using the 60-day Medicare lifetime reserve)

Post Hospital **Skilled Nursing Facility Care** for a Medicare Approved Stay in a Medicare Approved Facility

All costs for first 20 days of a benefit period.*

All but $105 a day for 21st through 100th day of a benefit period.*

*BENEFIT PERIOD: A new benefit period begins after you have been out of a hospital or skilled nursing facility for 60 days in a row.

Blood

All but first three pints during a calendar year, unless blood is replaced.

Home Health Care

When first qualify for benefits, skilled nursing care can be provided on fewer than seven days each week or less than eight hours each day over a period of 21 days (or less). Thereafter, skilled nursing or home health aide services must combine to total less than 8 hours per day and 28 or fewer hours each week. These guidelines are now subject to the prospective payment system, effective 10/1/00, for home health agencies, which allow a set amount of money for each 60 days care is needed. This 60 day period is called an "episode of care." The payment is based on what kind of health care an average person in a similar medical situation would need. Visits are paid for a nurse or home health aide as long as skilled care is needed at least once every 60 days. (Drawing blood is no longer considered a skilled service.) Also pays for part-time services for physical therapy, speech therapy, nutritional counseling, respiratory therapy. Patient must be homebound. (Homebound rules were relaxed in 2002 to allow special occasions such as graduations, family reunions and funerals.) Medical equipment paid at 80%.

Hospice
(Available to patients certified terminally ill.)

Unlimited benefits. No deductible for physician services, nursing care, medical appliances and supplies, counseling, and home health aide and homemaker services. Pays all but 5% of cost of outpatient drugs or $5 per prescription, whichever is lower. (Inpatient respite care is limited to five days per stay, and hospice does not pay for ongoing eight-hour shifts of non-skilled home care.)

Medicare Part B

PHYSICIANS' CHARGES:	Medicare pays:
Services of a **Physician, Nurse Practitioner and Physician Assistant**	80% of reasonable charges after $100 annual deductible, except 50% for mental health visits.
Outpatient Services and Medical Supplies (Other Than Blood and Immunosuppressive Therapy Drugs), Ambulance	Reasonable charges are determined by Medicare. Sometimes they are called Medicare-approved charges or Medicare-eligible expenses.
Blood	80% of Medicare-approved amount after $100 deductible after 1st three pints unless replaced.
Home Health Care	Covers home health care if the patient does not have Part A. These services are still subject to the "episode of care" payment method set forth by the prospective payment system effective for home health providers 10/1/00.
Preventive Services	Covers annual mammograms after age 40 and pap smears and pelvic exams at least every three years. Covers colorectal cancer screening and blood glucose testing strips. Covers diabetes services and supplies, including self-management tests, and bone mass measurements for certain conditions. Prostate cancer screening.

Co-payment and Part B deductible apply, except no deductible for mammograms, pap smears or pelvic exams. No co-payment or deductible for PSA (Prostate Specific Antigen) test.

MISCELLANEOUS: **Medicare Pays:**

Immunosuppressive Drugs   80% of reasonable charges after
(Drugs after Organ Transplant) $100 deductible.
and Some Oral Cancer Drugs

Medicare pays only for services it determines to be medically necessary and only the amount it determines to be reasonable.

Reimbursement to hospitals is based on a pre-established amount based on the diagnosis of the patient's condition, which is called a prospective payment system. If you are discharged earlier than expected, the hospital makes money. If you stay longer than the standard, the hospital loses money. For this reason, doctors are under tremendous pressure to get the patient out of the hospital as soon as possible. The Balanced Budget Act of 1997 also requires nursing homes and home health agencies to be paid under a prospective payment system, beginning 10/1/00 for home health agencies and phased in for nursing homes between 7/1/98 and 2002.

Reimbursement to physicians is based on a national fee schedule that began 1/1/99 and was fully implemented by 2002. Doctors who "accept assignment" do not bill patients for amounts above the fee schedule. After 1/1/98, patients may enter into private contracts with doctors who do not participate in Medicare at least two years after the contract as long as the claim is not filed with Medicare or with Medicare supplemental insurance.

Expenses Not Covered By Medicare

Medicare does not provide benefits for:

▲ private duty nursing at home or in the hospital

▲ skilled nursing home costs beyond 100 days unless you stop receiving skilled care 60 days in a row

▲ custodial or intermediate nursing home costs (non-skilled care)

▲ physician charges above Medicare's approved amount

▲ most outpatient drugs*

▲ care received outside the U.S., except under certain conditions in Canada and Mexico

▲ Medicare may not pay for services given by privately practicing speech pathologists

▲ dental care or dentures, checkups except preventive services as named on the preceding page, most routine immunizations (except flu shots, pneumonia vaccines and Hepatitus B are covered), homemaker services, cosmetic surgery, routine foot care, examinations for and the cost of eyeglasses or hearing aids

---

* At least 29 states have a drug assistance program.[3] Check with your State Agency on Aging for more information. In early 2003, there are three main sources for outpatient drug coverage through private insurance. Sixty-two percent of Medicare beneficiaries had some level of drug benefits in 1999, either through retiree health plans, the high option "H, I and J" Medicare supplement plans, or through a Medicare+Choice plan.[4]

Medicare Supplement Policies

~~~~~~~~~~~~~~~~~~~~~~~~~~~~~~~~~~~~~~~

Medicare supplement policies, sometimes referred to as "Medigap" coverage, are individual policies from private insurance companies that are designed to pay the coinsurance amounts, deductibles and other gaps **after Medicare benefits have been provided.** And that's the caution—Medicare supplements are designed to pay only after Medicare has made a payment. With a few exceptions, they typically do not pay for services not covered by Medicare. Medicare supplemental insurance policies can be valuable, however, as Medicare alone will not pay most of a patient's medical expenses.

Do You Need a Medicare Supplement?

Medicare supplements are purchased by a fourth of Medicare beneficiaries to fill gaps in benefits under the traditional Medicare program,[5] but there are four types of people who do not need a Medicare supplement:

▲ *Low-income individuals* can get the Medicare Part A and Part B deductibles and coinsurance payments and the Part B premium paid by their state Medicaid program. "Low-income" means your annual income is below the national poverty level and your assets (not counting your home) are less than $4,000 ($6,000 for couples).

The 2002 federal income guidelines for this program were $759 a month for individuals, and $1,015 a month for couples. These amounts are higher for Alaska ($944 individual/$1,265 couple) and Hawaii ($870 individual/$1,165 couple). Note: All of these amounts include an additional $20, which is called "a monthly Supplemental Security Income disregard," which just means these are the true amounts of income you can have to qualify for this program.

Call your local Medicaid office if you think you might qualify, and to obtain current income amounts. Ask for information about the Qualified Medicare Beneficiary (QMB) program. (See **Who to Call for Help**, p. 250)

Note: If your income is too much to qualify for the QMB program, you may still be able to qualify for the Specified Low-Income Medicare Beneficiary (SLIMB) program, which will pay your Part B premium of $58.70 per month in 2003. Your assets still have to be low, but your 2002 income could be as much as $906 for an individual and $1,214 for a couple (Alaska: $1,128 individual/$1,513 couple; Hawaii: $1,040 individual/$1,394 couple).

▲ *Individuals who are allowed by their employers to continue group health insurance after retiring* usually do not need a separate Medicare supplement policy. Retiree group insurance usually has better benefits (i.e. pre-scription drugs, hearing aids, vision aids, etc.) than an individual Medicare supplement.

▲ *Individuals or spouses who work past age 65* can be cov-ered by an employer's group health plan if the employer has 20+ employees and should elect to do so as group plans are normally better than individual Medicare supplement policies. Upon retirement, the individual can purchase a Medicare supplement policy if the employer does not provide group coverage to retirees.

▲ *Individuals who are enrolled in a Medicare managed care plan* (See **Managed Care Medicare Plans,** p. 240.)

People who either don't meet the low income requirements of the Qualified Medicare Beneficiary program or who are not cov-ered by an employer or former employer or who are not enrolled in a Medicare managed care plan (See p. 240) may consider pur-chasing a good individual Medicare supplement policy, unless they decide to self-insure balances to Medicare.

Can You Self-Insure Balances to Medicare?

Individuals with significant assets who wish to self-insure bal-ances to Medicare can do so as today balances after Medicare's payment are small. Some people elect to do this because they feel the money they have been using for Medicare supplemental insurance is better spent to pay long-term care insurance pre-mium, because long-term care is a much bigger risk than bal-ances to Medicare. A General Accounting Office report showed that the average amount spent by Medicare supplement policy-holders in 1998 was about $2,700, much higher than the average out-of-pocket expense of only $1,255 for people with no supplemental coverage to Medicare. (The $2,700 includes the average Medicare supplement premium of $1,300.)[6]

Disabled Individuals Under Age 65

Disabled individuals under age 65 who qualify for Medicare should contact their state's Department of Insurance for information about Medicare supplement policies. (See *Open Enrollment* on p. 232 for legislation effective 1/1/95 to help disabled people at age 65.)

Federal Guidelines for Medicare Supplements

The insurance industry developed very good Medicare supplement policies throughout the history of the Medicare program. But there has also been abuse of this sensitive market. For this reason, older Americans need to be extremely careful when selecting their Medicare supplement insurance policy.

Largely because of these problems, the federal government implemented guidelines in 1992 that require state insurance regulators to require insurance companies operating in their state to simplify the Medicare supplement enrollment process. The federal guidelines say insurance companies can now sell only ten standard policies. (Massachusetts, Minnesota and Wisconsin standardized their Medicare supplement plans earlier and didn't have to conform to the national standardized plans. Residents of these states should contact their state insurance departments to find out their state's version of Medicare supplement coverage.)

The ten policies are designated A-J. All insurance companies that sell Medicare supplement insurance have to offer Plan A, also called the "basic policy." The other plans are optional. The basic benefits (Plan A) consist of the following core benefits:

▲   Coverage for the Part A coinsurance amount ($210 per day in 2003) for the 61st through the 90th day of hospitalization in each benefit period.

▲   Coverage for the Part A coinsurance amount ($420 per day in 2003) for each of Medicare's 60 non-renewable lifetime hospital inpatient reserve days used.

▲   After all Medicare hospital benefits are exhausted, coverage for 100% of the Medicare Part A eligible hospital expenses. Coverage is limited to a maximum of 365 days of additional inpatient hospital care during the policyholder's lifetime. The benefit is paid either at the rate Medicare pays hospitals under the Prospective Payment System or another appropriate standard of payment.

▲   Coverage under Medicare Parts A and B for the reasonable cost of the first three pints of blood or equivalent quantities of packed red blood cells per calendar year unless replaced in accordance with federal regulations.

▲   Coverage for the 20% coinsurance amount for Part B services after the $100 annual deductible is met.

The chart on the next page summarizes the standard Medicare supplement plans.

Summary of Standard Medicare Supplement Plans

A	B	C	D	E	F*	G	H	I	J*
Basic Benefits	Basic Benefits	Basic Benefits	Basic Benefits	Basic Benefits	Basic Benefits	Basic Benefits	Basic Benefits	Basic Benefits	Basic Benefits
		Skilled Nursing Coinsurance	Skilled Nursing Coinsurance	Skilled Nursing Coinsurance	Skilled Nursing Coinsurance	Skilled Nursing Coinsurance	Skilled Nursing Coinsurance	Skilled Nursing Coinsurance	Skilled Nursing Coinsurance
	Part A Deductible	Part A Deductible	Part A Deductible	Part A Deductible	Part A Deductible	Part A Deductible	Part A Deductible	Part A Deductible	Part A Deductible
		Part B Deductible			Part B Deductible				Part B Deductible
					Part B Excess (100%)	Part B Excess (80%)		Part B Excess (100%)	Part B Excess (100%)
		Foreign Travel Emergency	Foreign Travel Emergency	Foreign Travel Emergency	Foreign Travel Emergency	Foreign Travel Emergency	Foreign Travel Emergency	Foreign Travel Emergency	Foreign Travel Emergency
			At-Home Recovery			At-Home Recovery		At-Home Recovery	At-Home Recovery
							Basic Drugs ($1250 Limit)	Basic Drugs ($1250 Limit)	Extended Drugs ($3000 Limit)
				Preventive Care					Preventive Care

* $1,620 high deductible option for Plans F and J issued in 2003.

229

Features of a Good Medicare Supplement Policy

∿∿∿∿∿∿∿∿∿∿∿∿∿∿∿∿∿∿∿∿∿∿∿∿∿∿∿∿∿∿

With standardized policies, it is much easier to select a good Medicare supplement insurance policy. Nevertheless, the following features are still important considerations when evaluating which Medicare supplement policy you should purchase.

If you already have Medicare and a Medicare supplement policy, this chapter can help you evaluate your current policy. The federal Medicare supplement guidelines only apply to policies sold after their implementation in 1992.

Guaranteed Renewable—This means the policy can never be cancelled as long as you pay the premiums and as long as you answered all the questions in the application truthfully. It can't be cancelled even if you have a lot of claims or even if the insurance company stops selling Medicare supplement insurance. "Conditionally renewable" means your policy can be cancelled under certain conditions, such as if the insurance company cancels all of the policies like yours in your state. If this happens and you have health problems, you may not be able to qualify medically for another policy. Federal guidelines require that policies be "guaranteed renewable." If your present policy was issued prior to 1992 and is "conditionally renewable," you should ask an insurance agent about changing to a "guaranteed renewable" policy.

Rating of the Insurance Company—Even if a policy is guaranteed renewable, if the insurance company goes broke, your policy might not stay in force. Buy policies from insurance companies with an A. M. Best Rating of "B+" or higher. Lower ratings (B, C, etc.) put you at risk of losing your policy if the company experiences financial difficulties. See p. 72 for information on how to check an insurance company's ratings and assets.

Pre-existing Conditions—If you replace your old Medicare supplement policy with a new one, the new policy has to cover you immediately for health problems you already have unless the replacement occurs in the first six months after purchasing your first Medicare supplement policy. This means no waiting period for pre-existing conditions for most replacements. If you are just becoming 65 and buying your first Medicare policy, the longest you have to wait for coverage for pre-existing conditions is six months. (See *Open Enrollment* on the following page.)

Underwriting—Unless it is your first policy, Medicare supplement policies you apply for can decline you or charge you more if you have health problems. To get a replacement Medicare supplement policy, you must answer questions about your health. Some companies need time to review your answers and many companies get more information from your doctor. Other companies give your insurance agent the authority to issue you a policy immediately if you can answer "no" to the health questions on the application. In these cases, your agent will leave the policy with you as soon as you complete and sign the application and pay your premium.

Open Enrollment—Federal guidelines guarantee that for six months following enrollment in Part B of Medicare, persons age 65 or older can't be declined or charged more for a Medicare supplement because of health problems. Insurance companies cannot impose a waiting period for pre-existing conditions during the initial open enrollment period if you have had at least six months of health insurance coverage before you apply for the Medicare supplement policy. If you've had less than six months, you get credit for the amount of time you have had health insurance coverage.

On January 1, 1995, federal law extended open enrollment for six months at age 65 to those persons who were first enrolled in Part B of Medicare prior to age 65 by reason of disability or end stage renal disease. If you purchase a Medicare supplement policy as a disabled person prior to age 65, you probably will be able to get Plan A or B. This law means you can get a better policy (Plans C–J) at age 65.

If you or your spouse continue to work past age 65 so that you are covered under an employer's group plan, you can delay enrollment in Part B of Medicare until you are no longer covered under the group plan. When you know your group coverage is ending, you can apply for Part B of Medicare (with no penalty) and you will have the six-month open enrollment period to obtain an individual Medicare supplement policy regardless of any health problems you may have. You will not have a pre-existing waiting period under your new Medicare supplement policy because you will have had health insurance for at least six months prior to the effective date of the Medicare supplement.

Ticket to Work and Work Incentives Improvement Act of 1999 -- If you have a Medicare supplement then go to work for a company that offers a group health plan, you can ask the Medicare supplement carrier to "suspend" your policy until you notify the insurance company of the date that you are no longer covered under the group health plan. Your premium and your coverage will be reinstated on that date without medical questions.

Premiums—Many insurance companies allow you to save money if you pay once a year (annually) or twice a year (semi-annually) versus paying monthly or quarterly. If you decide to cancel the policy for any reason, the insurance company does not have to, but may refund the balance of the premiums not used. The three most common methods for premium calculation for Medicare supplement policies are 1) community rating—all policyholders pay the same rate regardless of age, 2) issue age rating—premium is based on the age you apply for the policy and 3) attained age rating—age 65 premium is usually lower than Methods 1 and 2 but increases either annually or in age bands such as every five years as you get older. With Methods 1 and 2, premiums go up only to reflect inflation in the cost of benefits, i.e., as Medicare deductibles and co-payments increase, the policy has to pay out more in benefits so you may see a slight increase from year to year. Method 3 has rate increases as you get older because premiums are actually rising with your age, in addition to medical inflation. (A few states, like Missouri, prohibit sales of attained-age policies.)

"Free-Look" Period—You have 30 days after you receive your policy to send it back and get your money back. You can either return it to the agent or send it to the insurance company with a letter saying you do not accept the policy and you wish to have your money returned. Call your state's Department of Insurance if you have any problems getting your money back. (See p. 250.)

Multiple Policies—You don't need more than one Medicare supplement policy. The reason some people have taken out more than one is because they think they can get all of their bills paid if they have more than one policy. This is an unwise use of your money. There are excellent policies on the market today that will take care of most of your expenses with just one policy. Also, federal guidelines don't allow an insurance company to sell you a Medicare supplement policy in addition to one you already have. This means if you buy a new Medicare supplement policy, you agree to cancel the one(s) you already have.

Benefits—An ideal policy will pay both the Part A deductible ($840 per hospital stay in each 60-day benefit period) and the Part B deductible ($100 per calendar year). It will also pay all the coinsurance for additional hospital days and for skilled nursing facility days.

Excess Physician Charges—If your doctor does not accept Medicare assignment, you owe the difference between the actual charge and the amount Medicare approves. However, the doctor can charge no more than 115% of the Medicare-approved amount. Medicare supplement policies are available that will pay these balances. Again, you don't need multiple policies to get these excess charges paid. Plans F, I and J of the standardized plans pay 100% of the excess charges.

Miscellaneous Benefits—Some policies pay extra benefits in addition to Medicare deductibles and coinsurance and excess physician charges. Plans C–J of the standardized plans include at least one of the following extra benefits and Plan J includes all of them.

High Deductible Plans—The Balanced Budget Act of 1997 created a $1,500 deductible option for Plans F and J for policies issued in 1998 and after. The 2003 deductible is $1,620. This means that covered expenses are paid at 100% after the deductible is met. (The deductible increases each year based on the Consumer Price Index.)

Foreign Travel Emergency —If you become injured or get sick unexpectedly during the first 60 days of a trip out-side the United States, the standardized plans C–J will pay 80% of hospital, physician and medical care, subject to a $250 annual deductible and a lifetime maximum of $50,000, if the care would have been covered by Medicare had it been provided in the United States.

Preventive Care—Standardized Plans E and J pay up to $120 per year for such things as an annual physical exam-ination, cholesterol screening, hearing test, diabetes screening and thyroid function test. This benefit can also cover mammograms, Pap smears, and/or flu shots if Medicare stops paying for them.

At Home Recovery—Standardized Plans D, G, I and J pay up to $1,600 per year for short-term, at-home assistance with activities of daily living (bathing, dressing, going to the bathroom, taking medicine, eating, etc.) up to seven visits per week. The visits can last up to four hours and must be received either while you are receiving Medicare-approved home health services or no more than eight weeks after the last Medicare-approved home health visit.

Basic Drugs—Standardized Plans H and I pay 50% of the cost of outpatient prescription drugs up to a maximum annual benefit of $1,250 after a $250 annual deductible.

Extended Drugs—Standardized Plan J pays the same as the Basic Drugs benefit except the annual maximum is $3,000.

Claims—Medicare supplements usually can't pay unless Medicare pays first. This means that the Medicare supplement insurance company needs to see a copy of the Medicare Summary Notice (MSN) before processing the claim.

If your doctor participates in the Medicare program (accepts assignment of benefits) and you have assigned the benefits of a qualified Medicare supplement policy to your doctor, the company that processes Medicare claims for your state will automatically send your physician's claim to the Medicare supplement insurance company for processing. You don't have to handle the paperwork of claims filing if your doctor accepts Medicare assignment.

If your doctor does not accept assignment, you may be solely responsible for filing your Medicare supplement claims. There are a few insurance companies that provide electronic claims filing whether or not the doctor accepts assignment. Your insurance agent can tell you how each company works that you are considering.

Appeals—If you are not satisfied with how the Medicare supplement policy handled your claim, contact the insurance company or your agent. If you are still not satisfied, you can call the Department of Insurance in your state for help. (A list of insurance departments by state starts on p. 251.)

Managed Care for Medicare Supplements

`^^^^^^^^^^^^^^^^^^^^^^^^^^^^^^^^^^`

Medicare Select—A new way of handling Medicare supplement insurance was introduced in 1992 in 15 states. In 1995 it was authorized to be sold nationally for three years and approved indefinitely in 1998.

The original Medicare Select states were Alabama, Arizona, California, Florida, Illinois, Indiana, Kentucky, Massachusetts, Minnesota, Missouri, North Dakota, Ohio, Texas, Washington and Wisconsin.

The Medicare Select program allows policyholders to pay a lower premium in return for using a list of hospitals and doctors, called "preferred providers," specified by the insurance company or health maintenance organization (HMO) that underwrites the supplemental policy. The benefits when you use the designated providers are the same as the 10 standard Medicare supplement plans (A–J).

Emergency health care furnished by providers not on the list is also covered. If it's not an emergency and you use a doctor or hospital not on the list, your Medicare supplement claim can be denied or the payment can be reduced. The Medicare benefit is paid as usual, so whether or not you use a health care provider on the list only affects your Medicare supplement benefit, not the Medicare payment.

Even though premiums for Medicare Select plans average more than $200 less than standard Medicare supplements, only about 9% of Medicare beneficiaries had one in 1999. Some of the small participation can be attributed to lack of availability. About 15 states do not have insurance companies within the state selling Medicare Select plans.[7] Call your Department of Insurance for information on Medicare Select plans in your state. (See p. 251)

Managed Care
Medicare Plans

~~~~~~

Managed Care Medicare Plans—In addition to the new Medicare Select plans and the regular Medicare supplement plans, many states have managed care Medicare plans, also called Coordinated Care Plans or HMOs (Health Maintenance Organizations). These plans contract with specific health care providers (hospitals, doctors, skilled nursing facilities, physical therapists, etc.) to provide all the services covered by Medicare. Instead of being responsible for the Medicare deductibles and co-payments, the patient pays the HMO small co-payments (i.e., $5–$15 per doctor visit) and a small monthly premium. You still must pay the $58.70 monthly Part B premium, unless the plan in which you are enrolled chooses to pay part or all of it, which is allowed after January 1, 2003.

People enrolled in Medicare HMOs don't need a Medicare supplement because all of the services are handled by the HMO, including some preventive services not covered by the traditional Medicare program (prescription drugs, eye and ear exams, dental care, foot care, routine checkups, and so forth).

Depending on the type of plan, the patient either has to receive all non-emergency services from the health care providers on the list to be covered at all or else expect a lower benefit to be paid to providers not on the list. (You may hear the second type referred to as a "point-of-service" option, which just means you pay more out of your pocket to go to a provider outside the HMO's provider network.)

About 13% of people on Medicare belonged to a managed care Medicare plan in 2002.[8] Congress is hoping many more people will join because these plans promote cost containment of health care costs. That's why there's lower premium for those plans and that's why they pay for more services than the traditional Medicare program.

The managed care plans have an annual open enrollment to allow new enrollees to enter the program. At the present time, people who are enrolled in a managed care plan can go back to the traditional Medicare program at any time.

Some people return to traditional Medicare because managed care plans control how much treatment you can have, and people with chronic conditions sometimes prefer the traditional Medicare program. Rather than lose money on Medicare patients who need a lot of care, some HMOs have stopped serving all Medicare beneficiaries because they feel the government doesn't pay HMOs enough to care for chronically ill patients adequately. That's because the government has been paying managed care plans the same amount of money every month for all Medicare patients in the HMO's geographical service area, regardless of health condition. (When an HMO drops out of Medicare, the members do not lose their Medicare benefits. They just return to the traditional Medicare program.)

Congress recognized this problem and as of January 1, 2002,

Coordinated Care Plans began to receive funding based on demographic risk factors such as age, health conditions and sex, as well as geographic area.

New Medicare+Choice Plans

By November 1999, Medicare beneficiaries received information from the Centers for Medicare and Medicaid Services (formerly the Health Care Financing Administration) about several new choices for Medicare beneficiaries who are entitled to Part A and enrolled in Part B of Medicare. These plans are called **Medicare+Choice plans**. The first opportunity for enrollment in one of these new plans was November 1999. If you didn't make a choice, you were left in the traditional Medicare program. But don't worry. You will get another opportunity to enroll in any of the new plans that are available in your area each November.

Enrollment and Disenrollment

To help people become familiar with the new Medicare+Choice plans, there is a phased-in enrollment period. Plans are required to have an "open enrollment," which means any eligible Medicare beneficiary as described above can join, regardless of health conditions, during a Special Election Period from October 1st through December 31st, unless the plan has reached its membership capacity. Plans also are required to accept people when they first become eligible for Medicare, no questions asked.

In the first few years of this new program, Medicare beneficiaries can disenroll at any time and return to traditional Medicare or switch to another Medicare+Choice plan.

What Kind of Choices Will You Have?

As this new program develops, there will be several Coordinated Care Plans for you to choose from in addition to the traditional Medicare program, like the HMOs explained earlier. Some of these will require you to use a specific list of providers to receive any benefits, but the benefits you receive will be at little or no cost to you. Others with the "Point of Service" option mentioned on page 216 will allow you to use providers not on the list if you pay more out of your pocket. Other choices include:

Preferred Provider Organizations—You will be given a list of doctors and hospitals to choose from, but you are allowed to use providers not on the list and simply receive lower benefits. (The first plan of this kind is being tested in 23 states as of August, 2002.)[9]

Preferred Sponsor Organizations—This choice allows you to deal directly with the provider of care, such as a particular hospital chain or a group of doctors, without an insurance company's involvement. In other words, the provider is assuming the financial risk of providing services to Medicare patients.

Private fee-for-service plans—These plans do not limit your choice of providers, but are allowed to bill you up to 15% above the plan's payment for a service. Private fee-for-service plans can charge you a premium amount above the Medicare Part B premium and can charge deductible and coinsurance amounts that are different than those under the Original Medicare Plan. In other words, the insurance company, rather than the Medicare program, decides how much you pay for the services you receive.

Private contracts with doctors—You will be able to contract privately with doctors who choose to drop out of Medicare for two years. (Contracting privately means you and the doctor agree upon a charge and you can't file the claim with Medicare or a Medicare supplement.)

Religious fraternal benefit societies—Members of these organizations will be able to form their own health care programs.

Another exciting choice was a Medical Savings Account (MSA) for the first 390,000 Medicare beneficiaries who set one up between now and December 31, 2002. Unfortunately, there isn't an approved MSA for Medicare beneficiaries as of early 2003. In the event that an approved plan becomes available, here is how it is proposed to work:

An MSA is an exciting choice because it can mean that the government will pay some or maybe even all of your long-term care insurance premium.

First, you choose a high deductible plan to pay your acute care expenses, like doctor and hospital bills. The maximum deductible in 2000 was $6,300, indexed to increase annually. The government will pay the premium for the acute care plan on a monthly basis. In addition, the government will deposit the difference between the premium for your acute-care plan and the amount the government is providing for each Medicare beneficiary into an account for you. Here's an example using a Medicare allowance of $500 a month:

Medicare's annual allowance ($500 x 12) :	$6,000
Acute-care high deductible plan premium:	- $2,000
Amount Medicare deposits into an account for you	$4,000

This deposit will be made in a lump sum in the first month of your enrollment in the program. Neither the initial deposit nor the growth will be taxable income to you, as long as you use the money for "qualified medical expenses," according to the IRS. That includes expenses that go toward your high deductible, because you aren't allowed to purchase a Medicare supplement to cover that expense. It also includes items beyond what the traditional Medicare program covers such as prescription drugs, eyeglasses, hearing aids, etc.

The really exciting news is that you can also use the money the government has deposited into your MSA for long-term care insurance! Your policy must be tax-qualified. See **Features of a Good Long-Term Care Insurance Policy** on p. 34 for the definition of a tax-qualified policy.

The only choices available today are the Medicare HMO, the Preferred Provider Organization in 23 states, the Private Fee-for-Service plan, and the ability to contract privately with doctors. To see what is available in your state or to watch for new programs, such as the Medical Savings Accounts, see *Want to Know More?* p. 248.

You Do Not Have to Switch

These are all exciting choices, but you do not have to switch to any of these new programs. You may remain in traditional Medicare if you like.

Benefits

All of the Medicare+Choice plans must provide at least the same benefits as Part A and Part B of the traditional Medicare program, including flu shots and pneumonia vaccines and preventive mammograms. Medicare+Choice plans also must:

▲ offer female beneficiaries direct access to specialists for pelvic exams, Pap smears and mammograms without first obtaining a referral from a primary physician;

▲ assess new enrollees to see if they need immediate medical attention of any kind;

▲ allow for direct access to specialists for complex medical conditions; and

▲ pay for diagnostic testing at emergency centers to determine if you need immediate attention and then pay for emergency treatment to stabilize your medical condition for a maximum co-pay of only $50 that you will be responsible for if you need emergency services outside of your plan's provider network. ("Severe pain" is an accepted medical reason to seek emergency help outside the provider network.)

In addition, Medicare+Choice plans are allowed to include additional benefits that aren't covered by traditional Medicare such as prescription drugs, dental and foot care, and preventive services such as routine physicals and eye and ear exams.

In 2003, Medicare+Choice plans will be allowed to waive the 3-day prior hospital stay requirement for skilled nursing facility care if it is cost-effective. This means a patient could be admitted to a skilled nursing facility after a one or two-day hospital stay or directly from home.

For any services you receive in the new Medicare+Choice plans, your cost sharing is limited to no more than the out-of-pocket costs of the deductibles and co-pays of traditional Medicare and probably will be less.

What If I Don't Like a Medicare+Choice Plan?

Congress passed a safety net in the Balanced Budget Act of 1997 to help people try the new managed care plans. If you try one and don't like it, you can go back to the traditional Medicare program within one year of your enrollment in the managed care plan, and you can get your Medicare supplement policy back "guaranteed issue." This means you can't be turned down or made to wait for pre-existing conditions. People who try a managed care plan as soon as they are eligible for Medicare get the same deal.

What if My Medicare+Choice Plan
Withdraws From My Area?

This can happen. If it does, your Medicare+Choice plan is required to notify you by October 2nd and to provide services to you through December 31st of that year. You can remain in your plan through the end of the year or return to Original Medicare or enroll in another Medicare+Choice plan in your area if available. If you return to Original Medicare, you will have the right to buy a Plan A, B, C or F Medicare Supplement policy with no health questions if you apply within 63 days after your Medicare+Choice coverage ends. Also, there's a really good chance you can keep your doctor, as over 90% of Medicare+Choice doctors participate in Original Medicare.[9]

Want to Know More?

As of September 2002, there were nearly five million Medicare beneficiaries enrolled in 155 Medicare+Choice plans throughout the country. About 63.5 percent of people covered by Medicare live in counties served by at least one Medicare+Choice plan.[10] For more information on the Medicare+Choice program in your state, you may call 800-633-4227 (TDD-1-877-486-2948) or visit the official Medicare website (www.medicare.gov) to order the publication *Medicare & You, 2003*. In addition to listing a number of valuable publications that you can order or print out to educate yourself thoroughly on Medicare+Choice, the website even allows you to enter your zip code and view a list of Medicare managed care plans available in your area. A new feature on the website is "Nursing Home Compare", which allows you to review quality ratings and many other characteristics of all the nursing homes in your area.

The Silver Lining in the Managed Care Opportunity

As you wade through the maze of Medicare changes in the next few years, please bear one thing in mind. The real risk today is long-term care. The average amount spent by Medicare beneficiaries in 1998 for out-of-pocket health expenses plus Medicare supplement premium was only about $2,700.[11] That amount is much smaller for members of Medicare+Choice plans, because the government is using lower out-of-pocket costs to create incentives for you to switch from traditional Medicare to managed care. And, the less you spend for your "acute care" coverage like hospital and doctor bills, the more money you have available to spend on long-term care insurance, which covers the greatest health care risk you face and for which you are not covered by Medicare, private health insurance or Medicare+Choice plans.

Appendix B:
Who to Call for Help

Directory of State Insurance Departments, Medicaid and Aging Agencies

ALABAMA

Alabama Insurance Department
201 Monroe Street
Ste. 1700
Montgomery, AL 36104
(334) 269-3550
Insurance Counseling
1-800-243-5463

Alabama Medicaid Agency
501 Dexter Avenue
Montgomery, AL 36103
(334) 242-5600
(800) 362-1504

Commission on Aging
770 Washington Avenue
RSA Plaza
Ste. 470
Montgomery, AL 36130
1-877-425-2243

ALASKA

Alaska Division of Insurance
333 Willoughby Avenue
State Office Building
9th Floor
Juneau, AK 99801
(907) 465-2515
Insurance Counseling
1-800-478-6065

Alaska Medicaid Agency
P.O. Box 110660
Juneau, AK 99811-0660
(907) 465-3355

Alaska Commission on Aging
P.O. Box 110209
Juneau, AK 99811-0209
(907) 465-3250

AMERICAN SAMOA

Insurance Department
Office of Governor
Pago Pago, AS 96799
011-684-633-4116

Medicaid Agency
Department of Health
LBJ Tropical Medical Center
Pago Pago, AS 96799
011-684-633-4590

Territorial Administration on Aging
Government of American Samoa
Pago Pago, AS 96799
011-684-633-1252

ARIZONA

Arizona Insurance Department
2910 N. 44th Street
Ste. 120
Phoenix, AZ 85018
(602) 912-8444
Insurance Counseling
1-800-432-4040

Medicaid Agency
801 East Jefferson Street
Phoenix, AZ 85034
(602) 417-4000

Aging and Adult Administration
1789 W. Jefferson Street, #950A
Phoenix, AZ 85007
(602) 542-4446

ARKANSAS

Arkansas Insurance Department
1200 West Third Street
Little Rock, AR 72201
1-800-282-9134
Insurance Counseling
1-800-224-6330

Medicaid Agency
Division of Medical Services
Department of Human Services
Donaghey Plaza South
P.O. Box 1437, Slot 1100
Little Rock, AR 72203-1437
(501) 682-6789

Division of Aging and Adult Services
P.O. Box 1437, Slot 530
Little Rock, AR 72203-1437
(501) 682-2441

CALIFORNIA

California Insurance Department
300 South Spring Street
South Tower
Los Angeles, CA 90013
1-800-927-4357
Insurance Counseling
1-800-434-0222

Medicaid Agency
714 P Street, Room 1253
Sacramento, CA 95814
(916) 654-0391

California Commission on Aging
1600 K Street, 4th Floor
Sacramento, CA 95814
(916) 322-5630

COLORADO

Colorado Insurance Division
1560 Broadway
Ste. 850
Denver, CO 80202
(303) 894-7499
Insurance Counseling
1-800-544-9181

Medicaid Agency
Department of Health Care Policy &
    Financing
1575 Sherman Street
Denver, CO 80203-1714
(303) 866-2993

Division of Aging and Adult Services
1575 Sherman Street
Ground Floor
Denver, CO 80203
(303) 866-2800

COMMONWEALTH OF THE
NORTHERN MARIANA
ISLANDS

Department of Community &
    Cultural Affairs, Civic Center
    Commonwealth of the Northern
    Mariana Islands
Saipan, CM 96950
011-607-234-6011

Medicaid Agency
Department of Public Health &
  Environmental Services
  Commonwealth of the Northern
  Mariana Islands
P.O. Box 409 CK
Saipan, MP 96950
011-670-664-4884

CONNECTICUT

Connecticut Insurance Department
P.O. Box 816
Hartford, CT 06142-0816
Insurance Counseling
1-800-203-3447

Medicaid Agency
Department of Social Services
25 Sigourney Street
Hartford, CT 06106-5116
(860) 424-5116

Elderly Services Division
25 Sigourney Street
Hartford, CT 06106
(806) 424-5277

DELAWARE

Delaware Insurance Department
841 Silver Lake Blvd.
Dover, DE 19904
(302) 739-4251
Insurance Counseling
1-800-366-9500

Medicaid Agency
Department of Health and Social
  Services
1901 North DuPont Highway
New Castle, DE 19720
(302) 255-9040

Division of Services for Aging &
  Adults
1901 N. DuPont Highway
2nd Floor Annex Admin. Bldg.
New Castle, DE 19720
(302) 577-4791

DISTRICT OF COLUMBIA

Insurance Department
810 First Street, NE
Ste. 701
Washington, DC 20002
(202) 727-8000
Insurance Counseling
(202) 676-3900

Medicaid Agency
Medical Assistance Administration
825 North Capital St., NE
5th Floor
Washington, DC 2002
(202) 442-5988

Office on Aging
441 4th Street, NW
9th Floor
Washington, DC
(202) 724-5622

FEDERATED STATES OF
   MICRONESIA
State Agency on Aging
Office of Health Services
Federated States of Micronesia
Ponape, ECI 96941

FLORIDA
Florida Department of Insurance
200 E. Gaines Street
Tallahassee, FL 32399-0300
(850) 413-3100
Insurance Counseling
1-800-963-5337

Medicaid Agency
Agency for Health Care
   Administration
2727 Mahan Drive
Tallahassee, FL 32308
(850) 488-3560

Department of Elder Affairs
Building B-Suite 152
4040 Esplanade Way
Tallahassee, FL 32399
(850) 414-2000

GEORGIA
Georgia Insurance Department
2 Martin L. King, Jr., Drive
704 West Tower
Atlanta, GA 30334
(404) 656-2070

Medicaid Agency
Department of Community Health
2 Peachtree Street, NW
Atlanta, GA 30303
(404) 656-4507

Division of Aging Services
Department of Human Resources
2 Peachtree St., NW
Ste. 9-385
Atlanta, GA 30303-3142
(404) 657-5258

GUAM
Guam Insurance Department
P.O. Box 23607
FMF Barrigada, GU 96921
011-671-475-1825
Insurance Counseling (808) 586-7299

Medicaid Agency
Bureau of Health Care Financing
Department of Public Health & Social
   Services
P.O. Box 2816
Agana, GU 96910
011-671-735-7269

Division of Senior Citizens
   Department of Public Health &
   Social Services
P.O. Box 2816
Agana, GU 96932
011-671-477-2930

HAWAII
Hawaii Department of Commerce &
   Consumer Affairs
Insurance Division
P.O. Box 3614
Honolulu, HI 96811
(808) 586-2790
Insurance Counseling
1-800-669-8387

Medicaid Agency
Department of Human Services
P.O. Box 339
Honolulu, HI 96809-0339
(808) 586-4996

Executive Office on Aging
No. 1 Capital District
250 S. Hotel Street
Rm. 406
Honolulu, HI 96813-2831
(808) 586-0100

IDAHO
Idaho Insurance Department
700 W. State Street
Boise, ID 83720-0043
(208) 334-4250
Insurance Counseling
1-800-247-4422

Medicaid Agency
Division of Medicaid
Department of Health and Welfare
Americana Building
P.O. Box 83720
Boise, ID 83720-0036
(208) 364-1802

Commission on Aging
3380 Americana Building
Ste. 120
Boise, ID 83706
(208) 334-3833

ILLINOIS
Illinois Insurance Department
320 W. Washington St.
4th Floor
Springfield, IL 62767-0001
(217) 782-4515
Insurance Counseling
1-800-548-9034

Medicaid Agency
Department of Public Aid
201 South Grand Avenue, East
3rd Floor
Springfield, IL 62763-0001
(217) 782-2570

Department on Aging
421 E. Capitol Avenue, No. 100
Springfield, IL 62701-1789
(217) 785-3356

INDIANA
Indiana Insurance Department
311 W. Washington Street
Ste. 300
Indianapolis, IN 46204-2787
Insurance Counseling
1-800-452-4800

Medicaid Agency
Medicaid Policy and Planning Family
    & Social Services Administration
P.O. Box 7083
402 W. Washington Street
Indianapolis, IN 46207-7083
(317) 233-4454

Division of Aging & Home Services
402 W. Washington St.
P.O. Box 7083
Indianapolis, IN 46207-7083
(317) 232-4861

IOWA

Iowa Insurance Department
330 Maple Street
Des Moines, IA 50319-0065
(515) 2181-5705
Insurance Counseling
1-800-452-4800

Department of Elder Affairs
200 10th Street
3rd Floor
Des Moines, IA 50309-3609
(515) 242-3333

KANSAS

Kansas Insurance Department
420 S.W. 9th Street
Topeka, KS 66612-1678
(785) 296-3071
Insurance Counseling
1-800-860-5260

Medicaid Agency
Department of Social &
    Rehabilitation Services
915 Harrison Street
Topeka, KS 66612
(785) 296-3959

Department of Aging
New England Bldg.
503 South Kansas
Topeka, KS 66603-3404
(785) 296-4986

KENTUCKY

Kentucky Insurance Department
215 W. Main Street
Frankfort, KY 40601
1-800-595-6053
Insurance Counseling
(502) 564-7372

Medicaid Agency
Department of Medicaid Services
275 East Main Street
6th Floor
Frankfort, KY 40621
(502) 564-4321

Office of Aging Services
Cabinet for Human Resources
275 East Main Street, 5 West
Frankfort, KY 40601
(502) 564-6930

LOUISIANA

Louisiana Insurance Department
950 N. 5th Street
P.O. Box 94214
Baton Rouge, LA 70804-9214
Insurance Counseling
1-800-259-5301

Medicaid Agency
Bureau of Health Services Financing
1201 Capitol Access Road
P.O. Box 91030
Baton Rouge, LA 70821-9030
(225) 342-5774

Office of Elderly Affairs
412 N. 4th Street
Baton Rouge, LA 70802
(225) 342-7100

MAINE

Maine Bureau of Insurance
34 State House Station
Augusta, ME 04333
(207) 624-8475
Insurance Counseling
1-800-750-5353

Medicaid Agency
Bureau of Medical Services
State House Station 11
Augusta, ME 04333-0011
(207) 624-7539

Bureau of Elder and Adult Services
State House, Station 11
Augusta, ME 04333
1-877-353-2771

MARYLAND

Maryland Insurance Administration
525 St. Paul Place
Baltimore, MD 21202-2272
(410) 468-2000

Medicaid Agency
Department of Health and Mental
   Hygiene
201 West Preston Street
Baltimore, MD 21201
(410) 767-4664

Department on Aging
301 West Preston Street
Ste. 1007
Baltimore, MD 21201
(410) 767-1100

MASSACHUSETTS

Massachusetts Insurance Division
One South Station
Boston, MA 02210-2208
(617) 521-7777

Medicaid Agency
Division of Medical Assistance
600 Washington Street
Boston, MA 02111
(617) 210-5690

Executive Office of Elder Affairs
1 Ashburton Place
5th Floor
Boston, MA 02108
1-800-882-2003

MICHIGAN

Michigan Insurance Bureau
525 W. Ottawa
Lansing, MI 48909
(517) 373-1820

Medicaid Agency
Medical Services Administration
Department of Community Health
Sixth Floor
Lewis Cass Bldg.
320 South Walnut St.
Lansing, MI 48913
(517) 373-3573

Office of Services to the Aging
P.O. Box 30676
Lansing, MI 48909-8176
(517) 373-8230

MINNESOTA

Minnesota Insurance Department
85 Seventh Place East
Ste. 500
St. Paul, MN 55101-2362
(612) 296-4026

Medicaid Agency
Minnesota Department of Human
   Services
444 Lafayette Rd.
St. Paul, MN 55155-3852
(651) 297-3933

Board on Aging
444 Lafayette Rd.
St. Paul, MN 55155-3843
(651) 296-2770

MISSISSIPPI

Mississippi Insurance Department
1001 Woolfolk State Office Bldg.
501 N. West St.
Jackson, MS 39201
(601) 359-3569
Insurance Counseling
1-800-948-3090

Medicaid Agency
Division of Medicaid
Office of Governor
Suite 801, Robert E. Lee Bldg.
239 N. Lamar St.
Jackson, MS 39201-1399
(601) 359-6050

Council on Aging & Adult Services
750 N. State St.
Jackson, MS 39202
1-800-948-3090

MISSOURI

Missouri Department of Insurance
301 West High St.
Jefferson City, MO 65102-0690
Insurance Counseling
1-800-390-3330

Medicaid Agency
Division of Medical Services
Department of Social Services
615 Howerton Court
P.O. Box 6500
Jefferson City, MO 65102-6500
(573) 751-3425

Division of Aging
Department of Social Services
P.O. Box 570
Jefferson City, MO 65102
(573) 751-6400

MONTANA
Montana Insurance Department
126 N. Sanders
Mitchell Bldg., Rm. 270
Helena, MT 59620
(406) 444-2040
Insurance Counseling
(402) 471-2201

Medicaid Agency
Medicaid Services Bureau
1400 Broadway
Helena, MT 59601
(406) 444-4540

Senior & Long-Term Care Division
111 N. Sanders Street
Rm. 210
Helena, MT 59604
(406) 444-4077

NEBRASKA
Nebraska Insurance Department
Terminal Bldg.
941 "O" Street, Ste. 400
Lincoln, NE 68508
(402) 471-2201

Medicaid Agency
Medicaid Division
Nebraska Dept. of HHS
P.O. Box 95044
Lincoln, NE 68509-5044
(402) 471-2306

Department on Aging
State Office Bldg.
301 Centennial Mall South
Lincoln, NE 68509-5044
(402) 471-2306

NEVADA
Nevada Division of Insurance
788 Fairview Drive
Ste. 300
Carson City, NV 89701
(775) 687-4270
Insurance Counseling
(702) 486-3545

Medicaid Agency
Nevada State Welfare Division
505 East King St.
Rm. 600
Carson City, NV 89710-3708
(775) 684-4000

Division for Aging Services
3416 Goni Rd.
Bldg. D
Ste. 132
Carson City, NV 89706
(775) 687-4210

NEW HAMPSHIRE
New Hampshire Insurance
  Department
56 Old Suncook Rd.
Concord, NH 03301
(603) 271-2261
Insurance Counseling
1-800-852-3388

Medicaid Agency
Medicaid Administration Bureau
Department of Health and Human
  Services
6 Hazen Drive
Concord, NH 03301-6521
(603) 271-4353

Division of Elderly & Adult Services
129 Pleasant St.
Concord, NH 03301-3857
(603)271-4680

NEW JERSEY
New Jersey Insurance Department
P.O. Box 325
Trenton, NJ 08625-0325
(609) 292-5360
Insurance Counseling
1-800-792-8820

Medicaid Agency
Department of Health and Senior
  Services
P.O. Box 360
Trenton, NJ 08625-0712
(609) 292-7837

Division of Senior Affairs
P.O. Box 807
Trenton, NJ 08625-0807
(609) 943-3437

NEW MEXICO
New Mexico Insurance Department
P.O. Box 1269
Santa Fe, NM 87504-1269
(505) 827-4601
Insurance Counseling
1-800-432-2080

Medicaid Agency
Medical Assistance Division
New Mexico Human Services
  Department
P.O. Box 2348
Santa Fe, NM 87504-2348
(505) 827-2185

State Agency on Aging
228 East Palace Avenue
Santa Fe, NM 87501
1-800-432-2080

NEW YORK
New York Insurance Department
25 Beaver Street
New York, NY 10004
(212) 480-6400
Insurance Counseling
1-800-333-4114

Medicaid Agency
NYS Department of Health
Office of Medicaid Management
Empire State Plaza
Rm. 1466, Corning Tower Bldg.
Albany, NY 12237
(518) 474-3018

State Office for the Aging
New York State Plaza Agency
Building #2
1-800-342-9871

NORTH CAROLINA

North Carolina Insurance Department
P.O. Box 26387
Raleigh, NC 27611
(919) 733-2032
Insurance Counseling
1-800-443-9354

Medicaid Agency
Division of Medical Assistance
Department of Health and Human
   Services
1985 Umstead Drive
P.O. Box 29529
Raleigh, NC 27626-0529
(919) 857-4011

Division of Aging
2101 Mail Service Center
Raleigh, NC 27699-2101
(919) 733-3983

NORTH DAKOTA

North Dakota Insurance Department
600 East Blvd. Dept. 401
Bismarck, ND 58505-0320
1-800-247-0560
Insurance Counseling
1-800-247-0560

Medicaid Agency
Medical Services Division
600 East Blvd.
Bismarck, ND 58505-0250
(701) 328-2321

Department of Human Services
Aging Services Division
600 South 2nd Street, Ste. 1C
Bismarck, ND 58504-5729
1-800-451-8693

OHIO

Ohio Insurance Department
2100 Stella Court
Columbus, OH 43215-1067
(614) 644-2658
Insurance Counseling
1-800-686-1578

Medicaid Agency
Office of Medicaid
Department of Human Services
30 East Broad Street
31st Floor
Columbus, OH 43215-3414
(614) 644-0140

Department of Aging
50 W. Broad Street
9th Floor
Columbus, OH 43215-3362
(614) 466-5500

OKLAHOMA
Oklahoma Insurance Department
P.O. Box 53408
Oklahoma City, OK 73152-3408
(405) 521-2828
Insurance Counseling
1-800-763-2828

Medicaid Agency
Oklahoma Health Care Authority
4545 North Lincoln Blvd.
Ste. 124
Oklahoma City, OK 73105
(405) 522-7300

Department of Human Services
Aging Services Division
312 NE 28th Street
Oklahoma City, OK 73125
(405) 521-2327

OREGON
Oregon Department of Consumer &
   Business Services
350 Winter Street NE
Rm. 440
Salem, OR 97301
(503) 947-7980
Insurance Counseling
1-800-722-4134

Medicaid Agency
Department of Human Services
Office of Medical Assistance Programs
500 Summer Street, NE
E37
Salem, OR 97310-1079
(503) 945-5772

Department of Human Resources
Senior & Disabled Services Division
500 Summer Street, NE
E02
Salem, OR 97301-1073
1-800-282-8096

PALAU
State Agency on Aging
Department of Social Services
Republic of Palau
P.O. Box 100
Koror, Palau 96940

PENNSYLVANIA
Pennsylvania Insurance Department
1326 Strawberry Square
Harrisburg, PA 17120
(717) 787-3898
Insurance Counseling
1-877-881-6388

Medicaid Agency
Medical Assistance Programs
Health and Welfare Bldg.
Rm 515
P.O. Box 2675
Harrisburg, PA 17105-2675

Department of Aging
555 Walnut St.
5th Floor
Harrisburg, PA 17101-1919
(717) 783-1550

PUERTO RICO
Office of the Commissioner of
  Insurance
P.O. Box 8330
Fernandez Juncos Station
Sancturce, PR 00910-8330
(787) 722-8686
Insurance Counseling
(809) 721-8590

Medicaid Agency
Office of Economic Assistance to the
  Medically Indigent – Department
  of Health
Call Box 70184
San Juan, PR 00936
(787) 250-7429

Governor's Office of Elderly Affairs
P.O. Box 50063
San Juan, PR 00902
(787) 721-5710

REPUBLIC OF THE MARSHALL
  ISLANDS
State Agency on Aging
Department of Social Services
Republic of the Marshall Islands
Marjuro, Marshall Islands 96960

RHODE ISLAND
Rhode Island
233 Richmond Street
Providence, RI 02903-4233
(401) 222-2223
Insurance Counseling
1-800-322-2880

Medicaid Agency
Division of Medical Services
Department of Human Services
600 New London Avenue
Cranston, RI 02920
(401) 462-6500

Department of Elderly Affairs
160 Pine Street
Providence, RI 02903
(401) 222-2858

SOUTH CAROLINA
South Carolina Department of
  Insurance
300 Arbor Lake Dr.
Ste. 1200
Columbia, SC 29223
(803) 737-6160
Insurance Counseling
1-800-868-9095

Medicaid Agency
Department of Health and Human
  Services
P.O. Box 8206
Columbia, SC 29202-8206
(803) 898-2500

Division on Aging
202 Arbor Lake Dr.
Ste. 301
Columbia, SC 29223-4535
(803) 898-2850

SOUTH DAKOTA
South Dakota Division of Insurance
118 West Capitol
Pierre, SD 57501
(605) 773-3563
Insurance Counseling
1-800-822-8804

Medicaid Agency
Department of Social Services
700 Governors Drive
Pierre, SD 57501
(605) 773-3165

Office of Adult Services and Aging
700 Governors Drive
Pierre, SD 57501
(605) 773-3165

TENNESSEE
Tennessee Department of Commerce
   & Insurance
500 James Robertson Pkwy
Davy Crockett Tower
Nashville, TN 37243
(615) 741-2241

Medicaid Agency
Department of Finance and
   Administration Bureau of TennCare
729 Church Street
Nashville, TN 37247
(615) 741-0213

Commission on Aging
Andrew Jackson Bldg.
500 Deadrick Street
9th Floor
Nashville, TN 37243
(615) 741-2056

TEXAS
Texas Department of Insurance
333 Guadalupe Street
Austin, TX 87801
(512) 463-6169
Insurance Counseling
1-800-252-3439

Medicaid Agency
Health and Human Services
Commission
P.O. Box 13247
Austin, TX 78711
(512) 424-6549

Department on Aging
4900 N. Lamar
4th Floor
Austin, TX 78751
(512) 424-6840

UTAH
Utah Insurance Department
State Office Bldg. Rm 3110
Salt Lake City, UT 84114-6901
1-800-538-3800
Insurance Counseling
1-800-439-3805

Medicaid Agency
Department of Health
Division of Health Care Financing
P.O. Box 14100
Salt Lake City, UT 84114-1000
(801) 538-6111

Aging Services Administration Office
120 North 200 West
Rm. 325
Salt Lake City, UT 84103
(801) 538-3910

VERMONT
Vermont Department of Banking &
  Insurance
89 Main Street, Drawer 20
Montpelier, VT 05620-3101
(802) 828-3301
Insurance Counseling
1-802-828-3302

Medicaid Agency
Office of Health Access
Department of Social Welfare
103 South Main Street
Waterbury, VT 05671
(802) 241-3985

Agency of Human Services
Department of Aging & Disabilities
103 South Main Street
Waterbury, VT 05671
(802) 241-2400

VIRGINIA
Virginia Bureau of Insurance
1300 E. Main Street
Richmond, VA 23219
(804) 371-9206
Insurance Counseling
1-800-552-3402

Medicaid Agency
Department of Medical Assistance
  Services
600 East Broad Street
Richmond, VA 23219
(804) 786-4231

Department for the Aging
1600 Forest Avenue
Suite 102
Richmond, VA 23229
(804) 662-9354

VIRGIN ISLANDS
Virgin Islands Insurance Department
Kongens Gade No. 18
St. Thomas, VI 00802
(340) 774-7166
Insurance Counseling
1-800-552-3402

Medicaid Agency
Bureau of Health Insurance and
  Medical Assistance
210-3A Altona
Suite 302 Frostco Center
St. Thomas, VI 00802
(340) 774-4624

Senior Citizen Affairs Division
Department of Human Services
19 Estate Diamond Fredericksted
St. Croix, VI 00840
(809) 774-0930

WASHINGTON
Washington Insurance Department
P.O. Box 40255
Olympia, WA 98504-0255
(360) 725-7000
Insurance Counseling
1-800-397-4422

Medicaid Agency
Medical Assistance Administration
P.O. Box 45505
Olympia, WA 98504-5505
(360) 902-7604

Aging & Adult Services
    Administration
Department of Social & Health
    Services
P.O. Box 45130
Olympia, WA 98504-5130
1-800-737-0617

WEST VIRGINIA
West Virginia Insurance Commission
1124 Smith Street
Charleston, WV 25301
(304) 558-3354
Insurance Counseling
1-800-642-9004

Medicaid Agency
Bureau of Medical Services
Department of Health & Human
    Resources
7011 MacCorkle Avenue SE
Charleston, WV 25304
(304) 926-1703

WV Bureau of Senior Services
1900 Kanawha Blvd. East
Holly Grove Bldg. 10
Charleston, WV 25305-0160
(304) 558-3317

WISCONSIN
Wisconsin Insurance Department
121 E. Wilson Street
Madison, WI 53702
(608) 266-3585
    Insurance Counseling
1-800-242-1060

Medicaid Agency
Division of Health Care Financing
Department of Health & Social
    Services
One West Wilson Street
Room 350
Madison, WI 53701
(608) 266-8922

Bureau of Aging and LTC Resources
One West Wilson Street
Madison, WI 53707-7851
(608) 266-2536

WYOMING
Wyoming Insurance Department
Herschler Bldg.
3rd Floor East
122 West 25th Street
Cheyenne, WY 82002
(307) 777-7401
Insurance Counseling
1-800-856-4398

Medicaid Agency
Health Care Access & Resources
    Division
Department of Health
Hathaway Bldg. Ste. 154
2300 Capitol Ave.
Cheyenne, WY 82002
(307) 777-7531

Aging Division
6101 Yellowstone Rd.
Rm. 259B
Cheyenne, WY 82002
1-800-442-2766

Useful Websites

The following is a list of web sites that we at *LTC Consultants* have found to be helpful. We feel that these web sites can be useful to anyone who wants to learn more about long-term care and long-term care insurance.

Alzheimer's Association: www.alz.org

American Association of Homes and Services for the Aging: www.aahsa.org

American Association of Retired Persons: www.aarp.org

American Medical Pharmaceutical Outlet: www.medshelp4u.com

American Psychological Association: www.apa.org

Assisted Living Federation of America: www.alfa.org

Assisted Living Info: www.assistedlivinginfo.com

Benefits Checkup: www.benefitscheckup.org

Careguide: www.careguide.com

Center for Long-Term Care Financing: www.centerltc.com

Consumer Consortium on Assisted Living: www.ccal.org

ElderCare Online: www.ec-online.net

e-Eldercare: www.e-eldercare.com

ElderWeb Online Eldercare Sourcebook: www.eldercareweb.com

Federal Administration on Aging: www.aoa.gov

Gerontological Society of America: www.geron.org

HOMECARE Online: www.nahc.org

LTC Consultants: www.ltcconsultants.com

Mature Market Institute: www.maturemarketinstitute.com

Medicare & Medicaid Info: www.cms.gov

The Medicine Program: www.themedicineprogram.com

National Alliance for Caregiving: www.caregiver.org

National Association of Professional Geriatric Care Managers:
www.caremanager.org

National Center for Assisted Living: www.ncal.org

National Council on Aging: www.ncoa.org

National Family Caregivers Association: www.nfcacares.org

National Senior Citizen's Law Center: www.nsclc.org

Nationwide Nursing Home Directory:
www.nursinghomeinfo.com

Senior Alternatives: www.senioralternatives.com

Senior Care Resources: www.seniorcarehelp.com

Seniorlink Select: www.seniorlinkselect.com

Visiting Nurse Association of America: www.vnaa.org

Well Spouse Foundation: www.wellspouse.org

Appendix C:
Sources

Sources for Introduction:

1. O'Shaughnessy, Carol, Congressional Research Service, "Long-Term Care: Who Will Care for the Aging Baby Boomers?" Senate Hearing 107-106 to Senate Special Committee on Aging, June 28, 2001

2. "MetLife Market Survey on Nursing Home and Health Care Costs, 2002", MetLife Mature Market Institute, Released April, 2002

3. Dychtwald, Ken, PhD, **AgePower**, Penguin Putnam, 1999

4. Morris, Ellen Birkett, "Employers Finding Ways to Help 'Sandwich Generation'", *Business First* (The Conference Board), Week of January 3, 2000 (weekly publication)

Sources for Chapter 1:
Long-Term Care and Your Financial Security

1. Miller, Jessica, "The Changing Face of Long-Term Care," *CARING* Magazine, August 1998, p. 24

2. "MetLife Market Survey on Nursing Home and Home Health Care Costs, 2002", MetLife Mature Market Institute, Released April, 2002 (Nursing home costs include semi-private room rate plus an estimated 20% for miscellaneous charges, such as prescription drugs and care-related supplies)

3. *Ibid*

4. *Ibid*

5. Heffler, Stephen, et al, "Health Spending Projections For 2001-2011: The Latest Outlook", Office of the Actuary, Centers for Medicare and Medicaid Services, *Health Affairs*, March/April 2002, p. 208 (5.8% projected growth rate for home health and nursing home care 2001-2011)

6. Nashville, Tennessee annual cost surveys 1990-2001 provided by John Hancock Financial Services, Nashville, TN

7. Alecxih, Lisa Maria B., Zeruld, Sharon and Olearczyk, BrieAnne, The Lewin Group, "Characteristics of Caregivers: Based on the Survey of Income and Program Participation", National Family Caregiver Support Program, Selected Issue Briefs, 2001, Last Updated 4/1/02, p. 18

8. Jones, A. *The National Nursing Home Survey: 1999 Summary*, National Center for Health Statistics, Vital Health Stat 13(152), 2002, Table 25, p. 30

9. Leahy, Michael, "Something to Remember", *The Washington Post Magazine*, January 12, 2003, pp. 13, 22

10. "Statistical Data on Alzheimer's Disease," Alzheimer's Association, 2000

11. Koppel, Ross PhD, "Alzheimer's Disease: The Costs to U.S. Businesses in 2002," Alzheimer's Association, June 2002, p. 3

12. *Family Caregiving in the U.S., Findings from a National Survey*, AARP/National Alliance for Caregiving, 1997

13. *The NewsHour with Jim Lehrer/* Kaiser Family Foundation/ Harvard School of Public Health National Survey on Nursing Homes", October 2001 (conducted April-June 2001), p. 11

14. Franklin, Mary Beth, "Knowing the Score," Kiplinger's Personal Finance Magazine, March 2000, p. 95

15. Who Buys Long-Term Care Insurance? 1994-1995 Profiles and Innovations in a Dynamic Market, Health Insurance Association of America/Life Plans, Inc., p. 2 (Confirmed with LifePlans, Inc., February, 2002)

16. Brown, Dr. Robert, Associate Professor of Neurology, Mayo Medical School, Mayo Clinic, Rochester, Minnesota, February, 2000

17. Dychtwald, Ken PhD, **Healthy Aging: Challenges and Solutions,** Aspen Publishers, 1999, p. 199

18. "The Looming Budgetary Impact on Society's Aging", Congressional Budget Office Long-Range Fiscal Policy Brief, July 3, 2002

19. O'Shaughnessy, Carol, Congressional Research Service, "Trends in Long-Term Care Financing in Selected Countries", Testimony before the Senate Special Committee on Aging, June 20, 2002, p. 1

20. "Centenarians in the United States," Census Bureau, July 1999 p. 2

21. "Minor Memos," *Wall Street Journal*, December 31, 1999, p. 1

22. Friend, Tim, "Science Finds No Limit on Life Span," *USA Today*, March 17, 1999

23. Brendle, Anna, "102-Year-Old Professor Hailed as Oldest U.S. Worker", National Geographic News, September 26, 2002

24. Skatssoon, Judy, "Baby Boomers to Reach 120", *The Australian*, November 15, 2002

25. Laditka, Sarah B., "Modeling Lifetime Nursing Home Use Under Assumptions of Better Health," *The Journals of Gerontology: Psychological and Social Sciences*, July 1998, pp. S177-S187

26. Urrea, Yvette, "Friends of Paralyzed Surfer Set Up Fund," *North County Times*, March 31, 2000, pp. A1, A9

27. Tilly, Jane, et al, "Long-Term Care Chart Book: Persons Served, Payers, and Spending," The Urban Institute in Collaboration with the Congressional Research Service, May 5, 2000, p. 12

28. Jones, A. *"The National Nursing Home Survey: 1999 Summary, National Center for Health Statistics,* Vital Health Stat 13(152), 2002, Table 25, p. 30

29. "Traumatic Brain Injury: Programs Supporting Long-Term Care Services in Selected States," General Accounting Office, February 1998, GAO/HEHS-98-55, pp. 1, 4

30. Schrop, Joannie M., "Stroke Busters: New Treatments in the Fight Against Brain Attacks," *U.S. News & World Report*, March 15, 1999, p. 62

31. Donelan, et al. "Challenged to Care: Informal Caregivers in a Changing Health System", *Health Affairs*, July/August 2002, p. 225

32. Dychtwald, Ken, PhD, **AgePower,** Penguin Putnam, Inc. Publishers, 1999, p. 146

33. Morris, Ellen Birkett, "Employers Finding Ways to Help 'Sandwich Generation'", *Business First* (The Conference Board), Week of January 3, 2000 (weekly publication)

34. National Council on Aging/John Hancock Long-Term Care Survey, 1999

35. Saluter, Arlene F. and Lugaila, Terry A., "Marital Status and Living Arrangements: March 1998," Current Population Reports, Census Bureau Report P20-496/PPL-100 (Update)

36. Carter, Jessica. "Workshop to Help Those Who Care for Loved Ones," *Daily News Journal*, Murfreesboro, Tennessee, April 18, 2000, p. 1B

37. McConnell, Eleanor S., Pieper, Carl F., Sloane, Richard J., Branch, Laurence G., "Effects of Cognitive Performance on Change in Physical Function in Long-Stay Nursing Home Residents", *Journal of Gerontology: MEDICAL SCIENCES*, December, 2002, p. M778

38. Spillman, Brenda C and Pezzin, Liliana E., *"Potential and Active Family Caregivers: Changing Networks and the 'Sandwich Generation'"*, The Urban Institute; John Hopkins University School of Medicine, *The Milbank Quarterly*, Vol. 78, No. 3, 2000

39. *Contra Costa Times*, Walnut Creek, California, March 29, 1996, Reporter: Julie Appleby

40. *Parade Magazine*, March 1, 1998

41. "Women-Owned Businesses in the United States, 2002", Center for Women's Business Research, 2001, pp. 1,2

42. Donelan, et al. "Challenged to Care: Informal Caregivers in a Changing Health System", *Health Affairs*, July/August 2002, p. 225

43. *Family Caregiving in the U.S., Findings from a National Study*, National Alliance for Caregiving/AARP, 1997, p. 33

44. Schrop, Joannie M., "Stroke Busters: New Treatments in the Fight Against Brain Attacks," *U.S. News & World Report*, March 15, 1999

45. Centers for Medicare and Medicaid Services, 2001 statistics, Released 1/03

46. *Contra Costa Times*, Walnut Creek, California, March 29, 1996, Reporter: Julie Appleby

47. "The Nursing Facility Sourcebook, 2001", American Health Care Association, p. 71

48. Centers for Medicare and Medicaid Services, 2001 statistics, Released 1/03

49. Spillman, Brenda C., PhD and Kemper, Peter PhD, "Lifetime Patterns of Payment for Nursing Home Care," Agency for Health Care Policy and Research, as published in *Medical Care*, Vol. 33, No. 3, 1995, p. 291 and Wiener, Joshua M., Sullivan, Catherine M. and Skaggs, Jason, The Brookings Institution, "Spending Down to Medicaid: New Data on the Role of Medicaid in Paying for Nursing Home Care," as published by *AARP, The Public Policy Institute*, June 1996, p. 21.

50. Centers for Medicare and Medicaid Services, 2001 statistics, Released 1/03

51. "The 2000 Annual Report of the Board of Trustees of the Federal Old-Age and Survivors Insurance and Disability Trust Funds", Table II.F19 – "Comparison of OASDI Covered Workers and Beneficiaries by Alternative, Calendar Years 1945-2075", Intermediate Projection

52. Walker, David M., U.S. Comptroller General, "Long-Term Care: Aging Baby Boom Generation Will Increase Demand and Burden on Federal and State Budgets", General Accounting Office, GAO-02-544T, 3/21/02, p. 7

53. "New State-By-State Analysis Of Nation's Medicare Program: Proposed 17% Cut To Medicare, Scheduled For October 1st Implementation, To Slash Patient Care By $2.88 Billion", American Health Care Association Press Release, 2002

54. *Long-Term Care Insurance in 2000-2001,* Health Insurance Association of America, 2003, p. 3

55. A conservative estimate based on historical growth and number of existing groups documented in Douglas, Jennifer, *U.S. Group Long-Term Care Insurance 2002 Sales and In Force,* Life Insurance Market Research Association (LIMRA), 2003

56. Centers for Medicare and Medicaid Services, 2001 statistics, Released 1/03

57. Swedish Embassy, Washington, DC, January, 2003

58. *Who Buys Long-Term Care Insurance in 2000? A Decade of Study of Buyers and Nonbuyers,* prepared for Health Insurance Association of America by LifePlans, Inc., October 2000, p. 17

59. *Ibid*

60. "A Health Care Safety Net," *Fortune*, Kuhn, Susan E., October 14, 1996, p. 299

61. "Out-of-Pocket Health Care Costs Among Older Americans," *The Journals of Gerontology: Psychological and Social Sciences*, January 2000, Volume 55B, No. 1, p. S51

62. "Living Longer and Better, Long-Term Care: A Crucial Piece of the Retirement Puzzle," *Fortune*, October 1998 Special Investor's Issue, p. S3

63. Vanac, Mary, "Plan Now for Later," *Akron Beacon Journal*, August 30, 1999

64. Chatzky, Jean Sherman, "The Big Squeeze," *Money*, October 1999, p. 138

Sources for Chapter 2:
Features of a Good Long-Term Care Insurance Policy

1. Kaiser Family Foundation/Harvard School of Public Health/United Hospital Fund of New York/Visiting Nurse Service of New York, "The Wide Circle of Caregiving - Key Findings from a National Survey: Long-Term Care from the Caregiver's Perspective", June 2002, p. 2

2. Okrent, David R. "Medical Deductions for the Elderly, Part II, Expenses and Premiums Related to Long-Term Care", *The ElderLaw Report*, Panel Publishers, March 2002, p. 2

3. Shellenbarger, Sue, "When Your Parents Need a Baby Sitter: Adult Day Care Centers in Short Supply" *Wall St. Journal*, December 19, 2002, p. D1

4. "Discovering Assisted Living", American Association of Homes and Services for the Aging, 2002

5. "MetLife Market Survey on Nursing Home and Health Care Costs, 2002", MetLife Mature Market Institute, Released April, 2002

6. "Facts and Trends: The Assisted Living Sourcebook, 2001, National Center for Assisted Living, p. 4

7. Namazi, Kevin H. and Chafetz, Paul K., editors, *Assisted Living: Current Issues in Facility Management and Resident Care*, Auburn House, Westport, CT, 2001 as reported in *The Gerontologist*, June 2002, p. 426

8. Jones, A. *The National Nursing Home Survey: 1999 Summary. National Center for Health Statistics* Vital Health Stat 13(152), Table 15, June 2002

9. "MetLife Market Survey on Nursing Home and Home Health Care Costs, 2002", MetLife Mature Market Institute, Released April, 2002. (Nursing home costs include semi-private room rate plus an estimated 20% for miscellaneous charges, such as prescription drugs and care-related supplies)

10. Olsen, Laura Katz, "The Public and Private Worlds of Women and Elder Care in the U.S.", Hallym International Journal of Aging, Vol. 2/No. 1, 2000, p. 19

11. *Ibid*, p. 15

12. Cohen, Marc A., PhD, "Benefits of Long-Term Care Insurance: Enhanced Care for Disabled Elders, Improved Quality of Life for Caregivers, and Savings to Medicare & Medicaid", prepared for Health Insurance Association of America by LifePlans, Inc., September 2002, p. 3

13. Donelan, et al. "Challenged to Care: Informal Caregivers in a Changing Health System", *Health Affairs,* July/August 2002, p. 226

14. Heffler, Stephen, et al, "Health Spending Projections For 2001-2011: The Latest Outlook", Office of the Actuary, Centers for Medicare and Medicaid Services, *Health Affairs,* March/April 2002, p. 208 (5.8% projected growth rate for home health and nursing home care 2001-2011)

15. *Ibid*

16. Jones, A. *The National Nursing Home Survey: 1999 Summary. National Center for Health Statistics* Vital Health Stat 13(152), Table 1, June 2002

17. Leon, Joel, PhD, and Marainen, Murtaugh, Christopher M., Spillman, Brenda C., Warshawsky, Mark J., "In Sickness and in Health: An Annuity Approach to Financing Long-Term Care and Retirement Income", *The Journal of Risk and Insurance,* 2001, Vol. 68, No. 2, p. 229

18. Douglas, Jennifer, *U.S. Group Long-Term Care Insurance 2002 Sales and In Force,* Life Insurance Market Research Association (LIMRA), 2003

19. "Fourth Annual Long Term Care Insurance Survey", *Broker World,* July 2002, p. 8

20. "MetLife Market Survey on Nursing Home and Home Health Care Costs, 2002", MetLife Mature Market Institute, Released April, 2002 (Nursing home costs include semi-private room rate plus an estimated 20% for miscellaneous charges, such as prescription drugs and care-related supplies)

21. *Ibid*

22. Cohen, Marc A., PhD, "Benefits of Long-Term Care Insurance: Enhanced Care for Disabled Elders, Improved Quality of Life for Caregivers, and Savings to Medicare & Medicaid", prepared for Health Insurance Association of America by LifePlans, Inc., September 2002, p. 6

Sources for Chapter 3:
Long-Term Care: The New Employee Benefit

1. Dychtwald, Ken, PhD, **AgePower**, Penguin Putnam, Inc. Publishers, 1999, p. 146

2. A conservative estimate based on historical growth and number of existing groups documented in *Long-Term Care Insurance in 2000-2001*, Health Insurance Association of America, January 2003, p. 5

3. Morris, Ellen Birkett, "Employers Finding Ways to Help 'Sandwich Generation'", *Business First* (The Conference Board), Week of January 3, 2000 (weekly publication)

4. Donelan, Karen, et al., "Challenged to Care: Informal Caregivers in a Changing Health System, *Health Affairs,* July/August 2002, p. 222 and *Family Caregiving in the U.S.,* Findings from a National Survey, National Alliance for Caregiving/AARP, 1997, p. 8

5. Ash, Patricia E., *U.S. Group Long-Term Care Insurance: 2001 Sales and In Force,* Life Insurance Market Research Association (LIMRA), 2002

6. "1999 Long-Term Care Survey," National Council on the Aging/John Hancock, p. 8

7. Dutton, Gail, "Benefits Soften Up," *HRfocus,* November 1998, p. 10

8. "The MetLife Study of Employee Benefits Trends", MetLife, December 2002, p. 8

9. Pincus, Jeremy, "Employer-Sponsored Long-Term Care Insurance: Best Practices for Increasing Sponsorship," Employee Benefit Research Institute Issue Brief, April 2000, p. 9.

10. *USA Today, Weekend,* November 20-22, 1998

11. Galinsky, Ellen and Bond, James T., "The 1998 Business Work-Life Study: A Sourcebook," Families and Work Institute, p. 48

12. *Work and Elder Care: Facts for Caregivers and Their Employers*, U.S. Department of Labor, Women's Bureau, No. 98-1, May 1998, p. 3

13. Neal, Margaret B, PhD and Wagner, Donna L., PhD, "Working Caregivers: Issues, Challenges, and Opportunities for The Aging Network", Administration on Aging, National Family Caregiver Support Program, 2000, p. 3

14. "1999 Long-Term Care Survey," National Council on the Aging/John Hancock, p. 2

15. *Long-Term Care Insurance in 2000-2001*, Health Insurance Association of America, 2003

16. *LTC Consultants* Policy Comparison, October 2002

17. Family Caregiving in the U.S., Findings from a National Study, National Alliance for Caregiving/AARP, 1997, p. 32 and "The MetLife Juggling Act Study: Balancing Caregiving with Work and the Costs Involved," Mature Market Institute, Metropolitan Life Insurance Company, November 1999, p. 2

18. Neal, Margaret B, PhD and Wagner, Donna L., PhD, "Working Caregivers: Issues, Challenges, and Opportunities for The Aging Network", Administration on Aging, National Family Caregiver Support Program, 2000, p. 1

19. O'Shaughnessy, Carol, Congressional Research Service, "Long-Term Care: Who Will Care for the Aging Baby Boomers?" Senate Hearing 107-106 to Senate Special Committee on Aging, June 28, 2001

20. *Family Caregiving in the U.S., Findings from a National Study*, National Alliance for Caregiving/AARP, 1997, p. 33

21. *Ibid*

22. *The MetLife Study of Employed Caregivers: Does Long-Term Care Insurance Make a Difference?* MetLife Mature Market Institute, March 2001

23. *The MetLife Study of Employer Costs for Working Caregivers*, MetLife Mature Market Group, June, 1997, p. 3

24. Shellenbarger, Sue, "Work & Family: We Take Better Care of Our Elderly Parents Than Most Realize," *Wall St. Journal*, March 12, 1997

25. *Family Caregiving in the U.S., Findings from a National Study*, National Alliance for Caregiving/AARP, 1997, p. 12

26. *Ibid*

27. Schmidt, Jo Horne, "Who's Taking Care of Mom and Dad?" *Journal of the American Society of CLU & ChFC*, November, 1997, p. 83

28. *The MetLife Study of Employed Caregivers: Does Long-Term Care Insurance Make a Difference?* MetLife Mature Market Institute, March 2001

29. Koppel, Ross, PhD, "Alzheimer's Disease: The Costs to U.S. Businesses in 2002", Alzeimer's Association, June 2002, p. 3

30. Telephone call from *LTC Consultants* to Human Resources department of Lancaster Labs, 1/10/03

31. "Elder Care and Death is an Avalanche Issue," *USA Today*, April 29, 1997, p. 2A

32. *National Family Caregivers Association/Fortis Final Report*, 1997

33. *USA Today, USA Snapshots*, June 16, 1997 (based on the National Council on Aging/John Hancock study)

34. "1999 Long-Term Care Survey," National Council on the Aging/John Hancock, p. 3

35. "The MetLife Juggling Act Study: Balancing Caregiving with Work and the Costs Involved," Mature Market Institute, Metropolitan Life Insurance Company, November 1999, p. 8

36. Family Caregiving in the U.S., Findings from a National Study, National Alliance for Caregiving/AARP, 1997, p. 17

37. Alecxih, Lisa Maria B., Zeruld, Sharon and Olearczyk, BrieAnne, The Lewin Group, "Characteristics of Caregivers: Based on the Survey of Income and Program Participation", National Family Caregiver Support Program, Selected Issue Briefs, 2001, Last Updated 4/1/02, p. 8

38. "Financial Commitments to Family Members Especially Prevalent Among Surveyed Hispanics", Second Annual "Retirement Reality Check" survey, Allstate, November 14, 2002

39. Dychtwald, Ken, PhD, **AgePower**, Penguin Putnam, Inc. Publishers, 1999, p. 146

40. *The Breakthrough Intercessor*, an intercessory prayer ministry founded by Catherine Marshall, author of **Christy**, Lincoln, Virginia

41. *Family Caregiving in the U.S., Findings from a National Study*, National Alliance for Caregiving/AARP, 1997, p. 25

42. *Who Buys Long-Term Care Insurance? 1994-1995 Profiles and Innovations in A Dynamic Market*, Health Insurance Association of America/Life Plans, Inc., pp. 18-19 (Confirmed with LifePlans, Inc., February 2002)

43. O'Shaughnessy, Carol, Congressional Research Service, "Long-Term Care: Who Will Care for the Aging Baby Boomers?" Senate Hearing 107-106 to Senate Special Committee on Aging, June 28, 2001

44. Jones, A. *The National Nursing Home Survey: 1999 Summary. National Center for Health Statistics* Vital Health Stat 13(152), Table 25, June 2002

45. *Albany Times-Union*, March 8, 1998

46. Chavez, Tim, "Their Love Story is One of Survival and Triumph," *The Tennessean*, February 13, 1999, p. 1B and personal interview with Kristi and David Denton by Phyllis Shelton, 2002

47. Alligood, Leon, "Love Conquers All", *The Tennessean*, February 14, 1999, p. 1B

48. Written testimony from David C. Sharp, Montgomery Village Care and Rehabilitation Center, Montgomery Village, Maryland to Phyllis Shelton, January 22, 2003

49. Shelton, Phyllis R., President, *LTC Consultants*

50. *Long-Term Care Insurance in 2000-2001*, Health Insurance Association of America, 2003, p. 4

51. Heffler, Stephen, et al, "Health Spending Projections For 2001-2011: The Latest Outlook", Office of the Actuary, Centers for Medicare and Medicaid Services, Health Affairs, March/April 2002, p. 208 (5.8% projected growth rate for home health and nursing home care 2001-2011)

52. Kaiser Family Foundation/Harvard School of Public Health/United Hospital Fund of New York/Visiting Nurse Service of New York, "The Wide Circle of Caregiving - Key Findings from a National Survey: Long-Term Care from the Caregiver's Perspective", June 2002, p. 2

53. Jones, A. *The National Nursing Home Survey: 1999 Summary. National Center for Health Statistics* Vital Health Stat 13(152), Table 1, June 2002

54. Nilsson, Ingrid, Assistant to the Minister of Economic and Financial Affairs at the Swedish Embassy in Washington, D.C., January 30, 2003

55. *The MetLife Study of Employed Caregivers: Does Long-Term Care Insurance Make a Difference?* MetLife Mature Market Institute, March 2001

Sources for Chapter 4:
The Partnership for Long-Term Care

1. "MetLife Market Survey on Nursing Home and Home Health Care Costs, 2002", MetLife Mature Market Institute, Released April, 2002

2. "Raetzman, Susan, Craig, Lauren and McDougall, Cathy, "Reforming the Health Care System: State Profiles 2001", AARP, Public Policy Institute, p. 138

3. "Medicaid Long-Term Care Expenditures in FY 2001", Table N, The MEDSTAT Group, Cambridge, MA, May 10, 2002

4. "Medicaid Long-Term Care Expenditures in FY 2001, Table 1, Medicaid Expenditures for Long-Term Care Services: 1989-2001, The MEDSTAT Group, Cambridge, MA, May 10, 2002

5. Jones, A. *The National Nursing Home Survey: 1999 Summary,* National Center for Health Statistics, Vital Health Stat 13(152), 2002

6. "Partnership for Long-Term Care, National Evaluation Summary Statistics as of 12/31/00," Laguna Research Associates, San Francisco, CA, June 17, 2002, p. 6

Sources for Chapter 5:
The Medicaid Benefit for Long-Term Care

1. "State Budgets Under Stress: How are States Planning to Reduce the Growth in Medicaid Costs?" The Kaiser Commission on Medicaid and the Uninsured", July 30, 2002, p. 5

2. "Medicaid Long-Term Care Expenditures in FY 2001, Table 1, Medicaid Expenditures for Long-Term Care Services: 1989-2001, The MEDSTAT Group, Cambridge, MA, May 10, 2002

3. Coleman, Barbara, Fox-Grage, Wendy and Folkemer, Donna, "State Long-Term Care: Recent Developments and Policy Directions", U.S. Department of Health and Human Services, July 2002, p. 4

4. "Medicaid Long-Term Care Expenditures in FY 2001", The MEDSTAT Group, Cambridge, MA, May 10, 2002, p. 1

5. Margolis, Harry S., Esq., *The ElderLaw Report,* Aspen Publishers, June 1998, p. 7 (*Golf v. New York State Department of Social Services*—CT. App. N.Y., Nov. 7, 1998 WL 151293, Apr. 2, 1998) and July/August 1998, p. 15 (*Chambers v. Ohio Department of Human Services*—U.S. Ct. App. 6th Cir., No. 96-3046, May 27, 1998)

6. "Indiana Cracks Down on Senior Fraudsters", Corporation for Long-Term Care E-Alert, 8/23/02

7. Margolis, Harry S., Esq., "Purchase of Annuity Is Improper Asset Transfer", *The ElderLaw Report,* Aspen Publishers, May 2000, p. 7 *In re: Perkins* (Ohio Dept. of Human Services, Admin. App., Case No. 5040240805, Appeal Nos. 9932080 & 9936198, Docket No. 2000-AA-0085, Feb. 28, 2000)

8. "New Minnesota Law Makes Annuity Purchase a Medicaid Transfer", *Elder Law Answers,* 10/8/02 (amends Section 256B.059 of the Minnesota Statutes, eff. 7/1/02)

9. Margolis, Harry S., Esq., "N.D. High Court Rules State May Recover from Spouse's Estate" *The ElderLaw Report,* Aspen Publishers, March, 1999, p. 5 (North Dakota Dept. of Human Services v. Thompson N.D. Sup. Ct., Civil No. 980050, 1998 WI. 887673, Dec. 22 1998); "Medi-Cal May Recover Against Property Deeded With Retained Life Estate", *ElderLaw Answers.com,* 5/29/02: "Minnesota Appeals Court Rules that State Can Recover Against Home Owned by Spouse", *ElderLaw Report,* 2002

10. *Ibid.* "Recipient's Assets Conveyed to Wife Are Recoverable from Her Estate," June 2000, pp. 5–6 (In the Matter of the Estate of Wirtz, N.D. Sup. Ct., No. 990275, 2000 WI, 291154, March 21, 2000)

11. *Ibid.* "HCFA Says Annuities May Be Recovered from Estates", March 1999, p. 5

12. Wilcox, Melynda Dovel. "Will Nursing-Home Bills Haunt Your Estate?" *Kiplinger's Personal Finance Magazine*, April 1998

13. "Nevada Class Action Seeks to Block Liens on Homes of Spouses", *ElderLaw Answers.com*, 4/29/02

14. Centers for Medicare and Medicaid Services, 2001 statistics, released 1/03

15. "Facts and Trends of The Nursing Facility Sourcebook, 2001", American Health Care Association, p. 76

16. Walker, David M., U.S. Comptroller General, "Long-Term Care: Aging Baby Boom Generation Will Increase Demand and Burden on Federal and State Budgets", General Accounting Office, GAO-02-544T, 3/21/02, p. 7

17. Wiener, Joshua, PhD, Tilly, Jane, Dr. P.H., and Alecxih, Lisa Maria B., M.P.A, "Home and Community-Based Services in Seven States", *Health Care Financing Review*, Spring 2002, p. 95

18. Allen, Kathryn G., "Long-Term Care: Implications of Supreme Court's *Olmstead* Decision Are Still Unfolding", General Accounting Office, GAO-01-1167T, p. 16

19. Cohen, Marc A., PhD, Miller, Jessica, MS, Murphy, Elisa, MS, Weinrobe, Maurice, PhD, "A Descriptive Analysis of Patterns of Informal and Formal Caregiving among Privately Insured and Non-Privately Insured Disabled Living in the Community" LifePlans, Inc., p. 33

20. Wiener, Joshua, Ph.D, Tilly, Jane, Dr. P.H., and Alecxih, Lisa Maria B., M.P.A, "Home and Community-Based Services in Seven States", *Health Care Financing Review,* Spring 2002, p. 95

21. Graham, Ellen. "Work and Family: Should You Buy Insurance for Extended Elder Care?", *Wall Street Journal,* March 31, 1999, p. B1

22. Franklin, Mary Beth. "Knowing the Score," *Kiplinger's Personal Finance Magazine,* March 2000, p. 96

23. Quinn, Jane Bryant, "Shame on the Rich: Making Themselves Poor", *The Washington Post,* June 3, 2001, p. H02

24. *Who Buys Long-Term Care Insurance in 2000? A Decade of Study of Buyers and Nonbuyers,* prepared for Health Insurance Association of America by LifePlans, Inc., October 2000, p. 17

Sources for Chapter 6:
Alternatives for Financing Long-Term Care

1. "Accelerated Death Benefits, 1998," American Council of Life Insurance and LIMRA International, 1999, p. 7

2. "Accelerated Death Benefits, 1998," American Council of Life Insurance and LIMRA International, 1999, p. 20

3. Case study provided by The Heritage Group, Oklahoma City, OK, a firm that specializes in life settlements

4. Chodes, Gary, "A Revolution in Higher-End Life Insurance," *Accounting Today*, November 8–21, 1999

5. Baskies, Jeffrey A. and Slafsky, Neal A., *Trusts & Estates*, June 1997

6. "Statistical Data on Alzheimer's Disease," Alzheimer's Association, 2003

7. Heffler, Stephen, et al, "Health Spending Projections For 2001-2011: The Latest Outlook", Office of the Actuary, Centers for Medicare and Medicaid Services, *Health Affairs*, March/April 2002, p. 208 (5.8% projected growth rate for home health and nursing home care 2001-2011) and "MetLife Market Survey on Nursing Home and Home Health Costs, 2002", MetLife Mature Market Institute, Released April, 2002

8. Cohen, Marc A., PhD and Miller, Jessica, MS, "The Use of Nursing Home and Assisted Living Facilities Among Privately Insured and Non-Privately Insured Disabled Elders", LifePlans, Inc., p. 38 and Cohen, Miller, Murphy, Weinrobe, "A Descriptive Analysis of Patterns of Informal and Formal Caregiving among Privately Insured and Non-Privately Insured Disabled Elders Living in the Community", LifePlans, Inc. p. 34

Sources for Appendix A:
Senior Benefits

1. Miller, Jessica, "The Changing Face of Long-Term Care", *CARING* Magazine, August 1998, p. 24

2. "The Medicare Program: Medicare at a Glance", The Henry J. Kaiser Family Foundation, October 2002, p. 1

3. "Medicare Chart Book, The Henry J. Kaiser Family Foundation, Fall 2001, p. 64

4. Laschober, Kitchman, Neuman, and Strabic, "Trends in Medicare Supplemental Insurance and Prescription Drug Coverage, 1996-1999", *Health Affairs,* February 27, 2002

5. Murray, Lauren A. and Eppig, Franklin J., "Insurance Trends for the Medicare Population, 1991-1999", *Health Care Financing Review*, Spring 2002, p. 10

6. "Medigap Insurance: Plans are Widely Available But Have Limited Benefits And May Have High Costs", General Accounting Office, GAO-01-941, July, 2001, p. 17

7. *Ibid* p. 9

8. "Protecting Medicare Beneficiaries When Their Medicare+Choice Organization Withdraws", Centers for Medicare and Medicaid Services, October 2002, p. 1

9. *Ibid*

10. *Ibid*

11. "Medigap Insurance: Plans are Widely Available But Have Limited Benefits And May Have High Costs", General Accounting Office, GAO-01-941, July, 2001, p. 17

ACKNOWLEDGMENTS

We gratefully acknowledge receiving help from the following publications and groups: *Medicare and You, 2003*, **Long-Term Care: Your Financial Planning Guide,** 2001 edition, The American Health Care Association, The National Association of Insurance Commissioners, the State of Tennessee Department of Commerce and Insurance, the following organizations and individuals who are there for you when you need them, and most of all, to the wonderful staff of *LTC Consultants* without whom nothing would ever be printed!

Centers for Medicare
    and Medicaid Services . . . . .Anna Long, Roy Trudel

U.S. Dept. of Health and Human
Services National Center for
    Health Statistics . . . . Genevieve Strahan

The Agency for Health Care
    Research & Quality . . . . .Bill Spector, Ph.D.

United States Office
    Personnel Management . . . . .Frank Titus,
John Cutler, Laura Lawrence, Holly Schumann, Terry Schleicher

Bureau of the Census Population
    Division . . . . .Terry Lugaila

The Urban Institute . . . . .Brenda Spillman, Ph.D.

Visiting Nurse Service of NY . . . . Christopher M. Murtaugh, Ph.D.

LifePlans, Inc. . . . . .Marc Cohen, Ph.D.,
                                             Jessica Miller

Health Insurance Association of
America . . . . .Susan Coronel,
Greg Dean, J.D.

Life Insurance Market Research
Association (LIMRA) . . . . .Patricia Ash,
Jennifer Douglas

Mr. Long-Term Care . . . . .Martin Bayne

Long-Term Care Group . . . . .Eileen Tell

National LTC Partnership Office . . . . . .Mark Meiners, Ph.D.

California Partnership for
Long-Term Care . . . . .Sandra Pierce-Miller

Connecticut Partnership for
Long-Term Care . . . . .David Guttchen,
Mary Pettigrew, Jim Palma

Indiana Partnership for
Long-Term Care . . . . .Mary Ann Hack

New York State Partnership for
Long-Term Care . . . . .Bob Borrelli

Brandeis University . . . . .Christine Bishop, Ph.D.

Osborne & Associates . . . . .Tim Osborne, CPA

Tennessee Department of Insurance . . . . .Howard McGill

Centennial Adult Care Center . . . . .Stephen Zagorski

Corp. for Long-Term Care Certification . . . . .Harley Gordon,
Attorney-at-Law

Center for Long-Term Care

   Financing . . . . .Steve Moses

Elder Law Attorney . . . . .Harry Margolis, Esq.

Elder Law Attorney . . . . .Dana Shilling, J.D.

Elder Law Attorney . . . . .Timothy Takacs, Esq.

Florida Medicaid .Lynn Raichelson

Georgia Medicaid . . . . .Alan Hill

New York Medicaid .Barbara Barnes

American Republic . . . . .Dick Garner

Bankers Life & Casualty . . . . .Ray Nelson

CNA . . . . .Clint Butler

Golden Rule . . . . .Scott Berghuis

John Hancock . . . . .Matt Carpenter,

                                   Holly Leugers

MetLife Mature Market Institute . . . . . . .Sandra Timmerman

New York Life . . . . .Beth Ludden

The Heritage Group . . . . .Tom and Jane Moran

LTC Consultants

   National Trainers . . . . .David Miller,

             Catherine Dove, Lauryl Chalfin, Bill Comfort, Jr.

   Insurance Professionals . . . . .Don Hansen,

                                 Lisa McAree

National Association of

Reverse Mortage Lenders . . . . .Peter Bell

Milliman USA . . . . .Dawn Helwig

LifeCare . . . . .Jim Glickman

MedStat . . . . .Brian Burwell

Association of Health

Insurance Advisors .Diane Boyle,

Mike Kerley

National Association of Health Underwriters . . . .Janet Trautwein

Sandi Kruise Insurance Training . . . . .Sandi Kruise

and the biggest thanks of all goes to my wonderful spouse who endures my annual research and writing cycle!!

16. Homemaker Services
        $100⁰⁰

17. Alternate Payer Designation
        Yes

18. Impairement Reinstatement

19. Bed   Reservation
        up to 60 days

20. World Wide Coverage
        Yes for 1 yr.

   21. Med. Alert System
        Yes

   22. Ambulance
        No
   23. Med. Equipment

21. Ted p. 75

22. Company Assets

23. Ratings p.

24. Pre Existing Conditions

25. Free Look Period

26. Meaning of "Tax Qualified"